This book is to be returned on or before

NEW
CLASSIC
CUISINE

NEW CLASSIC CUISINE

ALBERT AND MICHEL ROUX

With a chapter on wine by
MICHAEL BROADBENT
illustrations by
PAUL HOGARTH
and photographs by
ANTHONY BLAKE

Macdonald Orbis

To Antonin Carême (1784-1833)
The pharaoh of patisserie and cooking;
the greatest chef the world has known

The authors would like to express their thanks to all the people listed here, without whose efforts this book would have been impossible to prepare: Robyn Joyce, for her invaluable help and support throughout every crisis; Victor Ceserani MBE, formerly head of the School of Hotel Keeping and Catering, Ealing College of Higher Education, who read all the recipes for us; Christian Germain from the Château de Montreuil, Montreuil Sur Mer, France, formerly head chef at *The Waterside Inn* who tested and tasted most of the recipes; Richard Nurick from Hawkins and Nurick for his advice on wine; Isabelle Ferretjans for typing the manuscript; and finally Kate Whiteman for her sympathetic translation.

Translated by Kate Whiteman

A Macdonald Orbis BOOK

First published in Great Britain in 1983 by
Macdonald & Co (Publishers) Ltd
London & Sydney
A member of Maxwell Pergamon Publishing Corporation plc
Headway House, 66-73 Shoe Lane,
London EC4P 4AB.

ISBN 0-356-09392-1

This book was designed and produced by
Quarto Publishing plc, 6 Blundell Street, London N7 9BH

Art director Alastair Campbell
Production director Edward Kinsey
Editorial director Jeremy Harwood
Senior editor Nicola Thompson
Art editor Caroline Courtney
Assistant editor Sabina Goodchild
Assistant designers Alex Arthur,
Hilary Krag

Filmset in Great Britain by
QV Typesetting Limited, London

Colour origination by
Hong Kong Graphic Arts Service

Printed in Hong Kong by
Leefung-Asco Printers Limited.

CONTENTS

FOREWORD

I am confident that a cookery book put together by the Roux brothers will prove an important addition to the shelf of recipe books for those who are interested in the finer arts of cooking.

I first met Albert Roux in the early 1950s when he came over from Paris as chef to Mr and Mrs Peter Cazalet at Fairlawne in Kent. It was a hospitable house and Mr Roux found plenty of scope for his undoubted talents. He was and remains a man dedicated to his profession, a perfectionist, satisfied by nothing but the best. He has always derived great pleasure from discussing his culinary arts and skills with those who sought to learn from him.

After some years at Fairlawne he and his brother Michel, who had also learnt and practised his trade in large family houses in Paris, came together to start up a small restaurant in Lower Sloane Street, Le Gavroche. No one who knew them doubted that their business would flourish and indeed it did. The Roux brothers now devote their time to looking after their clients in five establishments, one of which has the ultimate accolade of three Michelin stars, and another has two. A remarkable success story.

What perhaps distinguishes the Roux brothers from most restaurant owner/chefs is that they were both brought up in the kitchens of private houses where they learnt what is a distinctive form of cooking. Their careers have covered all that is best in private house and restaurant cooking and this, together with their particular individuality and dedication to their work, is reflected in their book.

Soames

INTRODUCTION

Two brothers united by one ideal bordering on an obsession — to cook — dedicate this book to those who love the pleasures of the table and are prepared to seek out the good and the fine. It is a summary of all our culinary expertise — a total of 50 years of practical experience in the kitchen.

The origins of *New Classic Cuisine* go back to 1974, when we opened *The Waterside Inn*, our restaurant on the Thames at Bray. We then decided not to expand our business further. We wanted to perfect the service offered in the restaurants we already owned and to delve deeper into our culinary researches. Above all, we wanted to work on this book, which captures much of our past and a little of the future. It is compiled from years of notes and our hope is that the result will bring our readers a sense of satisfaction, which will last throughout their meals and bring a smile of pleasure to their lips.

Do we really need so many books on the same subject? Numerous cookery books have been published over the years and, recently, many of our colleagues — chefs and friends — have written volumes in which they summarize their work. Could this be a new fashion, some kind of snobbery, or does it stem from an urgent need to express their beliefs in print?

Personally, we are convinced that every lover of food should own several books written by master chefs. This is because cookery is such a wide and diverse subject, with an infinite number of subtle variations. Each great chef will reveal his own particular creativity, style and finesse in every dish he creates, while the ideas of each chef will differ and even be diametrically opposing. After all, which gourmet would spend a year eating lunches and dinners continuously in the same restaurant? The work of a great chef is the very essence of his being; no one chef's creations can be compared with those of another. For the gourmet, one of the pleasures is the fine art of seeking out and comparing the subtle differences between the styles of different masters.

Our travels, for study and pleasure, have stamped their mark on some of our work. They have taken us to all the countries of Europe, the United States, Canada, China, North Africa, the Middle East, the Caribbean, Indonesia and Australia. We have reached out to new horizons, discovered little-known spices and herbs and have tried out methods of cooking which were new to us, such as steaming, or cooking without heat, mainly using marinades.

All of this has increased our knowledge. From it, too, new principles have evolved, which have culminated in a 'blending' of the world's culinary techniques.

OUR RECIPES: Some are simple and inexpensive, while others are more refined and complicated to make. They have all been created and prepared at *Le Gavroche* and *The Waterside Inn*. We have indicated how long it should take to make each recipe, taking into account that all the ingredients and necessary equipment must be prepared and assembled in advance.

You may find that you achieve slightly different results each time you prepare a recipe. The final result depends as much on the quality of the ingredients as on the ingredients themselves, on the time and care taken to prepare the dish, on the mood of the moment and on the love lavished on a recipe during its making.

MARKETING, HERBS, SPICES, CHEESE: We would need a whole book to cover these subjects fully in all their beauty and complexity. Instead, we have limited ourselves to the basic facts. We have tried to give a brief indication of their importance and of their uses and we hope that these short chapters will help the gourmet to prepare a successful meal.

HOW TO SERVE THE DISHES: Because so many of our dishes are very delicate, we serve each element on individual plates. Some of our creations, however, are brought to the table in serving dishes made of silver, pottery or bi-metal. This is partly because an attractively presented dish is a pleasure to behold as a whole and partly because watching professionals serving at table is rather like watching a ballet. The service is the *grand finale* of the culinary spectacle. Poor waiters! Soon, we fear, they will be nothing more than fetchers and carriers to the great chefs, since more and more dishes will be assembled directly on the serving plates in the kitchen.

THE WINES: Wine is an indispensable companion to a meal. We suggest two possible wines to accompany each dish; these are our own simple choices. We are natives of Beaujolais, who devote a great deal of time to wine-tasting and who both adore wine. We have learnt more about this subject in London than anywhere else; here, we have met British wine experts who really love wine and are true connoisseurs. In addition, we augment our London experiences with visits to European vineyards.

Our own knowledge of the subject tells us that wine is a sister science to our own, so we have asked our friend, the wine expert, Michael Broadbent, to write about this complex and fascinating subject.

Finally, we must state our basic belief. Cooking is a living art. It has a past and a present and now it is looking resolutely towards the future.

ALBERT BY MICHEL

He rises at dawn and, as the hours go by, busies himself with his many and varied tasks, driven on by a never-failing supply of vitality and energy. Once or twice a week, for instance, his dawn task is to shop in the market. Not only does he regard this as a pleasure — he excels at it. Warmly greeted by our many suppliers, all anxious to offer him the very best of their produce, he normally finishes his marketing with the satisfaction of knowing that he has made one or more special and unusual purchases at a good price. These he will distribute among our chefs, at the same time giving them advice and instructions on how to prepare them to the best advantage. They are destined to be the special dishes of the day, to be enjoyed by our clientele.

Well before nine o'clock, he is back in our offices, busily opening the morning post, sorting and going through the mail. As soon as the staff arrive, he issues precise orders and instructions of the day — to be obeyed immediately, if not sooner. He generates a nervous energy all of his own.

If he has an outside appointment, he will change his clothes in the office to save time, swapping his casual shopping clothes for a formal city suit. He is often in central London before midday at a business meeting with a banker or lawyer to discuss some new project. His knowledge of law and finance and his talents as a negotiator are remarkable; it is a real pleasure to sit in on his deals. He has always had a persuasive manner. As a boy, even though I knew what a daredevil he could be, I was never able to refuse him anything — especially when he wanted to borrow anything of mine!

Yet, despite all this, he would rather be in his kitchens preparing a meal, so passionately does he love his pots and pans. There, he works with amazing speed and skill, doing in five minutes what others take 15 minutes to accomplish. He is always ready to help his young chefs, if they are behindhand, and will undertake any task, from the most complex down to the humblest. Such is his love of cooking that he is often to be found working at *Le Poulbot* or *Le Gamin*, as well as every day at *Le Gavroche*.

He spends his leisure time — when he has any — deep-sea fishing in Ireland, salmon fishing in Scotland, or perhaps in Norfolk for a few days' shooting. Walking in the fresh, pure air satisfies his deep love of nature; it also drives his inseparable labradors delirious with delight. Occasionally, he escapes to countries which are new to him. Always he returns stimulated by his experiences, revitalized and enriched with new ideas, which benefit all those around him.

His physical stamina, good nature, quick-wittedness and courage, his need for constant change and his respect for others all contribute to the affection and high regard in which he is held by our employees and circle of friends alike.

MICHEL BY ALBERT

If ever anybody's profession was decided at an early age, it was that of my brother. Looking back over the years, I think there were two factors at work.

When people asked him the inevitable question put to children — 'What are you going to do?' — his invariable answer was that he would do the same as his elder brother. As a child, too, he had a legendary appetite. He was always the first into the kitchen on coming home from school to find out what was for dinner, lifting the lids of the saucepans and sniffing eagerly — especially if our mother had cooked one of his favourite dishes, such as braised heart with carrot or chicken risotto.

During my apprenticeship in our local pastry shop, I remember him calling in to say hello on his way to school and I could see even then that he was eager to enter the profession. At the age of 14, he followed precisely in my footsteps, embarking on his own three-year-apprenticeship in pastry. These were three years of hard work, with an early morning start six days a week. On his day off, he would occupy our mother's kitchen to bake cakes to send to his big brother, then serving in the army in Algeria. Looking back, those little parcels were far more precious to me than anything money could buy — even if some of the cakes were inedible by the time they reached me — the result of three weeks' delay in the postal system, not through any fault in the cooking! They were made with undivided brotherly love, a love that has not diminished on either side over the years.

I am proud to say that I directed his first steps in the kitchen, for he came to work under me as a *commis chef* at the British Embassy in Paris. Then, as now, he was rarely satisfied with his own results, or the results of others. He is always striving for perfection. As a young man, he was never afraid to compete with older and far more experienced people in our profession.

This will to succeed has won him countless medals in France, of which the crowning glory was the title of *Meilleur Ouvrier de France* in patisserie. This title shows

what determination, skill and courage he possesses, since he won it a decade after abandoning patisserie as a full time job. His love of sugar work will inspire him to spend hours creating one perfect flower, accurate in every detail. His other love, not unconnected with food, is wine-tasting and his knowledge of wine has surprised quite a few people. Our staff and I always know when he has been to a wine-tasting, since he appears with a half-chewed cigar in his mouth and, needless to say, in a very jovial mood.

Even before we worked together at the British Embassy, both of us had decided that, one day, we would be associated in a restaurant of our own. It took us 12 years to achieve our ambition. From the embassy, Michel entered the service of Mademoiselle Cecile de Rothschild as a *commis chef*. After his return from his National Service, I was extremely proud that he was asked to return to Mademoiselle Cecile to become the youngest head chef the family had ever employed. He stayed with the household for five years and then joined me in opening *Le Gavroche*. The rest is culinary history.

Albert Roux par Paul Hogarth

CHAPTER ONE

THE CULINARY TRADITION

THE GREAT HOUSES OF FRANCE

The great private houses of France have been the cradle of learning for all the best French chefs. Having established ourselves as patissiers in pastry shops, it was natural for us to move on to become chefs in such establishments. Here, cooking is a very personal art, liberal and uncomplicated, with no set rules. It is also a joint creation, between the chef and his gourmet employer.

Life in a great house is extremely interesting for the chef, but at the same time very demanding. Just consider some of the extremes. On one day, we could be quietly preparing a simple dish, such as shepherds' pie — on the next, frenetically cooking a banquet for distinguished, aristocratic guests. Together with other staff, we also had to accompany our employers out of town and even abroad. This travelling lifestyle meant we often had to shop in strange markets and work in conditions that were frequently far from perfect. On arrival, for instance, we often had to plan lunch immediately. This would involve going to the local market, where some of the ingredients we would normally have used were simply not available. Having made the necessary substitutions, we would then have to cook on an unfamiliar stove, and it can take a day to assess a new stove. Cooking is not like painting — you cannot stand back, think, and then make alterations. Everything is in the timing; there is no potential for a play-back.

Time and money, however, are totally irrelevant to such a chef. Imagine cooking, as we did, a kilo of truffles in Champagne just as a garnish! Having been given a generous budget and carrying our *livres des depenses* (household reckoning books) to the market, our brief was simply to achieve culinary perfection. The ingredients were always of the finest quality, while the implicit assumption that we, the chefs, shared the refined and sophisticated tastes of a family like the Rothschilds meant that every dish had to bear the seal of excellence. As chefs, we were not just employees; we knew the family's tastes and what their demands would be. Our menus, always planned by chef and employer together, reflected this in their variations and permutations.

These are the reasons why it is so sad that the great houses are disappearing. No restaurant can ever take their place. Before the war, there were over 100 great houses in Paris alone, but, now, only about 20 remain. As life became more democratic, staff salaries and the burden of taxation brought this great tradition to an end. Today, the cost of employing sufficient staff to run such a household properly has become prohibitive. This is why nowadays, when people give big parties, they call in extra staff just for a day or two, instead of keeping an old-style permanent staff of butler, valets, housemaids, gardeners, caretakers, chauffeur, cooks and so on.

The staff of the houses that survive are doing much more than just a job — each one of them has an exceptional understanding of the many demands of sophisticated society. They have acquired the kind of tact and good manners that are rarely found today — all these things being absorbed from day-to-day contact with people of impeccable taste, who are not merely 'employers' in the accepted sense of the word.

Of the houses that still exist, the Rothschild households remain the finest. The exceptionally refined taste of this family is imprinted on their chefs — and there are many who bear that seal of excellence. Like others among our colleagues, we were determined to continue in this tradition when we founded our own establishment. Our lifelong ambition had been to create one of the finest restaurants in the world. In this aim, we were backed by a few of our ex-employers, led by the Cazalet family. There were 10 originally who supported us in opening *Le Gavroche* in 1967 and they brought their friends with them.

That was 17 years ago. We were then the first French chefs in Europe to introduce a high-class menu of 20 to 25 dishes. Nobody before had had the courage to do something like that. We also chose England as our base using French staff, but today 60 percent of our cooks are British.

But, above all, at both *Le Gavroche* and *The Waterside Inn*, you can feel the effects of our training in private houses. There is an attention to detail — both in the cooking and service — that you will not often find elsewhere, since, in our restaurants, our aim is to be the custodians of those great traditions that nurtured the classic chefs of the past.

WHAT MAKES A GREAT CHEF?

Many criteria can be used to judge the qualities which make a chef great. In our opinion, greatness is only attained after many years of hard work, although certain qualities are innate. Any great chef must have a thorough knowledge of classical cooking and all the basic culinary techniques, including those of patisserie. He must never hesitate to question or criticize a working method and, when necessary, openly to change or amend it for the better. Equally, we feel, it is essential to accept criticism, good or bad, from customers or colleagues in order to reach towards perfection.

As for ourselves, we believe we have worked with perseverance and determination to gain the respect of the public, the press, and, especially, our peers across Europe. Since we both reached the age of 20, we have taken part in the major gastronomic competitions, while, in addition, we have organized culinary demonstrations and lectures, as well as participating in the activities of selected professional societies.

Even though we ourselves are classed among the great chefs, we accept this classification with all humility. We never hesitate to appreciate the beauty and quality of our colleagues' work, which we always judge objectively — just as we do our own.

IN THE KITCHEN

From a single glance, we can sense immediately from the atmosphere which members of our *brigade de cuisine* might need our support, our encouragement, or to be pushed. By treating all our workers with the same consideration, we can obtain the best results in terms of their culinary standards, the speed at which they work, their physical strength and their enthusiasm. Should a crisis occur, it is important that we remain calm and composed, especially during the service!

Looking at a sauce or dish at any stage during its preparation, or at the finished product, is enough for us to judge its excellence; tasting is necessary simply to confirm this judgement. We share our culinary techniques and theories with our young staff as often as necessary and we always encourage and compliment them as appropriate.

Being a great chef is like being the conductor of a great orchestra. It is necessary to command not just respect and awe, but also love and affection. It is thus that we are continuously able to train 16-year-old apprentices, both British and French, to examination standards in the patisserie, kitchen and dining room.

NOUVELLE CUISINE

Cooking never stands still. From earliest times, this art has evolved in almost every corner of the world, but, over the centuries, the story has naturally differed from area to area and epoch to epoch. Climatic variations, abundant or meagre harvests, political stability, peace or war — all these factors have directly influenced the standard of living and purchasing power of the consumer and, indeed, whether he has had any food at all. Today, the so-called *nouvelle cuisine*, the evolutionary culinary ideas practised in some European countries, has emerged to suit the mood of the present time. This is due to various factors.

Firstly, there is the physical factor. Nowadays, even manual work demands far less physical effort than ever before. Everything is mechanized, with the introduction of automation and even robots to reduce effort. Since people use less energy, they need fewer calories, and so have come to dislike heavy food and thickened sauces. Time, too, has become more precious, especially at lunchtime. People spend less time eating their meals in order to engage in other activities.

In the world of today, new and unfamiliar foods are constantly appearing. Whether these are fruits, vegetables or spices — some exotic, others not — they were unknown in the West 10 or 20 years ago. Now, they are regularly imported from all over the world at reasonable prices, so inspiring chefs to adapt some recipes, or to create new ones. This is linked with the growth of foreign travel. As this has become widespread, not only have different civilizations and new landscapes been discovered; so, too, have new dishes, which have influenced eating habits and ideas about eating.

Chinese cooking, for instance, has deeply influenced the art of cooking in the West. The multiplicity of contrasting dishes served at one meal in a Chinese restaurant allows the chef to demonstrate all his skills. Many French restaurants, too, now serve a special menu — a *degustation* (tasting) consisting of 6 to 8 courses, served in tiny portions. This idea undoubtedly derives, at least in part, from Chinese cookery.

Finally, there is the influence of the great private houses. For many years, both of us worked as chefs in the great private houses of Europe. We have no doubts that many of our greatest chefs are still preparing dishes they found in old recipe books, written by private chefs, and have adapted such recipes to suit modern tastes. Naturally, these have been improved and perfected by some of the techniques mentioned in this book, but, above all, they have had individual artistry and personal style added. This is the secret of success.

Neither of us, therefore, believe in a *nouvelle cuisine*. Rather, we believe in the 'cuisine of today', which, like all fashions, is constantly changing, but is firmly rooted in the past.

New ideas must always be based on established techniques. Today, food is cooked quickly, colours are attractive and varied, vegetables are lightly cooked and crunchy, and every ingredient is well-defined. Sauces tend to be reduced and light in texture, with emulsions, *beurre blanc* and clear gravies predominating. What is apparent is that the classic ground rules of cooking are more important that ever before, since, in today's cuisine, there is no room for even the smallest mistake to pass unnoticed.

THE CUISINE OF TOMORROW

The cuisine of the future will have made giant strides forward — not always for the best, alas! We believe that certain factors will inevitably contribute to the decline of *haute cuisine*.

The first of these is the shorter working week. In a few years' time, the 35-hour working week will be standard throughout Europe. No cook working a mere 7 hours a day could possibly attend to kitchen basics as well as cook and serve a meal, in so short a time. The kitchens of the great restaurants will therefore have to adapt and change their working methods. There would be no point in staggering working hours and employing two sets of kitchen staff — the personal touch would be lost and so all hope of producing truly great cuisine.

The character of food will change as well. As far as fruit and vegetables are concerned, the ever-increasing use of fertilizers and bio-chemical additives create produce that is attractive in colour and of great size. Unfortunately, this will taste more and more insipid and have less and less nutritional value. Organically grown and naturally harvested fresh fruit and vegetables will become rarer and less commercially viable. Such produce will be grown only by people who love good, fresh food.

In dairy products, too, the trend towards pasteurization, homogenization, dehydration, sterilization, refrigeration and freezing of milk, butter, cheese and their by-products will continue. These processes are already encouraged by European governments, not only for reasons of health and hygiene, but also because they help to rationalize production.

Shorter working hours will mean more leisure time for hobbies, travel, sport, the arts and so on, but, paradoxically, we believe that less will be spent on food. People will patronize only cheap restaurants, serving fast food, snack bars and take-away cafés and these will proliferate.

So, in 20 years' time, the quality of an *haute cuisine* meal, whether prepared at home or eaten in a restaurant, will be quite different from the meals we expect today. The best restaurants, as far as food is concerned, will be family-owned and run. On average, they will seat only 40 diners, so that the *patron* can offer a personal service and be in total control. Some large hotels all over the world will continue to run internationally-renowned restaurants for reasons of prestige, even though they may make a loss.

Let us hope, at least, that eating in the year 2000 and beyond will still be a pleasure, rather than just a necessary means of absorbing protein. Let us pray that 'progress' will not make every meal identical, nor stamp out the pleasures of eating.

CHAPTER TWO

WINE

Food and wine are natural companions and have been so throughout history. However, it is the French we have to thank for elevating both the preparation of food and the making of wine into an art form. Beautiful dishes and fine wine are among the hallmarks of civilization. It is always pleasant to try them out — and blissful when the combination of food, wine and company is in perfect harmony.

The matching and pairing of food and wine is always a challenge. As a start, let me define four potential approaches. The aim should be to complement the finest cooking with the finest wine. Secondly, when faced with cuisine of the highest order — rich, yet delicate, and complex, yet subtle — you might decide to choose relatively straightforward wines as a respectfully muted complement to the food. Thirdly and conversely, when faced with an array of magnificent and perhaps rare wines, it might be better for the food to be low-keyed and unobtrusive. Finally, you could abandon all rules and just eat and drink copiously. This last approach should be ruled out, of course. Although it is occasionally good to be hungry, it is not sensible to drink to excess — too much alcohol and consequent acidity is bad for you, your head and your liver.

Speaking personally, my approach differs according to circumstance. At home, when I plan to serve a range of really interesting wines — especially some old and rare ones — the meal is planned so that the food will accompany, but not distract or detract from, the wines. These must be the main focus of attention, so, in relation to the wine, the food should be like a muted piano accompaniment to a *lieder* singer.

If, on the other hand, I am in some temple of gastronomy, the roles are reversed. Here, the central pleasure is the level of cooking. This can be as rare as the rarest wine and thus requires concentration to fully savour its delicacy and delight. Therefore, the wine should be appropriately low-keyed — good enough to do justice to the meal, but not dominant enough to steal the limelight.

SELECTION AND APPROACH

No matter what the price range, certain basic principles should be followed when selecting wine to proceed, accompany and follow a meal. The wines should not only be appropriate for the occasion, the menu and for the guests — they should not step on each other's toes. In other words, they should progress in the same logical way as

Left to right: *Bread (page 42); Pain aux noix (page 44); Pain de Mie (page 43).*

the various courses.

Take red wine, for instance. It is normal in wine circles to precede a really mature vintage — the star wine of the evening — with a younger, less fine wine of the same type. The latter prepares the nose and palate for the former, enabling the older wine to reveal its hidden depths and harmony more emphatically. Generally, however, light and dry wines should precede heavier and sweeter ones. A powerful wine with an assertive flavour is likely to make a fine, delicate wine taste thin and feeble, if this progression is reversed. Establishing the right contrast between wines is just as important as with food. At a multi-course banquet, for instance, a cool sorbet not only helps the palate to recuperate and change gear, as it were, so that it can do justice to a further succession of rich dishes — it also enables the host to switch the style of wine as well.

THE APERITIF

It is common knowledge that hard liquor dulls both palate and brain. If the aim is to enjoy a serious meal, with fine wine and food, then gin, whisky, vodka and their mixers should be kept out of sight. For myself, I have no doubt that the most perfect of all pre-dinner drinks is Champagne — the real thing, not a napkin-shrouded, gold foil necked, lesser version. In my drinking career, I have never come across a bottle of sparkling wine with the true character, finesse and length of flavour of a genuine Champagne.

There are basically three choices of Champagne — non-vintage, vintage and de luxe. For my money, I prefer an 8 to 12-year-old true vintage as a general drink, though an old Champagne — a 1955, 1959, or 1961, say — is even better. Champagne of this age is turning a golden colour, developing a honeyed bouquet and losing its aggressive young bubbles; it is becoming more of a wine, but with an uplift on the palate given to it by a more subtle sparkle. My favourite vintage *marques* are Bollinger, Pol Roger, Roederer and Krug.

Non-vintage Champagnes, particularly those with a year or so of 'landing age', can be extremely good. You can give Champagne this 'landing age' yourself by simply keeping it in your own cellar. Bollinger and Roederer are always reliably good. As far as de luxe Champagnes are concerned, the first thing to realize is that, whatever the *marque*, they will be expensive. I think de luxe Champagnes, with their fancy bottles and fancy prices, are mainly for the conspicuously wealthy, or for those who wish to appear so. The brand leader is undoubtedly Dom Pérignon, though I personally find its style too hard and austere. My favourite is Cristal Brut, though the vintages do vary. For me, the 1966 Cristal epitomizes Champagne at its most elegant and sublime.

Of the champagne-style wines which are not true Champagnes, I think the best are produced in the Loire. Schramsberg, the 'Krug' of the Napa Valley in California, is also excellent, as it should be for the price, but it is rarely given time to age. As far as the rest of the world's vast out-pouring of sparkling wine is concerned, I think they are best served mixed with orange juice as a poor man's Buck's Fizz. This, incidentally, is another of my favourite aperitifs.

The other classic aperitif is sherry. This should be dry and of high quality. Because of over-production and severe competition, the quality of sherry as a whole has, in my opinion, deteriorated but, paradoxically, the net result of this is that the best sherry has never been better value for money. The old-established family firms have scarcely wavered in quality, so my choice would be the two familiar names, Tio Pepe and La Ina. In common with other *fino* sherries, these should be bought when needed, not cellared or given bottle age. That fresh tangy smell and taste is vital. Serve them chilled.

White wines also make excellent aperitifs, especially on warm summer evenings. Almost any dry or dryish white wine, served chilled, can fulfil this function, though, personally, I think wines with a 'fat' flavour and body, a great white Burgundy, say, or a fine Californian Chardonnay, are best with a meal.

Light whites — wines low in alcohol and light in style, with refreshing acidity — are the best choice. Vinho Verde, from northern Portugal, is light, *pétillant* and inexpensive, but, for me, somewhat thin and lacking in savour. A young Moselle would probably be my favourite. German quality wines usually have a touch of residual sugar to balance their refreshing acidity and a low alcohol content. They are excellent value. However, the really cheap sugar-and-water German wines should be avoided. Vintages are important; keep an eye out for the lovely 1976s.

Other alternatives are Muscadet, Chablis and those twins from the upper Loire, Sancerre and Pouilly Blanc Fumé, though, personally, I prefer all of these with shellfish. The fruity, but pleasantly acidic, mid-Loire wines are under-appreciated; the Savennières and dry Vouvrays can be excellent.

In the absence of Champagne or the finest dry sherry, however, my favourite aperitif before a not-too-serious meal is a *Kir*, or vin blanc cassis. The essential ingredients are a good quality, fresh Cassis from Burgundy and a young, dry, acidic white wine, such as Bourgogne Aligoté, or a lesser Chablis. For a drink with a little more of an uplift, try a *Kir royale*, in which Champagne is substituted for the white wine. Personally, though, for the latter I would only use a decent sparkling wine. But, most essentially, serve it very cold.

FIRST COURSES AND FISH

There is no doubt that the old conventional notions are safe and reliable — white wine with fish, red wine with meat. However, there are exceptions and great fun can be had by trying some exotic mixtures.

With shellfish of all types, select a bone dry white wine. The classics are Muscadet, usually very reliable if unexciting, and Chablis. Do not neglect the fruity, tangy, acidic Sancerre and Pouilly Blanc Fumé. Smoked salmon, though, is incredibly difficult to match, since, if the wine is too light, its flavour is overpowered. Possibly a well-chilled Gewürztraminer stands up to this the best, though, as with other smoked fish, I think it a good idea to break rules and drink an ice-cold Dutch gin or Swedish schnapps, if the meal is not a great gourmet occasion.

With the lighter types of fish, try a dry white wine, with perhaps a little more body and less obvious acidity. A good white Burgundy immediately springs to mind, the choice ranging from the light, dry wines of the Mâconnais — Pouilly-Fuissé, Pouilly-Vinzelles and Saint-Véran — to the little-known, but good and not too expensive Montagny and Givry. Côte de Beaune whites, especially the classic Puligny-Montrachets and Meursaults, are at the top end of the scale. As alternatives, drink a good Alsace Riesling, a Grand Cru Chablis, or, for a completely different contrast, try sherry.

With the heavier types of fish, such as turbot, I suggest a mature white, good quality Burgundy — the 1978 vintage is one to look out for — or perhaps a good white

Rhône, an Hermitage blanc, or the rarer and more expensive Condrieu and Château Grillet. I find the last varies in style from vintage to vintage.

With soup, it all depends on personal taste. With fish soup, a dry *fino* sherry is excellent, with 'meatier' soup, amontillado sherry or dryish madeira; but no soup goes with white wine. With all meat or game pâtés, red wine is best. The richer and more countrified the pâté, the heavier the wine. A hefty terrine can be accompanied by a Côte Rôtie, for instance, though not if more delicate reds are to follow. The only exception is the smoothest, creamiest, richest pâté de foie gras, for which the perfect accompaniment is Sauternes, preferably of a lighter vintage. This, however, makes the next wine difficult to plan.

Asparagus, artichokes and avocados in whatever guise are extremely difficult to match with wine. Do not sacrifice a fine white Burgundy, but, if you must drink wine with them, choose a flavoury and somewhat acidic wine. I discovered only recently that a dryish sherry with a good flavour, such as La Ina, goes well with asparagus.

CHICKEN, POULTRY AND VEAL

Lighter poultry dishes and veal go well with almost any dry to medium dry white wine, or a light red. My specific choices would be a white Burgundy, white Rhône, an Alsace Riesling, or a Gewürztraminer, though the unusual, lightly spicy style of the latter is an acquired taste. If you favour the exotic, try an Alsace Muscat — it has a grapy aroma and flavour, but is often surprisingly dry.

Foremost among the light reds is a youngish, not too grand claret, such as a 1976 Château de Sales. A good quality Beaujolais Villages would also fill the bill, though too many, I fear, are pale, pink and a trifle tinny. If you are looking for originality, try a Loire red, a Chinon or Bourgueil, though, unless the vintage is a good one, these can be very tart.

MEAT

Here, the greatest range of wines, particularly fine wines, come into their own, the combinations being almost limitless. If you decide to play safe, claret, the English term for red Bordeaux, is the most versatile. Fine claret is the perfect accompaniment for many reasons: it has variety, subtlety, is hearteningly reliable in quality and, above all, possesses the perfect weight and balance to accompany food. For me, the perfect accompaniment for a fine claret is a lightly grilled, very pink lamb cutlet.

The richer the sauces and the heavier the meat, the bigger the wine. With beef, select one of the bigger Bordeaux vintages, or a good Burgundy from the Côte de Beaune, or Côte de Nuits. Burgundy is easy to drink, but hard to choose. At the lower end of the price scale, the softer, slightly sweeter, often smoother style can be immediately agreeable. However, a true Burgundy, a fine wine with pure *pinot* grape character and style, is completely different. Romanée-Conti and La Tâche are among the best, particularly when fully mature. The best of the older vintages are 1952, 1953, 1955, 1959, 1962 and 1966. Of the more recent vintages, the 1971 and 1972 are good, the 1976 hard, and the 1978 excellent, but still too young. Other good red Burgundies include the domaines of Clair-Daü, Drouhin-Laroze, the Nuits St Georges of Henri Gouges, the Chambertins of Rousseau (but avoid the 1977s), the Domaine Dujac and, perhaps the greatest, the Musigny and

Bonnes Mares of de Vogüé. Of the shippers and merchants, I personally recommend Joseph Drouhin, Louis Latour, Jadot and the domaines owned by Bouchard Père.

Really rich and heavy meat dishes, such as oxtail and heavier game, can be accompanied by big rich Burgundies, but above all, by fine classic Rhône wines. The reds of the Rhône tend to be taken for granted, and even the finest are not over-priced. It is strangely difficult to find a really good Châteauneuf-du-Pape; the best I have ever come across has been from the estate of Château Rayas. The outstanding shipper of Hermitage and Côte Rôtie is Paul Jaboulet Aîné. It is difficult to obtain old vintages, but they are worth looking out for.

SWEETS AND PUDDINGS

This is the most difficult of all food and wine relationships. With tarts, flans and sweet dishes, the French tend to serve Champagne. It certainly freshens the palate, but I personally think it spoils the Champagne. If you really want a fizzy wine, try an ice cold Asti Spumante. Its grapiness, semi-sweetness and sparkling uplift can provide a surprisingly attractive match. The most common choice is, not unnaturally, a Sauternes. The sweetness of the wine offsets the sugar element of the food, but the result is that the dessert's sweetness tends to dominate, turning a lovely rich wine into something which then appears dry and rather acidic. Oddly enough, meringues tend to go well with these sweet wines. Another exception is *crème brûlée*, as the bouquet of an old Sauternes is uncannily similar.

In my opinion, the great German sweet wines should be drunk on their own, as should Sauternes. Instead, try pairing off the dessert with Tokay Aszu-Escencia or Coteaux du Layon.

CHEESES

In theory, port goes with Stilton and red wine with all other cheeses. In practice, however, the richer, riper and runnier French cheeses will overpower many red wines and totally destroy the finest Burgundy. Claret and Burgundy are well suited to the more austere English cheeses, the most perfect combination being a full mature farmhouse cheddar with a fairly robust, but fine, claret, such as a Montrose 1970. With Brie and Camembert, I prefer a tougher young Rhône wine, such as a 1979 Côte Rôtie. Just occasionally, a really ripe brie and an overripe old claret go well together. A great white Burgundy suits a ripe camembert, while, as an alternative to port, try a late-harvest Zinfandel from the Napa Valley.

The final problem is whether to serve the cheese before or after the dessert. If you intend to serve a dessert wine, have the cheese and red wine first. If you are serving Stilton and port, this must come last.

DESSERT WINES

Old tawny port and nuts — brazils and cob-nuts — make a perfect combination. Genuine old tawnies, once undervalued and underpriced, are now coming into their own. These are either described as 'old tawny', or '10-' and '20-year-old'. One of the finest, but difficult to find, is Sandeman's 20-year-old. Delaforce and Croft produce gòod old tawnies, Taylor and Noval market excellent 10-year-olds.

Of the great classic fortified dessert wines, Madeira and the old sweet sherries have suffered a fall from grace. Only Bual and Malmsey madeira qualify as dessert wines and, at their best — preferably as old vintage and old *soleras* — they are a magnificent revelation. Really fine old dessert sherries are surprisingly scarce, too, though one or two rich old *olorosos* are available.

For something completely different, try Tokay Aszu-Escencia. This is not only delicious, but is reputed to have therapeutic — and, according to some, aphrodisiac — qualities. The 1964 vintage is still to be found, though at higher and higher prices. It is now fully mature and excellent.

LIQUEURS AND DIGESTIFS

Although spirits before a meal are frowned upon by purists, afterwards they become a completely different matter. The classic after dinner spirit is, of course, Cognac. It is a great pity that commercial interests, hand-in-hand with the French government, have effectively killed off vintage Cognac, though older brandies can still be bought regularly at auction and some old landed brandies are still available. These are brandies of a given vintage, which are shipped within three years and matured in cask.

THE TEMPERATURE OF WINE

When serving any wine, temperature is of considerable importance. Over-chilling, or serving too warm, can spoil a wine.

Champagne and sparkling wine should be served cold and kept chilled while serving. Dry, light wines should be served cool and kept cool. However, the finest white Burgundy, in my opinion, should be served approaching room temperature.

The three red wines which are best served cool are Beaujolais and the two Loire reds — Chinon and Bourgueil. Claret should be served at room temperature, but never heat it by putting a bottle in warm water or standing it in front of a fire. I judge the correctness of temperature by checking that there is little or no interchange of heat between my hand and the bottle. Burgundy can be served more or less directly from the cellar. Its temperature should be cooler than that of claret, as should the temperature of Rhône wines.

Dessert wines, such as Sauternes, Coteaux du Layon, and German wines of Beerenauslese and Trockenbeerenauslese quality, should be served cool.

The temperature of fortified wines follows the colours of the grape. Sherry is essentially a white wine and should be served cold, particularly the *finos* and *manzanillas*. Sercial madeira is chilled, while Verdelho, Bual and Malmsey are best at room temperature. White port should be chilled, but vintage should be at room temperature.

Brandies are warmed by cupping the glass in the hand. 'White' liqueurs, such as kümmel and kirsch, should be served cool, or even chilled. Cointreau is infinitely better, fruitier and has more flavour if served 'on the rocks'.

Ice buckets, though traditional, are messy and tend to over-chill wine. It is far preferable to use a *Vinicool* — an open-topped transparent-sided thermos flask. Cool your wine in a refrigerator to the right temperature and then put it in the *Vinicool*.

The vintage year and bottling dates are normally stated on the label. Having said this, the top de luxe *marques* can be excellent.

Armagnac is very fashionable in many good restaurants in France for obvious reasons. It is not dominated by a handful of huge firms. Small growers and distillers, who have not yet succumbed to the narrow dictates of commercialism, abound. Vintage armagnac is thus the rule rather than the exception. A few are somewhat coarse but the best are rich and full of character.

Historically, the French and Dutch were the liqueur makers *par excellence*, taking full advantage of the exotic fruit, sugar and rums all grown and made in their West Indies colonies. Crème de Noyau, from Martinique, for instance, used to be very popular a century ago, but, now, in common with other *crème* or sweet liqueurs, it is out of fashion, having been replaced by Drambuie, Benedictine and the like. Of the classic liqueurs, my favourites are Grand Marnier, kümmel, some of the 'dry' colourless liqueurs, such as Poire Williamine and kirsch, but only at its best and most refined.

Among the less common, but interesting, digestifs are Marc de Bourgogne and Fine de Bourgogne, the first being a distillation of the *marc*, or grape skins and residue, the second from wine. Like Calvados, (distilled from apples), these, however, are something of an acquired taste and the poor ones taste like rubber. Stick to the finest and oldest.

DECANTING WINE

Dry white wines are not generally decanted, since, firstly, they do not have a sediment and, secondly, decanting would warm them up too quickly. However, claret, particularly fine vintage claret, should be decanted. By decanting carefully, the sediment can be left in the bottom of the bottle and the wine served clear and bright. The act of decanting also aerates the wine, though, having taken part in blind tastings to prove the point, the effect is barely noticeable.

In my experience, it is in the glass that red wine develops.

If Burgundy is old and sedimented, it should either be decanted, or poured straight off into large glasses. A decanting cradle is an entertaining and effective way of dealing with the problem.

Of the fortified wines, only very old vintage madeira and vintage port should be decanted. In the case of port, this leaves behind the heavy sediment which has formed.

NEW WORLD WINES

This chapter has concentrated on describing traditional wines, but, thanks to the amazing strides made in viniculture, particularly in California, Australia and South Africa, many native wines of the same style can be substituted for the ones mentioned here. All these areas make fine dry whites, for example. Rieslings can be excellent, while Chardonnays often beat even the fine white Burgundies at their own game. Sweet wines are less successful on the whole, but superb dry sherry-style wine is a speciality of South Africa and South Australia.

Most port-style wines do not bear any resemblance to the real thing, though Hardy's and Chambers' — both Australian — are the nearest.

CHAPTER THREE

PLANNING YOUR MEAL

SHOPPING FOR FOOD

The prime factor in planning your menu must always be the choice of fresh foods available. Naturally, you need to have some basic theme in mind, but it will be your eyes and ears, your sense of smell and touch — and an element of experience too — which will finally decide your choice of menu as you do your marketing.

Always remember that no one shopkeeper, whatever his reputation, could possibly stock a complete selection of top-quality products, except at perhaps prohibitive prices. So you must wander from shop to shop before making your final choice. Never do this in a hurry; you are buying the very foundation of the meal and its success depends upon your purchases. Before you buy anything, have a quick look round to see what is on offer.

Always look for fresh foods in season, or for *primeurs* — those tiny, early season vegetables — then you can be sure of getting the best quality, even though the price may be high. Never be tempted to buy 'extras' you do not need. Remember that products like caviar, foie gras or truffles must always be of the finest quality and never, ever replaced by *ersatz* imitations. Either use an extravagant ingredient lavishly or do not use it at all.

If a recipe calls for a secondary ingredient which you have not been able to buy, use a similar ingredient instead and make whatever minor modifications you think are necessary for the recipe to work successfully. It is not easy to be creative, but, with a little flair and imagination, you can change a recipe here and there and still produce an excellent result.

The success of a meal also depends, of course, on harmony — on the colour of the sauces, the variety of textures in the different dishes and on simplicity — in a word, on *balance*. One final and equally important word of advice; choose your wines with care and serve them at the correct temperature. They must marry well with the food, not be ill-matched partners.

HOW TO CHOOSE MEAT AND FISH FOR QUALITY AND FRESHNESS

BEEF: The meat must be a deep red colour, finely grained, firm to the touch and marbled with fat in some places. Firm, white or slightly creamy-coloured fat indicates that the animal is young.

LAMB: Pale pink, finely grained flesh indicates a young animal; if it is darker and reddish-brown, the meat is mutton. As with beef, the fat should vary in colour from white to cream. The leg should be short and compact and have a covering of fat.

VEAL: The flesh should be white or very pale pink and soft to the touch, but not flabby; it should be moist, but not 'weeping'. The bones must be pinkish-white and fairly flexible to the touch.

PORK: The finely-grained flesh is tinged with pink and lightly marbled with fat, which is rather moist to the touch. There should be a thin layer of fat between the flesh and the skin, which must be thin, smooth and elastic.

POULTRY AND GAME: The skin should be smooth and not grainy; the beak and pinions should feel soft and 'give' when pressed with the fingers. The birds should have big feet and fat knees. If the tips of the large wing feathers of pheasant and partridge are pointed, that indicates a young bird. When choosing poultry or game, make sure that the spurs are rounded and the tip of the breastbone is flexible.

FISH: The eyes should be bulging and full of life; in other words, they should transfix you! The gills should be hard to open and the insides should have a good clear colour, ranging from pink to red. The fish should be stiff, as though suffering from a momentary paralysis; the skin must be taut and the flesh firm. They should give off a salty tang of fresh seaweed.

SHELLFISH: They must never be open when you buy them. When tightly closed and full of sea water, they feel heavy and smell of the sea.

CRUSTACEANS: They must be alive, vigorous, heavy and ready to run, swim or pinch or, better still, to escape back to their natural element — the rocks and the sea.

BASIC KITCHEN EQUIPMENT

This is a very comprehensive list. Although it might not be adequate for a professional restaurateur, it will certainly meet all the needs of a domestic kitchen. You can buy equipment according to how simple or complicated your cooking is going to be. For instance, there is no point in buying casseroles or Dutch ovens if you never braise, sauté or stew.

It never pays to buy cheap utensils. They wear out quickly or break and do not give the desired results. Finally, do resist those gadgets which are sold on street corners; they look interesting because they are new and different, but they tend to end up at the bottom of a drawer after being used only once.

SMALL ITEMS

2 pastry brushes (1 small, 1 medium)	1 lemon squeezer
4 to 6 wooden spatulas of different sizes, made of boxwood or beech	1 nutmeg grater

1 fish slice	1 olive stoner
1 large pepper mill	1 apple corer
1 salt grinder	1 funnel
1 trussing needle and kitchen string	1 corkscrew
1 carving board	1 zester
1 small chopping board	

KNIVES, PREFERABLY STEEL

1 large chopping knife	1 palette knife with a supple blade
1 sharpening steel or knife-sharpener	1 boning knife
1 medium knife, 20-25cm (8½-9½in)	1 meat cleaver
1 knife for filleting fish, with a supple blade	1 cannelizing knife
1 ham slicer, with a supple blade	1 larding knife
1 or 2 small paring knives	1 cooking fork
1 potato peeler	1 pair poultry shears

SMALL STAINLESS STEEL ITEMS

4 wire whisks, 20cm (8in), 25cm (10in), 30cm (12in) and 35cm (14in)	2 skimming ladles, 8cm (3in) and 10cm (5in) diameter
4 ladles, 6cm (2½in), 8cm (3in), 10cm (4in) and 12cm (5in) diameter	1 mandoline
1 cooking spoon	1 cheese grater
1 slotted spoon	

POTS AND PANS

It is essential to have a good variety of sizes of cookware, so that the pan you choose will be the right size for the dish you are cooking. All the pans should have lids and they should preferably be made of copper or heavy stainless steel. The food should fit comfortably on the cooking surface; if there is not enough space, it will not brown or cook evenly and if there is too much, it may brown too quickly and burn on the outside before the inside is properly cooked.

2 or 3 sauté pans (*sautoirs*) of various sizes, 20cm (8in) minimum, 40cm (16in) maximum	2 or 3 saucepans (*russes*) of various sizes, 15cm (6in) minimum, 25cm (10in) maximum
2 or 3 shallow pans (*sauteuses*) of various sizes, 20cm (8in) minimum, 35cm (14in) maximum	1 or 2 Dutch ovens with lids, from 30cm (12in) to 50cm (20in) maximum diameter

1 steamer, about 30cm (12in) diameter

1 or 2 enamelled or cast iron casseroles with lids, round or oval, in different sizes

1 oval fish pan, cast iron or heavy stainless steel, at least 30cm (12in) long

1 round grill pan, about 30cm (12in) diameter

1 or 2 pancake pans, cast iron or heavy stainless steel

2 or 3 frying pans of various sizes, minimum 20cm (8in), maximum 35cm (14in), cast iron or heavy stainless steel

3 or 4 roasting pans of various sizes, oval and rectangular, depending on your requirements and on the size of your oven, but not less than 15cm (6in) long

1 or 2 black metal flan tins, about 25cm (10in) diameter

4 oblong terrine dishes in cast iron or ovenproof porcelain

2 black metal, rectangular baking trays to suit the size of your oven

2 oval terrine dishes in cast iron or ovenproof porcelain

2 gratin dishes in cast iron or ovenproof porcelain

PASTRY-MAKING AND GENERAL EQUIPMENT

1 marble pastry slab, minimum size 75cm x 75cm (30in square)

kitchen scales weighing up to at least 5kg (11lb)

1 vegetable mill

1 mincer, hand or electric

1 blender or food processor

1 domestic ice-cream maker

1 set of plain round pastry cutters

1 set of fluted round pastry cutters

1 or 2 plastic forcing bags

1 set of mixed nozzels, plain and decorative

1 boxwood rolling pin

1 wooden-handled balloon whisk

1 rectangular pastry rack

1 round pastry rack

8 round dishes made of stoneware, glass or stainless steel, in various sizes

1 stainless steel or glass measuring jug

1 set of stainless steel skewers

1 very fine sieve

1 coarse sieve

1 conical wire sieve (*chinois*)

1 fine strainer

2 scoops or wooden-handled rubber scrapers

USEFUL HINTS

EGGS

HARD-BOILED EGGS: These are easy to peel if you tap them lightly under cold water as soon as they are cooked.

The water breaks the seal between the shell and the egg. You do not need an egg timer to cook soft-boiled eggs. Put them in a pan and cover with cold water. Set over high heat and bring to the boil. When the water boils, count to 10 and serve the eggs immediately — you will have 3-minute boiled eggs. Egg shells are very porous, so be careful never to store eggs near any foods which have a very strong smell, whether pleasant or unpleasant, (for example, truffles, melon and onions) as the eggs will absorb the odour. POACHED EGGS: Use very fresh, cold eggs for poaching. They will hold their shape better. FROZEN EGG WHITES: These will give a better result than unfrozen ones when beating in soufflés.

FISH AND SHELLFISH

Whole poached fish, such as pike and salmon, will absorb only as much salt as they need, so do not hesitate to salt a court bouillon lavishly.

TENCH AND CARP: If they are alive, plunge them into boiling water for a few seconds to suffocate them, then dip into cold water before preparing them for cooking. The livers of fish such as monkfish or red mullet may be served as an excellent and original hors d'oeuvre; they must be very fresh. CRAYFISH: If they are farmed, it is best to remove the intestines immediately after cooking, while the crayfish are still hot. If they come from a river, remove the intestines before cooking.

Keep all shellfish in a cool place after cooking, but not in the refrigerator, which will spoil their savour and taste.

FISH: Small pieces of skinned, poached fish are cooked when the flesh becomes very shiny and almost pearlized. To cut large raw fish into steaks, never saw at the fish but slice down sharply to make a clean cut. SCALLOPS: Soak in iced water for several hours before using; they will puff up and become firm. Before cooking the orange-coloured corals, prick them with a needle to prevent them from bursting during cooking. TO REMOVE THE INTESTINES FROM CRAYFISH: Pinch the shelled tails and twist and pull out. TO KILL LIVE LOBSTERS: Plunge a trussing needle deep into the head between the eyes before cooking.

GAME AND POULTRY

Never hang game for too long or allow it to become too 'high'. It will lose its savour and may taste bitter or unpleasantly pungent.

WOODCOCK: Since the bird excretes each time it flies, there is no point in drawing (cleaning) it. The intestines are clean and give the sauce that special taste which connoisseurs of game love. Do not use the gizzard, however. POULTRY: Always season the inside of poultry with a little salt and pepper; this will ensure that the seasoning is more evenly distributed. Once poultry is cooked, always turn it onto its breast until ready to serve; the drops of juice from inside the carcass will run into the breast meat and make it more succulent. Uncooked poultry is easier to cut and bone if it is very cold.

MEAT

MEAT: We recommend that you fry meat in clarified butter. This will prevent little black particles from forming and sticking to the meat; they may then find their way into the gravy or sauce. Never prick meat with a fork while it is cooking; some of the blood and vital juices will be lost. Roast meat should be salted halfway through cooking, braised meat just before cooking and grilled meats after cooking. Leave large joints of meat, such as rib of beef or leg of lamb to stand for 30 minutes before serving, covered with foil. They will be more evenly cooked, the meat will be more tender and less blood will run out when you carve the joint. Raw meat is easier to work with — when boning, cutting and so on — if it is very cold.

VEGETABLES

POTATOES: It is best to use floury potatoes, such as red Desirée or King Edwards for puréeing. For salads, use small, new potatoes and mix them with the vinaigrette while they are still warm. Serve potatoes as soon as they are cooked, scented with sprigs of chervil. A quarter of a lemon in the cooking water will prevent boiled potatoes from breaking up.

ASPARAGUS: Snap off the stalks at the point where they break easily. Never use a knife unless you want to even up a bundle before cooking. Asparagus is fresh when it snaps easily and is smooth and shiny. The tips should be narrower than the stalks.

ARTICHOKES: The same rules apply as for asparagus, but use a knife to even up the hearts.

LEEKS: If they are too large, the flavour is often too strong and may be bitter. Discard the greenest parts, or use them to make stock.

WILD MUSHROOMS: These tend to lose some of their delicacy and flavour after rain, so always choose very dry mushrooms. Peel or wipe them, or brush off the dirt, but do not wash them. If you *must* wash them, do not leave them to soak.

RADISHES: Do not hesitate to leave on and eat a few of the leaves, which are an excellent aid to digestion.

GREEN VEGETABLES (PEAS, BEANS, ETC): Sort them according to their size after trimming. Cook separately to ensure even cooking.

ALL VEGETABLES: With a little manual dexterity and a sharp knife, you can make vegetable 'flowers' to decorate the dishes you have prepared. Use carrots, potatoes, turnips, beetroot, leeks, tomatoes, onions, radishes etc.

SORREL: It will be much easier to snip if you roll up 2 or 3 leaves together like a cigar before snipping.

ONIONS: These will not make your eyes water if you peel them under running water.

CHESTNUTS AND SWEET CHESTNUTS: These are easier to skin if you slit the skin lightly with the point of a knife and then plunge them into boiling oil until the skin splits; alternatively, place the chestnuts in a very hot oven, about ($260\,°C/525\,°F/$ Gas 11) — this will have the same effect.

TO SKIN SWEET PEPPERS: Smear the peppers with oil and place in a very hot oven or under a hot grill, turning them until the skins blister and the peppers are lightly coloured on all sides. Hold under cold running water and rub lightly with your hands to remove the skins.

TO PEEL TOMATOES, PEACHES ETC: Plunge the fruit into boiling water for a few seconds, then into cold water. The skins will then slide off easily.

HERBS

CHOPPED GARLIC: This can be kept in oil for up to 2 weeks in the refrigerator. It will be more digestible if you remove the sprouting part.
CHOPPED SHALLOTS: These last for several days in the refrigerator if covered with dry white wine.
TARRAGON AND CHIVES: These should be snipped, not chopped, as chopping spoils the flavour and appearance.
PARSLEY: There are two types — single and curly. Single parsley may be used in sprigs or snipped. Curly parsley must be chopped, but it is left whole for frying as a garnish.

Dried herbs are much stronger than fresh ones so use them with discretion; 1 tbls of dried dill, for example, is equivalent to ½ cup of fresh dill. The flavour of dried herbs will vary in strength, depending on their age and whether they are home-dried or shop-bought, so use them to taste.

FRUIT AND NUTS

WALNUTS, PISTACHIOS AND ALMONDS: If you skin them and leave to soak in cold milk, they will taste as good as if they were fresh.
BANANAS: Like pears, they go black if kept in the refrigerator. Ideally, they should be stored in a cool, dark and airy place such as a basement or larder.
CITRUS FRUITS: Dry a few pieces of orange, lemon or tangerine peel; they add a delicious aroma to such dishes as Goulash and fruit compôtes. Oranges stuck with cloves will keep flies away. Put one near the cheeseboard or have one to hand while preparing fresh fish.
MELONS: They should feel heavy in the hand, indicating good quality. When a melon is ripe, the flesh around the stem should 'give' slightly when pressed and you should be able to pull away the stem.

PASTRY AND PATISSERIE

MAXIMUM KNEADING TIME FOR LEAVENED DOUGH AND PASTRY: This is when all the ingredients have been incorporated and kneaded together for some time. The bulk of the dough should come away from the sides of the kneading trough or the bowl of an electric mixer. The protein structure will have absorbed all the moisture and the dough will be very elastic.
KEEPING UNCOOKED DOUGH: Before putting it in the refrigerator, wrap the dough in a sheet of polythene or cling film to prevent it from drying out and forming a crust.
REFRIGERATING PUFF PASTRY: You must take puff pastry out of the refrigerator and leave it to come to room temperature for between 10 and 15 minutes before turning it so the fat has time to soften. If you do this, the fat will not break up when you turn the pastry and the pastry will be perfectly risen when baked.
PUFF PASTRY: When you have rolled it out, place it on a baking sheet dampened with water. This will prevent the pastry from moving about when you glaze it; it will also stop it from shrinking and spoiling its shape during baking.
LEAVENING YEAST-BASED DOUGH: When you are kneading dough in a warm room, the liquid ingredients (eggs, milk or water) should be cold,

so chill them in the refrigerator beforehand. The temperature of the dough after kneading should never exceed 24°C (75°F). After fermenting in a warm place, it is best to leave yeast-based doughs (croissants, brioches, Viennese pastries etc) to 'relax' at room temperature for 15 minutes before baking, so that they will puff up as much as possible during cooking.

HOW TO BEAT EGG WHITES: To obtain perfect, stiffly beaten egg whites, use only immaculately clean utensils, free from any trace of grease or fat; rinse them in cold water and dry thoroughly before using. Make sure that there is no trace of yolk in the whites. If they are very fresh, add a pinch of salt to break them down. Start by beating the whites at medium speed to make them frothy and absorb as much air as possible, then increase the speed to firm them up.

When flecks of beaten egg appear at the edges of the bowl, add a little sugar to prevent the whites from becoming grainy. They will then be firmer, which will make them easier to mix and handle. In other words, use salt for savoury and sugar for sweet soufflés. Frozen egg whites give the best results in making soufflés.

DURABLE GLAZES FOR PUFF PASTRY: (eg apple turnovers, Pithiviers, *galettes, dartois* bands etc.) Sprinkle the pastry with icing sugar at the end of cooking and put into a hot oven for a few seconds to obtain a varnish-like glaze. If you use a sugar syrup to glaze, use the pastry within a few hours, as the sugar will recrystallize and the glaze will become dull and pale.

TO COOK SUGAR: It is very important to dissolve the sugar completely in water without stirring before cooking, otherwise it may form lumps, caramelize or become grainy.

CONFECTIONER'S ALMOND PASTE OR MARZIPAN: If it is too crumbly or too hard, soften with fondant or glucose.

FONDANT: When you heat it, add a little syrup at 30° Baumé (1262 density) together with a small amount of glucose. This will soften the fondant and give it a beautiful shine. Never add uncooked egg white, as the fondant may ferment and cause bacteria to breed.

TO MAKE NOUGATINE: If the atmosphere is humid, add 50g (2oz) butter or fat for each kg (2lb 4oz) sugar immediately after mixing in the almonds. This will prevent the nougatine from 'sweating'.

MISCELLANEOUS

● Never wash omelette or *crêpe* pans; wipe them clean with newspaper or a cloth. If food is stuck to the pan, heat it and rub with a handful of coarse salt, newspaper or a cloth.

● Fresh breadcrumbs take only 10 minutes to make: cut off the crusts from a piece of half-stale white bread; dice the bread, add a spoonful of flour and process in a food processor or place in a cloth. Gather up the edges of the cloth and crush the bread with the palm of your hand. When it has crumbled, rub through a medium mesh sieve or sifter.

● Always add pepper at the end of cooking, so that it retains its full flavour.

● When adding salt to hot fish, meat or poultry aspics, always add more than you think is necessary; the salt will lose much of its strength as the liquid cools.

● A small spoon placed in the neck of a half-drunk bottle of Champagne will act as a cork and the Champagne will remain in perfect condition.

THE CHEESE COURSE

What a magical moment it is when the cheese is served — when the taste-buds respond with delight to the marvellous textures and tastes of the cheese. It is a glorious moment for the gourmet; it enhances the savour of the wine he has been drinking with his meal; it provides the perfect excuse to finish the bottle, to open another — or, better still, to produce a crusted vintage port.

The cheeseboard reveals whether you appreciate good food and therefore the good things of life. The cheeses must be chosen with great care and discernment. It is better to offer a very small selection of cheeses each at the peak of perfection, rather than proffer a cluster of little 'plastic' cheeses, weeping sadly.

HOW TO CHOOSE THE CHEESE

FARMHOUSE CHEESE: Always choose these above all others. They are made from untreated milk; pasteurization, which is so widespread today, unfortunately destroys much of the flavour of our cheeses. Before 1940, there were practically no pasteurized cheeses at all. Nowadays, cheeses made from ewe's or goat's milk in the traditional manner are still unpasteurized.

SMELL: Cheeses must smell; that is a mark of their quality. If they do not smell, you should not buy them.

FEEL: Soft-paste cheeses like Brie and Camembert must 'give' when you feel them. They should spring back when pressed with the thumb and must never be either hard or squashy.

RUNNINESS: An over-runny cheese has not dried out properly — do not buy it. Look for mellow, supple, creamy cheeses.

RIPENING: Cheese should be left to ripen in a cellar at a temperature of 7° to 10°C, (45°-50°F) with a humidity of 85% to 95% maximum. The cheese will be in perfect condition for eating if it is ripened in these conditions. It should then be eaten right away; it will only deteriorate if kept for even a few days.

PACKAGING: Avoid camouflages! Beware of pretty, 'folksy' packaging which prevents you from seeing, smelling and feeling the cheese. It is always better to choose a cheese which you can see.

AVOID: Fresh cream cheeses and processed cheese. They are fine for spreading in sandwiches, but do not merit a place on the cheeseboard.

SIMPLICITY: Stick to the classic cheeses, despite the enormous variety of cheeses in Europe. Do not get carried away, but ask your cheesemonger for his advice.

SERVING THE CHEESE

THE PLATTER: This can be made of wicker, glass, marble or china: ideally, it should be round and you should provide two knives — one for the mild cheeses and one for the strong flavours. Keep the platter covered with a damp cloth (preferably cheesecloth or muslin) until you are ready to serve the cheese.

ACCOMPANIMENT: Fruits such as pears, apples, nuts or grapes always go well with cheese.

BREAD: Offer home-made or wholemeal bread, or nut bread. Savoury biscuits or 'crackers' are generally popular with everybody, including us.

TO DRINK: As a general rule, you can serve almost any reasonably full-bodied red wine with cheese.

CHAPTER FOUR

THE BASIS FOR A MEAL

BREAD

Bread is a wonderful creation. In all its various shapes and sizes, be it pale or golden brown, soft or crisply crusty, bread smells good. It is the staple daily food for many people in Europe. Where would we be without bread?

French bread-making is world famous, yet the 'direct' method of baking was not practised until 1920. Nowadays, it is the most common method of baking bread. Although yeast is used, the 'direct' method needs no previous leavening and is therefore very practical.

French bread is so famous, so often imitated, yet it has no equal. The reason is simple: nothing goes into it but flour, water, salt and yeast. The making of bread is a complete subject in its own right, but we felt that we must at least list the different types of flour used in France:

TYPES 45 OR 55: Used for making baguettes and Viennese rolls.

WHEAT FLOUR, TYPES 45 OR 55: Used for wheat breads.

TYPES 80, 110 AND 150: Used for farmhouse loaves and wholemeal breads, which are very popular today.

VARIOUS FLOURS — RYE, SOYA, RICE AND CASSAVA: Used either as improving agents or as roughage. Rye flour, with the addition of a little wheat flour, is always used to make *pain de seigle* (rye bread).

The recipes in these chapters are for breads which we bake every day in our restaurant kitchens, using commercially available plain flour. They are very easy to make at home and are extremely more-ish!

INGREDIENTS

450g (1lb) plain flour

15g (½oz) salt

15g (½oz) live yeast

10g (⅓oz) sugar

250ml (10fl.oz) cold water

beaten egg (optional), to glaze

Makes: 15-20 rolls
Preparation time: 35 minutes, plus 2 hours 30 minutes rising time
Cooking time: about 12 minutes
Picture: page 23

BREAD

PREPARATION

Put the flour and sugar into the bowl or basin. In another bowl, mix the salt and yeast with the cold water (about 10°C/50°F). Pour the liquid into the flour, a little at a time, mixing with your hand until the ingredients are well blended. Cover the bowl with a cloth or baking tin and leave in a warm place (about 24°C/75°F) to rise. This will take about 2 hours. Knock back the dough by punching it with the heel of your hand 2 or 3 times (not more); this will release the gases. Turn the dough onto a marble or wooden surface. Using a sharp knife, divide the dough into even pieces of the size you require. Shape into rounds or pull into long rolls and arrange them on a baking sheet.

Leave in a warm, draught-free place for the bread to 'prove' (rise again). This will take about 30 minutes. Meanwhile, preheat the oven to 240°C/475°F/Gas 9.

BAKING

Just before putting the rolls in the oven, brush them with beaten egg, then make small slashes in the top of each roll. Either use a razor blade, (set in a cork so that you do not cut yourself) or make the marks with the points of a pair of kitchen scissors.

The oven must be very hot. A few small tins full of water placed in the bottom of the oven will give off enough steam to bake the bread properly. Bake the rolls for about 12 minutes. When you take them out of the oven, brush each one with a very slightly moistened brush to give the rolls a shiny finish.

Wrap the rolls in the foil and put them in the freezer as soon as they are cold; they will still taste freshly-baked if you use them within a few days. It is essential to warm them in a fairly hot oven (190°C/375°F/Gas 5) for about 5 minutes. By doing this, you can have fresh bread every day without having to bake it daily.

PAIN DE MIE

(White bread)

PREPARATION

Put the flour and sugar into a basin or bowl. Warm the milk and water to about 30°C (85°F). In another bowl, mix the salt and yeast with the lukewarm milk and water. Pour the liquid onto the flour, a little at a time, mixing with your hand until the ingredients are well blended. Add the eggs, one at a time, then the lukewarm melted butter. Continue to work the dough until it comes away from your hand; this will give it 'body' and elasticity. Cover the bowl with a cloth or baking tin and put it in a warm place (about 24°C/75°F) for the dough to rise. This will take about 2 hours. Knock back the dough by punching it with the heel of your hand 2 or 3 times (not more) to release the gas. Turn the dough onto a marble or wooden surface. Form a plait or divide the dough into 4 equal pieces and shape into balls. Generously grease a black metal rectangular loaf tin with a sliding lid, about 41cm (16in) long, 11cm (4½in) wide and 10cm (4in) deep. Place the plaited loaf in the tin, or put in the 4 balls one beside the other. Put the tin in a warm, draught-free place until the dough has risen to the top of the tin. This will take about 45 minutes. Preheat the oven to 220°C/425°F/Gas 7.

BAKING

Slide the lid onto the loaf tin. Place the tin in the oven and bake for 35 minutes. As soon as you remove the loaf from the oven, gently slide off the lid from the tin — make sure that the escaping steam does not scald you. Tip the loaf out of the tin onto a wire rack. Leave to cool completely before using.

If you wrap the loaf in foil and freeze it, it will taste just as good as when it was freshly baked. Heat the bread in a fairly hot oven (190°C/375°F/Gas 5) for a few minutes before serving.

You can mix the ingredients for the dough in an electric mixer with a dough hook, but be careful not to overwork the mixture.

INGREDIENTS

750g (1lb 9 oz) plain flour

20g (¾oz) salt

30g (1oz) live yeast

30g (1oz) sugar

3 eggs

60g (2oz) butter, melted

250ml (10fl.oz) milk, lukewarm

125ml (5fl.oz) water, lukewarm

Makes: 1 loaf
Preparation time: 20 minutes plus 2 hours 45 minutes rising time
Cooking time: 35 minutes
Picture: page 23

INGREDIENTS

500g (1lb 1oz) stone ground flour

1 tsp salt

25g (¾oz) live yeast

60g (2oz) butter

60g (2oz) brown sugar

250ml (10fl.oz) milk

4 tbls lukewarm water

35g (1½oz) shelled walnuts

Makes: 1 walnut loaf
Preparation time: 25 minutes, plus 1 hour 45 minutes rising time
Cooking time: 35 minutes
Picture: page 23

PAIN AUX NOIX

(Walnut bread)

This bread tastes better when it is slightly stale, or at least served on the day after it is cooked. It is delicious eaten with cheese. It also freezes very well.

If you can find a cylindrical, hinged loaf tin, the baked bread can be sliced into wafer-thin rounds resembling little cheese biscuits.

PREPARATION

Put the flour into the basin or bowl. In another bowl, mix the salt and yeast with the lukewarm water. Heat the butter in the saucepan until it turns golden brown. Strain the butter through the sieve into the milk and stir in the sugar and water, salt and yeast mixture. Pour the mixture into the flour, a little at a time, mixing with your hand or a spatula until the dough is very well mixed. Roughly chop the walnuts and add them to the dough. Cover the bowl with a cloth or a baking tin and leave in a warm place (about 24°C/75°F) for the dough to rise. This will take about 1 hour. Knock back the dough by punching it with the heel of your hand 2 or 3 times; this will release the gases. Roll out the dough into a long sausage shape. Generously butter a cast iron terrine dish or a rectangular black metal loaf tin, 32cm (13in) long, 8cm (3in) wide and 8cm (3in) deep. Place the dough 'sausage' in the tin. Leave in a warm, draught-free place to 'prove'. This will take about 45 minutes. Preheat the oven to 220°C/425°F/Gas 7.

BAKING

Bake the loaf in the preheated oven for 35 minutes. Turn out onto a wire rack to cool.

HERBS AND SPICES

Herbs and spices have always been important to man, especially to the country dweller, from earliest times to the present day. They have a multiplicity of uses; as subtle flavourings in cooking, as basic ingredients of many medicines and cosmetics, and in some parts of the world, they are even used as currency.

Cooks have always made use of herbs and spices in the culinary arts, from the simplest home cooking to the finest professional cuisines. We ourselves have always kept a little corner of the garden to grow herbs; here the air is permanently scented by a dozen or so herbs which we use in our cooking to add a note of sweetness, delicacy, bitterness or pungency, to achieve the desired effect. The blending of herbs and spices warms the spirit and delights our sense of taste and smell. Always use them sparingly; their flavour should never dominate a dish, but should blend subtly and sometimes add a touch of the exotic.

In the list that follows, we have not attempted to suggest all the possible ways of using herbs and spices; we have simply tried to guide you in your choice. Some aromatics may be used in many different dishes — it is up to you to discover new blends of flavours. It is always best to use fresh herbs in season. Dry your own fresh herbs to use when they are out of season. Lay them in a sunny place until they have dried, then pack in airtight containers or hermetically sealed jars. Store in a cool, shady place.

In our larder we also keep fresh basil covered with olive oil. Fresh tarragon steeped in vinegar is excellent for Béarnaise sauce.

HOW TO USE HERBS

BASIL: Use just as it is with raw tomato, in cold or lukewarm sauces like *sauce vierge*, with fish, soups and fresh pasta.

BAY-LEAVES: Use in sautés, stews, terrines or pâtés. Bay-leaves form part of a bouquet garni.

BORAGE: Put into soups. The flowers are cooked in fritters, for garnishes, or added to certain salads together with the young leaves.

CHERVIL: Put sprigs of chervil in salads, omelettes and soups. A delicate and decorative herb, used to garnish clear and cream soups.

CHIVES: Use in omelettes, green sauces, salads and *fromage blanc* or cottage cheese.

DILL: Use to marinate raw fish, with grilled fish, or in a mixed salad.

FENNEL: Use in soup or fish stock, on grilled meat and with pickled onions and gherkins.

GARLIC: Use in a purée, to flavour the gravy from a roast, tomato sauces, courgettes, ratatouille; rub it on croûtons of toasted bread; put in salad dressings.

HORSERADISH: Use as a relish with pot-au-feu; mix with cream to go with roast beef or smoked trout.

LEMON THYME: Use in carrots Vichy and with grilled or roast rabbit and lamb.

MARIGOLD: Use in sautés and soups.

MARJORAM: Use in stuffings, salads and soups.

MINT: Use to flavour peas, new potatoes, lamb, pork, *sauce paloise,* fresh or iced fruits and sorbets.

PARSLEY: Use as a garnish, in stuffings, with mussels and snails, in omelettes and with grilled fish. Parsley is the main ingredient of a bouquet garni.

ROSEMARY: For grilled lamb, stews, marinades, soups and

game.

SAGE: Use with game, in stuffings, with fish, pork and goose, in marinades and stuffed tomatoes.

SORREL: Use in soup, fish dishes, green sauce and omelettes.

TARRAGON: Use for decorative garnishes, or in omelettes. Béarnaise sauce, salads, *crudités* and eggs in aspic. It is used to flavour vinegar and this keeps it very well.

THYME: Useful for some soups, roast chicken; it forms part of a bouquet garni.

SPICES AND THEIR USES

QUATRE EPICES A mixture of ground white pepper, cloves, ginger and nutmeg, this is an ingredient in the sauce for chicken *bouchées*, and certain stuffings.

CARAWAY SEEDS: Served with strong cheeses, in sauerkraut, in bread and some cakes.

CARDAMOM: Also called Amomum, very rarely used in French cooking. An exotic and expensive spice, it is used like pepper in curries, rice dishes and many Asian dishes.

CAYENNE PEPPER: Much stronger than pepper. It is used like pepper in sauces, smoked fish and in the manufacture of cooked cheeses.

CINNAMON: Used to flavour many sweet dishes, stewed apples, chocolate sauce, mulled wines and punches.

CLOVES: An onion studded with cloves is used in making bread sauce, pot-au-feu, *blanquette de veau* etc. Cloves add a good flavour to stewed apples.

CORIANDER: Indispensable for dishes cooked *à la grecque*, game stock, certain biscuits and cakes.

CUMIN: Used like caraway with pork dishes and strong cheeses.

CURRY POWDER: A blend of spices which varies from region to region, it generally consists of ground red pepper, turmeric, cumin, coriander, black pepper, cloves, nutmeg and ginger. Used in the preparation of all different types of curry.

GINGER: Widely used in Asia, but not very much in Europe, where preserved ginger is used in some cakes and sweet dishes.

MACE: Used in sauces. Mace is also used for cakes, soups and pâtés.

NUTMEG: Used in white sauce, *duchesse* potatoes, spinach, black or white puddings and cheese soufflés.

PAPRIKA: Used in goulash, beef Stroganoff, chicken, *fromage blanc*, rice and veal. Paprika heightens the colour of grilled or barbecued shellfish.

PEPPER: Finds its way into practically every dish. Fresh (soft green) peppercorns are excellent in certain sauces.

POPPY SEEDS: Sometimes used for decorating bread, sprinkled over the crust.

SAFFRON: Used in mussel soup, *bouillabaisse*, mousseline sauce, rice and some fish sauces.

STAR-ANISE: Used in pastry-making, plum jam, herbal teas, bread and with chestnuts.

TURMERIC: Flavours and colours court bouillon, rice, white meats and exotic dishes.

VANILLA: Used in ice-creams, stewed fruit, rice puddings, petits fours, sweet soufflés etc.

STOCKS

Without any doubt, to us stocks are *indispensable*. A well-flavoured stock is the very foundation of sauces, gravies, aspics, moistening liquids; of braised dishes, sautés, soups and a multitude of recipes. Without them, the good cooking of which one never grows tired — the cuisine of yesterday, today and tomorrow — would disappear or could not possibly be the same.

Nowadays, stocks are light, aromatic, very personal concoctions, inexpensive and easy to make. They keep very well for a few days in the refrigerator or for several weeks in the freezer. Store them in small, covered containers, to use as you need them, then you will not have to make them more than once or twice a month. The stocks described here are those we use most often in our recipes. Above all, we recommend that you never cook up any old mixture of bones or carcasses, such as chicken with duck, or game with veal, in the hope of preparing a good stock. All you will end up with is a mish-mash with no pronounced flavour — in other words, a broth of no character.

COURT BOUILLON OR NAGE

A court bouillon or *nage* is used for cooking many kinds of shellfish. It can be prepared in advance and kept for 2 or 3 days in the refrigerator. If you want to incorporate some of the vegetables into a recipe, they may be cannelized or 'turned' into various shapes.

PREPARATION

Peel and wash the carrots, leek, celery, fennel, shallots and button onions and slice them into very thin rounds, 2-3mm (1/10in) thick.

COOKING

Place the finely sliced vegetables and the butter in a saucepan. Cover the pan and sweat the vegetables for 10 minutes. Pour in the vinegar, white wine and water; add the salt, bouquet garni and the unpeeled garlic clove. As soon as the mixture comes to the boil, lower the heat and simmer very gently for 20 minutes. Crush the peppercorns and tie them in a small piece of muslin. Add them to the liquid after 15 minutes. The vegetables should still be slightly crunchy when cooked.

INGREDIENTS

2 medium carrots

white part of 1 leek

½ celery stalk

½ fennel stalk

4 shallots

4 button onions

1 garlic glove

1 small bouquet garni

1 tsp peppercorns

2 tbls white wine vinegar

325ml (13fl.oz) dry white wine

30g (1oz) butter

1L (1¾pts) water

25g (1oz) coarse salt

Serves: 4 people
Preparation time: 20 minutes
Cooking time: 30 minutes

INGREDIENTS

1kg (2lb 2oz) veal knuckle bones

1 calf's foot, split

100g (4oz) carrots

100g (4oz) mushrooms

50g (2oz) onions

½ celery stalk

4 tomatoes

1 garlic clove

1 bouquet garni

1 sprig tarragon

200 ml (8fl.oz) dry white wine

about 2L (3½pts) water

Makes: 1L (1¾pts)
Preparation time: 15 minutes
Cooking time: 3 to 4 hours

VEAL STOCK

Demi-glaces or meat glazes will give a stronger flavour to sauces which may be too delicate or watery or not robust enough for your taste. They will keep for at least 2 weeks in the refrigerator. By reducing the strained veal stock to half its original quantity, you will obtain a *demi-glace*. Reducing it by three-quarters will give you a meat glaze. Reduce the stock slowly over a low heat, removing the scum frequently from the surface with the back of a ladle.

PREPARATION AND COOKING

Preheat the oven to 220°C/425°F/Gas 7. Coarsely chop the veal bones and place them in the roasting pan with the split calf's foot. Brown in the hot oven, turning from time to time with a large spoon. When they are lightly browned, transfer the bones to a saucepan.

Finely slice the carrots, mushrooms, onions, celery and garlic and put them in a roasting pan. Set the pan over medium heat for a few minutes, stirring the vegetables with a wooden spatula. Sweat the vegetables without letting them brown, then deglaze the pan with the white wine. Continue cooking until most of the liquid has evaporated. Add the vegetables to the veal bones, pour in the water to cover and bring the mixture to the boil. Lower the heat and simmer gently, skimming off the scum and grease as they accumulate on the surface.

Skin and deseed the tomatoes. After 10 minutes' cooking time, add them to the pan, together with the bouquet garni and the tarragon. You should have removed the scum and grease from the surface of the stock once or twice before adding the tomatoes. Continue to cook the stock for 3 to 4 hours.

Pass the stock through a muslin-lined sieve into a bowl. You should be left with about 1L (1¾pts) stock. Set the bowl aside in a cool place; do not refrigerate the stock until it is completely cold. It will keep in the refrigerator for about 10 days.

Preparation time: 15 minutes
Cooking time: 2½ hours

FONDS BLANC DE VOLAILLE

(White chicken stock)

You can make chicken stock without the veal knuckle or calf's tongue, but the addition of one of them will make your stock richer and more full-bodied; it can be rather watery if you only use the chicken. After it has improved your stock, you can happily serve the tongue as a dish in its own right; in a vinaigrette, for example, or with a fresh, herb-flavoured tomato *coulis*.

PREPARATION AND COOKING

Wash and finely slice the carrots, leek, celery and mushrooms. Heat the butter in the saucepan and sweat the vegetables. Add the boiling fowl or carcasses, together with the veal bone or tongue. Cover with cold water and bring to the boil. Lower the heat and simmer gently, skimming the surface frequently. After 10 minutes' cooking time, add the onion spiked with the clove and the bouquet garni.

Cook for a further 2 hours and 20 minutes, then strain the stock into a bowl through a muslin-lined sieve. Set aside in a cool place. As with all stocks, do not refrigerate until it is completely cold. The stock will keep in the refrigerator for 1 week, or for several weeks in the freezer.

INGREDIENTS

1kg (2lb 2oz) chicken carcasses, necks, wings and feet *or* 1 boiling fowl

1 veal knuckle bone or calf's tongue

100g (4oz) carrots

white part of 1 leek

½ celery stalk

100g (4oz) mushrooms

1 onion

1 clove

1 bouquet garni

20g (¾oz) butter

FONDS DE GIBIER

(Game stock)

PREPARATION AND COOKING

Chop or cut the game trimmings, carcasses or meat into small pieces. Heat the oil in the saucepan and brown the game pieces on all sides. Wash and coarsely dice the vegetables and add them to the pan. Lower the heat and sweat the vegetables for a few minutes. Pour in the red wine. Reduce the liquid by one-third, then add the veal stock and water and bring to the boil. Lower the heat and simmer the stock gently, skimming the surface frequently. After 10 minutes' cooking time, add the sage, juniper berries, coriander seeds and bouquet garni.

After 2½ hours' cooking time, you should be left with about 1L (1¾pts) of stock. Strain it through a muslin-lined sieve, skim off the fat from the surface and set aside in a cool place. Do not put the stock in the refrigerator until it is completely cold.

Duck stock can be made in exactly the same way; use only duck carcasses or trimmings and omit the coriander seeds. You could ask your

INGREDIENTS

1kg (2lb 2oz) game trimmings, necks, wings, knuckles etc (you can use any type of game bird, or hare, rabbit, etc.)

1 carrot

50g (2oz) onions

1 sprig sage

6 juniper berries

6 coriander seeds

1 bouquet garni

2 tbls peanut oil

500ml (1pt) full-bodied red wine

500ml (1pt) Veal stock (see page 48)

1L (1¾pts) water

Preparation time: 15
minutes
Cooking time: 2 to 3
hours

butcher to break up the bones and carcasses for you. Game stock will keep for 1 week in the refrigerator, or for several weeks in the freezer. By slowly reducing the stock to half its original quantity, you will obtain a game *demi-glace*.

INGREDIENTS

1kg (2lb 2oz) fish bones and heads (eg, sole, turbot, whiting, conger eel, or any white-fleshed fish)

50g (2oz) onions

white part of 1 leek

50g (2oz) mushrooms

50g (2oz) butter

100ml (4fl.oz) dry white wine

1 bouquet garni

2L (3½pts) water

Preparation time: 15
minutes
Cooking time: 30
minutes

FISH STOCK

PREPARATION AND COOKING

Remove the gills from the fish heads. Soak the bones and heads in cold water for 3 to 4 hours. Roughly chop the fish bones and heads. Wash and chop the vegetables and sweat them in the butter. Then add the chopped bones and heads and simmer for a few minutes. Pour in the white wine. Increase the heat and reduce the liquid by half, then cover the contents of the pan with water. Bring the mixture to the boil, skimming the surface frequently. After 5 minutes' cooking time, add the bouquet garni and simmer, uncovered, for 25 minutes. Carefully strain the stock into a bowl through a muslin-lined sieve. Leave to cool, then store in the refrigerator.

The stock will keep for 1 week in the refrigerator and for several weeks in the freezer.

TO MAKE FISH ASPIC: If the stock is very clear, the addition of a few leaves of gelatine will produce a fish aspic. A few slices of lemon squeezed into the aspic will give it a slightly sharp flavour.

TO MAKE A FISH *DEMI-GLACE:* Simmer the stock gently, skimming the surface frequently, until it has reduced by two-thirds. Use the *demi-glace* to enrich and add body to certain fish sauces.

MARINADES

We marinate meat for a number of reasons; sometimes to tenderize them, to bring out the flavour, to preserve them or even to change their character. A marinade, for example, can make lamb taste rather like venison or pork like wild boar.

Marinades can sometimes be used instead of traditional cooking methods; scallops and skinned, or thinly sliced fish will become partly cooked if they are covered for several hours with slices of lemon and/or lemon juice, crushed peppercorns and a sprinkling of oil. The two marinades given here are easy to make.

LIGHT, UNCOOKED MARINADE

This is suitable for small game, poultry, small fish and small pieces of meat which you intend to cook (especially to grill) the same day. Meat or fish should be placed in the marinade and turned from time to time. This marinade will be better if prepared the day before so that the flavours have time to marry together.

INGREDIENTS FOR A MARINADE FOR 6 SMALL ITEMS

2 lemons, peeled and sliced	1 glass dry white wine
1 finely sliced carrot	salt
1 finely sliced onion	coarsely ground pepper
4 tbls peanut oil	
6 coarsely crushed coriander seeds	

COOKED MARINADE

INGREDIENTS FOR A MARINADE FOR LARGE PIECES OF MEAT OR GAME

2 carrots	750ml (26fl.oz) water
2 onions	1 bouquet garni
1 celery stalk	1 sprig rosemary
20g (¾oz) butter	2 cloves
1L (1¾pts) full-bodied red wine	1 pinch peppercorns
100ml (4fl.oz) red wine vinegar	

PREPARATION

Finely slice the vegetables, put in a large saucepan and sweat in the butter. Add all the other marinade ingredients, bring to the boil, then simmer for 20 minutes. Leave to cool.

When the marinade is cold, put in the meat and marinate for 1 to 3 days. However, if you are going to serve the meat on the same day, put it into the marinade while it is still warm. Strain the marinade and keep it to use as the base for the sauce to accompany the meat.

SAUCES

Whether they be simple or complicated, sauces demand a great deal of care and practice. Their importance is such that a chef is not recognized as a Master unless he excels in the art of sauce-making.

The sauce chef mixes his ingredients like a chemist or an alchemist — rather like a sorcerer concocting his bubbling, steaming potion, he adds a pinch of this and a pinch of that. You can almost see a flame leap out of his casseroles and half light up his face. When the sauce is ready, the 'artist' has created a masterpiece, whose perfection he alone can discern by sight and smell; it gives him an overwhelming satisfaction, which shines out of his eyes. Now, he need only taste the sauce to correct the seasoning and to confirm that his creation is indeed a success.

Sauces are often put into two categories — brown and white. In order to make the so-called 'classic' sauces, and indeed all other sauces, it is essential to use good basic stocks, made from veal, chicken or fish.

SOME WORDS OF ADVICE

Once a sauce is cooked, you must keep it away from any heat source. Dot a few flakes of butter over the surface to prevent a skin from forming. If possible serve the sauce as soon as it is cooked.

Never throw away the carcass of any poultry you have just eaten, but put it to good use; chop it up and put it in a saucepan with a *mirepoix* of carrot and shallot or onion and a small bouquet garni. Pour in enough water to cover the carcass and bring to the boil. Lower the heat and simmer gently for 30 minutes, then strain through a muslin-lined sieve and keep it until you need it — and there you have some gravy or light stock which you can use as the base for a sauce, or to add body to gravy next time you serve a poultry dish.

Always reduce dry white or red wine by boiling before adding it to a sauce, casserole or dessert. The wine will become more full-bodied and flavourful, because the alcohol will have evaporated and the wine will lose its acid taste. Remember, though, that sweet, syrupy wines, like port, Sauternes, Barsac, Beaumes de Venise etc, have a delicate aroma and should be added to the sauce at the end of cooking; there is no need to boil them beforehand.

Compound butters, such as crayfish, anchovy, pistachio, shallot and Montpellier, are added to the sauce once it is cooked, with the pan off the heat; they are principally used in fish sauces.

Essences or infusions of vegetables or fruits, such as mushrooms, truffles, peaches and so on, add delicious nuances of flavour to a sauce, but must be used with discretion. They should be added about 20 minutes before the sauce is ready. Another useful hint is that a few drops of lemon juice or vinegar will liven up a dull, lack-lustre sauce.

THICKENING AGENTS OR LIAISONS

There are some methods of thickening sauces which we use more than others. Those which we use accentuate the taste, fine flavours, lightness and creaminess of the sauce, so that it not only tastes better, but above all, it becomes more digestible. There was a time when the consistency of a sauce was practically all that mattered. Happily, nowadays, different principles are practised in sauce-making.

OUR FAVOURITE THICKENING AGENTS

REDUCTION: This is done over high heat, until the sauce reaches the desired consistency (often syrupy).

BUTTER OR CREAM: Butter is stirred into a sauce in small pieces, cream 1 spoonful at a time. This may be done either over high heat, or with the pan off the heat, depending on the desired effect — whether the sauce is to be light, glossy etc.

SHELLFISH CORAL, BLOOD OR FOIE GRAS: These are mixed with a little softened butter or cream and added to the sauce off the heat. Never bring the sauce back to the boil, or it will curdle.

EGG YOLKS: Beat the eggs with a little milk or cream and add to the sauce off the heat. Do not bring the sauce to the boil, or it will curdle.

VEGETABLES: Make a gravy for deglazing by mashing with a fork any potatoes, carrots or garlic which have been cooked with a roast.

OTHER THICKENING AGENTS — TO BE USED AS NEEDED

ROUX: White or *blonde* roux are made by melting butter in a saucepan, adding flour and cooking together. If the roux is hot, the added liquid must be cold and vice-versa, otherwise the sauce will coagulate and go lumpy. You must cook the sauce for at least 30 minutes.

BEURRE MANIE: This is a mixture of 1 spoonful flour to 2 of butter, mashed together, uncooked, with a fork. It is added to the sauce, a little at a time, over high heat. The sauce will thicken immediately. Beat with a wire whisk to incorporate the butter.

SPRINKLING WITH FLOUR: Sprinkle flour over meat which has already been browned; this method is used for stews, casseroles, sautés etc. Stir with a spatula and place the dish in a hot oven (220°C/425°F/Gas 7) for a few minutes to allow the flour to cook before adding the liquid. The flour may be browned on a baking sheet beforehand. If this is done, it takes on a nutty colour and becomes much more digestible. It also means that you can add the liquid as soon as the flour is sprinkled over the meat.

ARROWROOT AND POTATO STARCH: Dissolve them in a little water or white wine. Add to the sauce over high heat; it will thicken very quickly. Simmer for 10 to 15 minutes.

BREAD SAUCE

INGREDIENTS

100g (4oz) onions (either 1 large or 2 medium onions)

2 cloves

80g (2½oz) thickly sliced white bread

15g (½oz) butter

350ml (14fl.oz) milk

50ml (2fl.oz) double cream

salt

freshly ground white pepper

This sauce is an excellent accompaniment when served with chicken, roast turkey or pheasant dishes.

PREPARATION

Peel the onion and cut in half. Finely chop one half and stud the other half with the cloves. Remove and discard the crusts from the bread and cut it into cubes.

COOKING

Put the chopped onion in a saucepan with the butter. Set over low heat and sweat until soft. Pour in the milk and add the clove-studded onion half. Infuse over very low heat for 20 minutes, then add the bread cubes, bring to the boil, lower the heat and cook gently for 30 minutes. Remove the onion half and cloves and discard them.

Stir the sauce gently with a small wire whisk. Add the cream, let the sauce bubble for 10 minutes and season to taste.

Serves: 4 people
Preparation time: 5 minutes
Cooking time: 1 hour

SAUCE BEARNAISE

(Béarnaise sauce)

PREPARATION

Peel, wash and finely chop the shallots.

THE REDUCTION

Put the tarragon, shallots, vinegar and crushed peppercorns into a shallow pan. Set over high heat and reduce the mixture by half. Set aside in a cool place.

COOKING

When the reduction is cold, add the egg yolks and proceed exactly as for Hollandaise sauce (see page 57), but heat the egg yolks at a fractionally higher temperature (65°C/150°F).

Add the chervil just a few minutes before serving, so that its flavour and colour are at their best. Do not strain the sauce, but serve it just as it is; we much prefer the coarser texture. Like Hollandaise sauce, Béarnaise sauce can be used as a base for other sauces, such as those listed below:

CHORON SAUCE: Add to the finished sauce 3 tbls tomatoes, chopped and sweated in butter to remove some of the excess moisture. Serve with grilled meats.

FOYOT SAUCE: Add 1 tbls melted meat glaze to the finished sauce. Serve with small cuts of grilled or braised meats.

PALOISE SAUCE: Replace the tarragon in the reduction with chopped fresh mint. Add chopped, uncooked mint to the finished sauce instead of the chervil. Like the other sauces, this goes well with all grilled meats, but is particularly good with lamb.

INGREDIENTS

2 medium shallots

5 tbls snipped tarragon

3 tbls wine vinegar (preferably red)

1 tsp white peppercorns, coarsely crushed

4 egg yolks

250g (9oz) butter

3 tbls snipped chervil

salt

Serves: 6 people
Preparation time: 15 minutes
Cooking time: 12 minutes

INGREDIENTS

2 crisp eating apples

1 banana

1 pineapple, weighing about 750g (1lb 9oz)

40g (1½oz) butter

1 onion, weighing about 50g (2oz)

40g (1½oz) flour

40g (1½oz) Madras curry powder

1½ tbls dessicated coconut

1L (1¾pts) Chicken stock (see page 48)

1 bouquet garni

salt

Serves: 8 people
Preparation time: 20 minutes
Cooking time: 1 hour

SAUCE CURRY

(Curry sauce)

PREPARATION

Wash and core the apples and cut into very fine slices. Peel the banana and cut into rounds. Remove the leaves from the pineapple; peel and core it and then cut the flesh into very fine slices. Peel, wash and chop the onion very finely.

COOKING

Melt 25g (1oz) butter in a shallow pan set over low heat. Add the onion and sweat until soft. Put in the fruit and cook gently for 10 minutes.

Meanwhile, lightly brown the flour in a hot oven. Sprinkle the browned flour over the mixture in the pan, add the curry powder and coconut and mix well with a spatula. Pour in the chicken stock, bring to the boil, lower the heat and simmer gently for 1 hour, skimming the surface as often as necessary. Add the bouquet garni after 10 minutes cooking time. Season to taste with salt.

Pass the cooked sauce through a conical sieve into a bowl and dot the surface with the remaining butter to prevent a skin from forming.

If you have any, it is much better to use grated fresh coconut than dessicated; it will give the sauce a rich, creamy, sophisticated flavour. You can use less or more curry powder according to your own personal taste.

INGREDIENTS

2 medium shallots

30g (1oz) butter

6 tbls snipped fresh tarragon

100ml (4fl.oz) dry white wine

1 tbls tarragon vinegar
Continued

SAUCE ESTRAGON

(Tarragon sauce)

This light, delicately flavoured sauce goes particularly well with a chicken mousseline, certain kinds of poached fish or baked sweetbreads. There is no need to strain the sauce; the texture of the shallots and tarragon is very pleasant.

PREPARATION AND COOKING

Peel, wash and finely chop the shallots. Sweat with 15g (½oz) butter in a saucepan set over low heat. Add the tarragon to the pan. Pour in the white wine and vinegar, increase the heat and reduce the liquid by three-quarters. Pour in the chicken stock, bring back to the boil and reduce until the liquid is slightly syrupy.

Lower the heat, add the cream and simmer for 2 minutes, then stir in the remaining butter and season to taste with salt and pepper.

500ml (1pt) Chicken stock (see page 48)

2 tbls double cream

salt and freshly ground white pepper

Serves: 6 people
Preparation time: 10 minutes
Cooking time: 30 minutes

SAUCE HOLLANDAISE

(Hollandaise sauce)

PREPARATION

First of all, prepare the *gastrique*; mix together in a shallow pan 2 tbls water, the crushed peppercorns and the white wine vinegar. Set the pan over high heat and reduce by two-thirds.

INGREDIENTS

1 tsp white peppercorns, crushed

1 tbls white wine vinegar

3 egg yolks

250g (9oz) melted butter

juice of ½ lemon

salt

Serves: 6 people
Preparation time: 8 minutes
Cooking time: 12 minutes

COOKING

Take the pan off the heat and, whisking continuously, beat into the *gastrique* 1 tbls water and the egg yolks. Place the pan over very gentle direct heat or, better still, in a bain-marie filled with very hot but not boiling water.

Continue beating, make sure that the whisk reaches right to the bottom of the pan, so that the egg yolks emulsify and do not begin to scramble. After 8 to 10 minutes, the mixture should be very creamy. Take great care that the temperature never exceeds 60°C (140°F).

Now, whisking continuously, beat in the melted butter, a little at a time. If the sauce becomes too thick, add 1 or 2 tbls lukewarm water, then continue to whisk in the butter. Season to taste, then add a few drops of strained lemon juice. Strain through a muslin cloth if you like a very smooth sauce. Serve at once, or keep the sauce in a bain-marie filled with warm water.

Hollandaise sauce is used as a base for several others, including those listed on the following page.

MOUSSELINE SAUCE: At the last moment, add 4 to 6 tbls whipped double cream to the Hollandaise sauce (about one-third quantity cream to 1 quantity sauce). Serve with poached vegetables, such as broccoli, asparagus, courgettes, cauliflower and so on.

MUSTARD SAUCE: At the last moment, add 2 tbls English mustard powder, made up with water or dry white wine. This sauce is excellent with any grilled fish, especially sardines.

MALTAISE SAUCE: Add to the finished Hollandaise sauce the warmed juice of 2 blood oranges (previously reduced by half) and 1 tbls blanched orange zest. This sauce is delicious as an accompaniment to asparagus and poached salmon.

SAUCE ALBERT

INGREDIENTS

150g (5oz) fresh horseradish, grated

200ml (8fl.oz) Chicken stock (see page 48) *or* 200ml (8fl.oz) cooking liquid from a Pot au feu (see page 202)

200ml (8fl.oz) double cream

40g (1½oz) fresh white breadcrumbs

1 egg yolk

1 tsp English mustard

Serves: 4 people
Preparation time: 15 minutes
Cooking time: 40 minutes

This sauce is the perfect accompaniment to pot au feu and all boiled meats. Bottled horseradish may be used instead of fresh, in which case, increase the quantity by one-third.

PREPARATION

Combine the horseradish and chicken stock or pot au feu liquid in a saucepan. Bring to the boil, then lower the heat and cook gently for 15 to 20 minutes. Rub the sauce through a fine sieve, using a pestle or a plastic pastry scraper. Return the sauce to the pan and stir in the cream. Set over low heat and reduce by one-third. Beat in the breadcrumbs, stirring continuously with a whisk.

Boil the sauce for a few minutes; it should have the consistency of thick gravy. Take the pan off the heat, stir in the egg yolk and mustard and season with salt and pepper.

SAUCE VIERGE AU BASILIC
(Olive oil sauce with basil)

INGREDIENTS

200ml (8fl.oz) olive oil

2 medium tomatoes

1 garlic clove

8 tbls snipped fresh basil

Continued

The bouquet of this sauce improves if it is made several hours in advance. The flavours become more pronounced when the sauce is slightly warm; place the bowl in a bain-marie for a few minutes before serving. We use this sauce with thinly sliced turbot; it goes extremely well with any small, poached fish or grilled lamb cutlets.

PREPARATION

Plunge the tomatoes into a saucepan of boiling water for a few seconds; refresh in iced water, peel and deseed. Cut the flesh into very small lozenge shapes and place in a bowl.

Add the peeled, crushed garlic, the snipped basil, chervil and parsley and the finely crushed coriander seeds, the olive oil, lemon juice, salt and pepper.

3 tbls snipped chervil

3 tbls snipped flat-leaf parsley

6 dried coriander seeds, crushed

juice of 1 lemon

fine salt

freshly ground white pepper

Serves: 6 people
Preparation time: 15 minutes

CHLOROPHYLL

(Chlorophyll: finely puréed green herbs for colouring)

Chlorophyll is useful for a multitude of dishes and is well worth the long and tedious preparation. Put the chlorophyll into small individual ramekins and pour over a drop of oil to form an insulating film. It will keep for about 2 weeks in the refrigerator. In hot weather, leave out the shallots, which may cause the mixture to ferment or may spoil the flavour after 4 or 5 days in the refrigerator.

INGREDIENTS

45g (1½oz) chervil

140g (5oz) parsley

50g (2oz) chives

45g (1½oz) tarragon

1kg (2lb 2oz) spinach

70g (2½oz) shallots

salt

2L (3½pts) water

Makes: 150g (6oz) (about 6 tbls)
Preparation time: 1 hour
Cooking time: 10 minutes

PREPARATION

Wash the spinach and herbs and remove the stalks. Peel and wash the shallots. Place all the above ingredients in a blender or food processor with 2L (3½pts) water and process for 5 minutes, slowly at first and then at medium speed.

Lightly stretch a muslin cloth over a saucepan and pour in the contents of the blender. Let all the liquid drain through, then gather up the edges of the muslin and twist it extremely gently to extract as much liquid as possible. Discard the pulp and wash out the muslin cloth in cold water.

COOKING

Season the green juice with salt and set the saucepan over medium heat. Stir gently with a wooden spatula until the first trembling of the liquid; this will cause some of the ingredients to coagulate and will clarify the remaining liquid. Remove the pan from the heat immediately — do not allow it to boil.

Stretch the washed muslin over a bowl and, using a ladle, gently spoon out the contents of the saucepan. Use a metal palette knife to scrape up the gooey purée (the chlorophyll) from the muslin.

SAUCE CUMBERLAND

(Cumberland sauce)

INGREDIENTS

1 medium shallot

4 tbls wine vinegar (preferably red)

⅓ tsp white peppercorns, coarsely crushed

100ml (4fl.oz) Veal stock (see page 48)

50ml (2fl.oz) port

2 tbls redcurrant jelly

1 tsp Worcestershire sauce

1 orange

zest of 1 lemon

salt

Serves: 6 people
Preparation time: 8 minutes
Cooking time: 20 minutes

T his sauce makes an excellent accompaniment to breast of duck and all cold game. We like it best served with cold roast partridge; the delicate flavour of the meat is enhanced by the robust character of this sauce, which also perfectly complements a hare terrine.

PREPARATION

THE SHALLOT: Peel, wash and finely chop. Put in a saucepan with the vinegar and the crushed peppercorns. Set over high heat and reduce by two-thirds.

COOKING

Remove and reserve the orange zest. Sqeeze the orange juice into the reduced shallot mixture, together with the veal stock, port, redcurrant jelly and Worcestershire sauce. Set the pan over high heat and, as soon as the mixture comes to the boil, lower the heat and simmer for 20 minutes. Pass the sauce through a conical sieve into a bowl and keep in a cold place. Meanwhile, cut the orange and lemon zests into *julienne* and blanch. Drain, pat dry and reserve.

Serve the Cumberland Sauce when it is very cold and half-set. Stir in a pinch of blanched orange and lemon zest just before serving.

SAUCE MAYONNAISE

(Mayonnaise)

INGREDIENTS

2 egg yolks

1 tbls Dijon mustard

500ml (1pt) vegetable oil

Continued

M ayonnaise can be the starting point for innumerable delicious sauces. Keep this sauce at room temperature and not in the refrigerator. You can make an excellent green sauce by adding 45g (1½oz) chorophyll (see page 59) to this quantity of mayonnaise.

½ tbls white wine vinegar *or* juice of ½ a lemon

1 tbls double cream (optional)

1 tsp fine salt

freshly ground white pepper, to taste

Makes: about ½L (1pt)
Preparation time: 10 minutes

PREPARATION

Combine the egg yolks, mustard, salt and pepper in a bowl and mix together with a wire whisk or wooden spoon. Gradually pour on the oil in a thin, steady stream, beating all the time. Stir in the vinegar or lemon juice and finally the cream, if you are using it.

LA ROUILLE

INGREDIENTS

250g (9oz) potatoes

1 garlic clove

fine salt

3 hard-boiled egg yolks

250ml (10fl.oz) olive oil

pinch of saffron

freshly ground white pepper

Serves: 6 people
Preparation time: 20 minutes

Serve the *rouille* with fish or mussel soup; it should be handed round separately in a sauceboat or small olive wood bowl. For garlic lovers, an extra clove may be crushed and added to the sauce.

PREPARATION

Preheat the oven to 180°C/350°F/Gas 4.

Peel and wash the potatoes and boil or steam until tender. Drain well and put in a roasting pan. Place in the preheated oven for 1 minute so that the potatoes dry out.

Peel the garlic clove and roll it in fine salt, then rub it round a bowl. Rub first the potatoes and then the hard-boiled egg yolks through a fine sieve into the bowl. Stir with a spatula until well mixed, then blend in the olive oil, stirring constantly. Season to taste with salt and pepper and, finally, add the saffron.

BEURRE D'ECREVISSES
(Crayfish butter)

Preparation time: 35 minutes
Cooking time: 20 minutes

Crayfish butter is principally used to enrich and heighten the flavour of sauces and soups. Shrimp, prawn and lobster butters are made in the same way. Put the butter into a ramekin or earthenware bowl and cover with greaseproof paper; it will keep very well for 1 week in the refrigerator or for several weeks in the freezer.

INGREDIENTS

24 live crayfish

butter, equivalent in weight to the crayfish heads, claws, bits of shell and creamy parts and the vegetables, after cooking

1 medium carrot

1 medium onion

1 tbls Cognac

200ml (8fl.oz) dry white wine

small pinch cayenne pepper

4 parsley stalks

1 sprig thyme

½ bay-leaf

salt

PREPARATION

THE CARROT AND ONION: Peel, wash and coarsely dice. Melt 1 tbls butter in a cocotte or saucepan set over low heat, put in the carrot and onion *mirepoix*, sweat until soft. Set aside.

THE CRAYFISH: Remove the intestinal vein from inside the tails by pinching them between your thumb and forefinger. Place the crayfish in the cocotte or saucepan, set over very high heat and sauté in 2 tbls butter. After 2 or 3 minutes, pour in the Cognac and ignite. Pour in the white wine and season with salt and cayenne pepper. Lower the heat, add the vegetable *mirepoix*, parsley stalks, thyme and bay-leaf and cook for 10 minutes. Keep in a cold place.

THE BUTTER: Remove the crayfish tails and keep them to garnish the finished dish or for use in another recipe (for example, in a salad, au gratin, or *à la nage*). Weigh the crayfish mixture. Put everything in a blender or mortar with an equal quantity of butter. Blend until you have a smooth, well-mixed paste. Push it through a fine sieve, using a pestle or wooden spoon. The butter is now ready for use.

INGREDIENTS

250g (9oz) butter

2 large garlic cloves

½ very small shallot

6 tbls parsley

6 whole hazelnuts (optional)

small pinch nutmeg

pinch freshly ground black pepper

1 tsp fine salt

Makes: 250g/9oz snail butter
Preparation time: 15 minutes

BEURRE A L'ESCARGOT

(Snail butter)

Snail butter is well known as an indispensable and inseparable companion to snails. Sauté some snails quickly in the hot butter and serve in a casserole to make a delicious and easy first course. The nuts add a special flavour and a pleasant 'bite' to the butter.

Snail butter will keep very well in the refrigerator if you put it in an airtight container; it will keep for even longer in the freezer.

PREPARATION

THE BUTTER: Cut into small pieces, place in a bowl and leave to soften in a warm place. Work it with a spatula until creamy.

THE GARLIC AND SHALLOT: Peel and chop them very finely. Add them to the butter.

THE PARSLEY: Wash and de-stalk. Chop and add to the butter.

THE HAZELNUTS: Skin them by placing in a very hot oven or under a hot grill for a few minutes. Rub with a cloth to remove the skins. Finely chop the nuts and add to the butter.

THE SEASONING: Using a spatula, work all the ingredients together until thoroughly mixed, then stir in the salt, pepper and nutmeg.

VINAIGRE DE FRAMBOISES

(Raspberry vinegar)

Raspberry vinegar is mainly used for deglazing certain sauces. Although it has an excellent, delicate flavour, be careful not to use it to excess! The quantity of sugar needed may vary by as much as 20%, depending on the sugar content of the fruit. Obviously, the sweeter the fruit, the less sugar you will need. To use the raspberry pulp in sauces for game, cook it in the same way as jam, with an equal quantity of sugar, then store in airtight jars.

INGREDIENTS

2kg (4lb 4oz) very ripe raspberries

1.5L (2¾pts) white wine vinegar

about 150g (5oz) lump sugar

250ml (10fl.oz) Cognac or 90% proof alcohol

Makes: just over 1L (about 2pts)
Maceration time: 48 hours
Cooking time: 1 hour

PREPARATION

THE MACERATION: Put 1kg (2lb 2oz) raspberries in an earthenware or china bowl and pour over the vinegar. Cover with a cloth or a plate and leave in a cool place for 24 hours.

The following day, put the remaining raspberries in another bowl. Place a fine sieve over this bowl and pour through the first maceration of raspberries, making sure that all the liquid drains through. Discard the raspberry pulp, or use it in a sauce for game. Macerate the second batch of raspberries in the same way; that is, cover the bowl with a cloth or plate and leave in a cool place for 24 hours.

COOKING

Place a fine sieve over a saucepan and drain the raspberries well, then discard them. Add the sugar lumps and Cognac or alcohol to the vinegar. When the sugar has dissolved, set the saucepan in a larger saucepan half-filled with hot water. Set the pans over high heat and bring to the boil, making sure that the bain-marie (but not the vinegar) boils for 1 hour. Skim the surface of the vinegar as often as necessary. It is important that the vinegar should not boil, so keep the temperature at about 90°C (200°F). Pour the vinegar into a bowl and keep in a cool place. Once cold, strain the vinegar through a piece of muslin and bottle it.

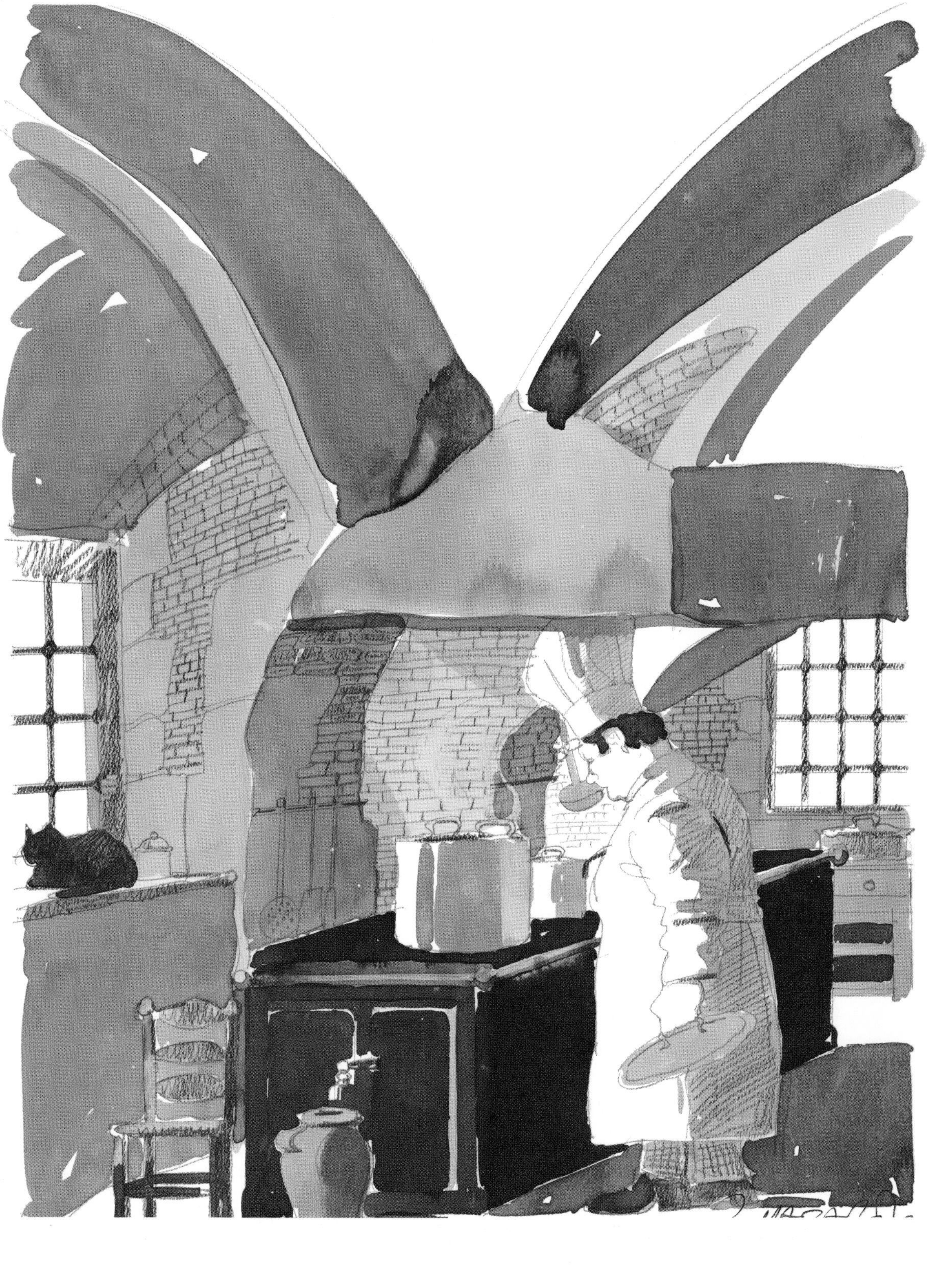

CHAPTER FIVE

SOUP

When we think of soup, it is the aroma which comes to mind above all — musky, powerful, light or delicate. It fills the kitchen with good smells as it cooks and filters out through the house. We think that adults particularly appreciate soup; it evokes vivid memories, sometimes bitter, sometimes amusing, sometimes even nostalgic of that constant, never-to-be forgotten parental exhortation to 'eat up your soup'.

There are soups suited to every occasion and to every season. On a hot summer evening, the perfect beginning to an al fresco supper could be a succulent chilled soup, simply made, yet an ideal and refreshing foretaste of the dishes to follow. On a cold winter's night, a rich, thick, hot soup can be a lifesaver — something full of flavour to warm the cockles of the heart after a day in the fresh air.

In country areas, soups are usually made from farm produce; cabbage, bacon, leeks, potatoes, cream etc. They are left to simmer away for hours on the stove and kept constantly bubbling. In some regions of France, half a glass of wine is poured into each plate; this is called making a *chabrol*. Recently, modern taste has tended towards smooth, cream soups or consommés, which are lighter and more delicate than the country broths.

Among the hundreds of different soups which exist, our own favourites include game and shellfish consommés, *velouté Germiny* (cream of sorrel), *crème Freneuse* (cream of turnip), *crème Argentueil* (cream of asparagus) and cream of watercress, not forgetting mussel and fish soups. We are often sufficiently carried away by greed to accept a second bowlful of good soup!

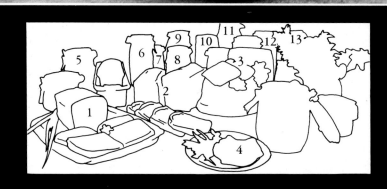

1 *Terrine de lapereau aux noisettes et pistaches (page 84);*
2 *Pâté en croute au suprême de volaille (page 80);*
3 *Terrine de poulet aux herbes (page 86); 4 Truffle;*
5 *Snails; 6 Raspberries; 7 Gherkins; 8 Onions; 9 Pieds de*
moutons; 10 Ceps; 11 Mousserons; 12 Tomatato concassé;
13 *Chanterelles (Preserving and bottling, page 92)*

INGREDIENTS

2 live hen lobsters, each weighing about 450g (1lb), with their eggs if possible

1 medium bouquet garni

4 garlic cloves

2 celery stalks

25g (1oz) parsley stalks

½ tsp freshly ground black pepper

500ml (1pt) dry white wine

1½L (2½pts) Fish stock (see page 50)

2 tomatoes

1 carrot

white part of 1 leek

small bunch of fresh mint

2 egg whites

1 branch chervil

salt

Serves: 4 people
Preparation time: 30 minutes
Cooking time: 40 minutes

CONSOMME DE CRUSTACES

(Shellfish consommé)

If you wish, you may garnish the soup with a few steamed baby vegetables, either 'turned' or shaped into balls; these complement this subtle, delicate consommé. You can serve the cold lobster meat as a salad with mayonnaise, surrounded by tiny, very lightly cooked vegetables or use it in Lobster salad with mangoes (see page 125). These make excellent hors d'oeuvre.

Hen lobsters still carrying their eggs (which they do in their tails) are considered to be at their most succulent and savoury. They have a better flavour than male lobsters.

PREPARATION AND COOKING

THE *NAGE*: Place the following ingredients in a saucepan, taking care to prepare them as in the recipe for *nage* or court bouillon (see page 47): the bouquet garni, 4 garlic cloves, 1 celery stalk, the parsley stalks and ground pepper. Pour in the white wine and fish stock, season with a little salt and bring to the boil over high heat. Cook for 10 minutes, skimming the surface if necessary.

THE LOBSTERS: Rinse them quickly in very cold water, plunge them into the *nage* and cook for 10 minutes. Draw the pan off the heat and leave the lobsters to cool in the *nage*.

THE CONSOMME: Strain the *nage* through the sieve and reserve. Split the lobsters and remove the intestinal vein. Take out the meat and reserve it for another use, but keep the claws to garnish the consommé. Pound the shells and heads, being careful to remove the gritty sac, which is just behind the head. Put the crushed shells and heads into a saucepan.

Wash and coarsely chop the tomatoes. Peel, wash and finely shred the carrot, celery stalk, leek and mint and put them all in the saucepan, mixing them in with the crushed lobster shells. Add the coral and egg whites, blending the mixture with your fingertips, or a spatula.

Pour in the strained *nage* and bring the mixture to the boil over high heat, stirring frequently with a spatula. As soon as the mixture comes to the boil, reduce the heat and simmer very gently for 30 minutes without stirring, so as not to cloud the consommé. The consommé should be as clear as pure spring water, so pass it through a fine sieve lined with muslin.

TO SERVE

Ladle the consommmé into bowls or soup plates and garnish with the finely diced flesh from the lobster claws. Sprinkle a few sprigs of chervil over each serving.

CREME CAROLINE

INGREDIENTS

325g (11oz) fresh or tinned sweetcorn kernels, drained

30g (1oz) onion

50g (1½oz) butter

850ml (34fl.oz) milk

1 pinch nutmeg

1 pinch paprika

1 tbls snipped chives

salt

Serves: 4 people
Preparation time: 10 minutes
Cooking time: 7-10 minutes

It is rare for us to use tinned produce rather than fresh; however we usually do use tinned sweetcorn for this recipe, as it tastes just as good as fresh and is always available.

PREPARATION AND COOKING

Peel, wash and finely slice the onion, then sweat it with the butter in a saucepan. Rinse the drained sweetcorn in cold water and add it to the onions. Cook gently for 2 minutes. Pour in the milk, season with some salt and nutmeg and bring to the boil. Lower the heat and cook for 5 minutes. Purée the mixture in a blender or food processor for a few minutes, then pass through a sieve into a bowl. Chill the soup in the refrigerator until it is very cold.

TO SERVE

Serve the soup in a chilled tureen or in individual soup bowls or plates. Sprinkle it with paprika and snipped chives.

CREME DE CONCOMBRE A LA MENTHE

(Minted cream of cucumber soup)

INGREDIENTS

2 cucumbers, total weight 1kg (2lb 2oz)

10 fresh mint leaves

250ml (10fl.oz) single cream

salt

Serves: 6 people
Preparation time: 15

This is a perfect summer soup, its cool simple flavour perfectly complementing a midsummer evening. The addition of mint subtly enhances the taste of the cucumber and it will delight everyone who tastes it. It is most important that it should be served extremely cold so that is is almost frozen.

minutes
Cooking time: 10
minutes

PREPARATION

Peel and deseed the cucumbers. Cut into even-sized chunks and steam for 10 minutes. Purée in a blender for a few minutes, then rub through a fine mesh sieve into a bowl. Set the bowl in crushed ice. Finely snip the mint and add it to the purée. Leave to steep for several hours, then stir in the cream. Season with salt, to taste.

INGREDIENTS

600g (1lb 4oz) watercress

120g (4oz) potatoes

650ml (26fl.oz) boiling water

2 slices White bread (see page 43)

60g (2oz) clarified butter

salt

freshly ground white pepper

3 tbls double cream

Serves: 4 people
Preparation time: 15 minutes
Cooking time: 7 minutes

CREME DE CRESSON

(Cream of watercress soup)

You can decorate this soup with a few blanched watercress leaves just before serving.

PREPARATION

THE VEGETABLES: Wash the watercress in several changes of water. Remove the stalks and any yellow or withered leaves. Peel and wash the potatoes and cut them into small, even-sided cubes.

COOKING

Sweat the watercress without fat in a saucepan set over high heat. Pour in the boiling, lightly salted water and add the potatoes. As soon as the potatoes are cooked (on no account let them go mushy), purée the mixture in a blender or food processor, then rub through a conical sieve. Season to taste with salt and pepper and keep warm.

Cut the bread into 5mm (⅛in) cubes. Heat the clarified butter in a frying pan and sauté the bread cubes over high heat until golden. Drain the croûtons and serve separately in a sauceboat.

TO SERVE

Serve in a tureen or individual bowls or soup plates. Spoon the cream into the bowls and pour in the hot soup.

CREME VICHYSSOISE

(Vichyssoise)

Apopular soup, this must be served very cold. If you have no chicken stock in the refrigerator, you can make the Vichyssoise entirely with water.

PREPARATION

THE VEGETABLES: Trim, wash and finely chop the leeks, keeping only the white parts and the first 2.5cm (1in) of the green parts. Peel, wash and finely slice the onions. Peel the potatoes and cut them into large even-sized chunks.

COOKING

Melt the butter in a saucepan and gently sweat the leeks and onions. Add the water, chicken stock and potatoes and leave to simmer for 20 minutes. Add the cream and cook for a further 5 minutes. Purée the mixture in a blender or food processor, then rub through a sieve into a bowl set in crushed ice. Stir the soup gently from time to time and season with salt. Sprinkle over the chives just before serving.

INGREDIENTS

700g (1lb 8oz) leeks
350g (12oz) onions
350g (12oz) potatoes
750ml (1½pts) water
750ml (1½pts) Chicken stock (see page 48)
400ml (16fl.oz) double cream
50g (2oz) butter
2 tbls snipped chives
salt

Serves: 8 people
Preparation time: 15 minutes
Cooking time: 25 minutes

GRATINEE NORMANDE

(Normandy onion soup)

The cider gives a slightly mellower flavour to the classic *soupe à l'oignon* and makes it more digestible. Be sure to make this soup in large quantities; greedy people are apt to give themselves away by asking for a second bowlful!

PREPARATION

THE ONIONS: Peel, wash and finely slice. In a sauté pan, sweat them with 25g (1oz) butter until pale golden. Add the bouquet garni, pour in 150ml (6fl.oz) cider and simmer for 5 minutes. Set aside.
THE VELOUTE: Melt the remaining butter in a saucepan. Stir in the flour and make a pale roux. Pour in the chicken stock and bring to the boil, stirring continuously with a wire whisk. Cook for 15 minutes,

INGREDIENTS

375g (12oz) onions (preferably the purple Breton type)
40g (1½oz) butter
1 very small bouquet garni
250ml (10fl.oz) sweet cider
2 tsp flour
650ml (25fl.oz) Chicken stock (see page 48)
8 thin slices French bread, preferably from a baguette
70ml (2½fl.oz) double cream

Continued overleaf

skimming the surface frequently. Preheat the grill to hot. Stir the onions into the velouté and simmer for 15 minutes, skimming if necessary. Season to taste with salt and pepper. Meanwhile, lightly toast the bread under the grill.

TO SERVE

Divide the remaining cider between 4 heatproof bowls and pour in the soup and the cream. Top with the toasted bread, then sprinkle over the grated Gruyère. Place under the hot grill until the cheese is melted and golden brown. Serve piping hot.

INGREDIENTS

25g (1oz) Gruyère cheese, grated

salt

freshly ground black pepper

Serves: 4 people
Preparation time: 10 minutes
Cooking time: 35 minutes
Picture: page 77

1kg (2lb 2oz) mussels preferably Bouchot

150g (5oz) onions

150g (5oz) leeks, white parts only

120g (4oz) carrots

½ celery stalk

75g (2½oz) butter

2 small bouquets garnis

⅓tsp white peppercorns, crushed

100ml (4fl. oz) dry white wine

1 fat clove garlic

100g (4oz) tomatoes

750ml (26fl. oz) Fish stock (see page50)

150ml (6fl. oz) double cream

pinch of saffron

2 branches chervil

salt

freshly ground black pepper

SOUPE DE MOULES

(Mussel soup)

A light soup, tasting of the sea, scented with saffron, this will tempt even non soup-eaters. The chervil may be replaced with a light sprinkling of lemon thyme flowers. It is best to use Bouchot mussels if you can find them, as they contain no sand and therefore need no cleaning and no de-bearding.

PREPARATION

THE VEGETABLES: Peel, wash and finely slice them all into a bowl. Then set aside in a cool place.

THE MUSSELS: Wash and scrape them. Heat 1 tsp butter in a large saucepan and sweat one-third of the onions and leeks. Add the mussels, 1 bouquet garni and the crushed white peppercorns. Pour in the white wine, cover the pan and cook over high heat. From time to time, stir the mussels or shake the pan, so that the mussels at the bottom go to the top. When they have all opened, drain the mussels in a conical sieve set over a bowl to catch all the cooking liquor. Decant the liquor and keep at room temperature. Remove the mussels from their shells, cutting away the 'beards' if necessary. Once you have done this, keep all the mussels in a bowl covered with a damp cloth.

Serves: 4 people
Preparation time: 30 minutes
Cooking time: 40 minutes

COOKING

Peel and crush the garlic clove. Peel, deseed and chop the tomatoes. Heat the remaining butter in a saucepan and sweat the remaining onions and leeks, the diced carrots and celery, the second bouquet garni, the crushed garlic and the tomatoes. Cover the pan and cook gently for 5 minutes. Pour in the fish stock and the mussel liquor and bring to the boil.

Reserve 20 mussels for the garnish. Put the rest into the soup mixture. Simmer gently for 20 minutes, then add the double cream and saffron. Let it bubble once, then pour the mixture into a blender or food processor. Blend for 5 minutes, or until the soup is smooth, then rub through a conical sieve. Correct the seasoning with salt and pepper. Return the soup to the saucepan and reheat it gently.

TO SERVE

Divide the reserved mussels between 4 bowls or soup plates, pour over the boiling hot soup and sprinkle with chervil. Serve immediately.

CHAPTER SIX

FIRST COURSES

The role of the first course is to stimulate the tastebuds of the diners, so it must be unusual, original, delicate and light and served in small portions. It must be neither too sweet nor too spicy; in a word, it heralds a well-balanced meal.

Among all the choice of starters, the highly prized and ever popular soufflé represents the pinnacle of rashness and courage on the part of the cook. It demands total discipline from the guests, who must go to the table at the precise moment that the soufflé goes into the oven. Waiting for a soufflé is like waiting for the theatre curtain to rise; the guest must wait quietly, with a sense of anticipation and curiosity, while the host or hostess must be attentive, a little nervous, and sometimes even completely on edge.

It is not unusual for a lunch menu to consist entirely of first courses; in that case, it is essential to provide a wide variety of tastes, textures and sauces. We have included many cold first courses in this chapter. They make life much easier for the cook, because they can be prepared several hours in advance and they are essential to the presentation and variety of any buffet.

PATES AND TERRINES

Wonderfully rich in texture, delicate and succulent, foie gras comes to us from geese and ducks. Two-thirds of all the foie gras in the world (2,000 tons a year) is produced in France; other major producers are Hungary, Yugoslavia, Israel and, recently, Japan.

Duck foie gras is even better than goose, especially if it is served fresh. It is often more luscious and has a finer flavour; 80% of all the foie gras sold is duck. The rearing of ducks and geese for foie gras is still done on a relatively small scale and has been practised for centuries. Geese are herbivorous birds, which like to wander freely in the pastureland, in large, open pens. From the age of 5 months, they are individually force-fed 3 times a day — a very labour-intensive business. The foie gras is at its full maturity after 4 weeks of feeding. Ducks are force-fed, from the age of 4 months, for 3 weeks before their liver reaches maturity. A goose liver weighs between 500g and 1200g (1lb 1oz and 2lb 8oz), but the ideal weight is about 800g (1lb 12oz). Duck livers weigh between 300g and 700g (10oz and 1lb 8oz) and their ideal weight is about 400g (14oz).

When you are choosing foie gras it should 'give' a little when pressed with the thumb — it must be neither too hard nor too soft. Make sure that it has no marks or blemishes. It should be creamy-white or pale yellow, depending on the type. Foie gras is so popular that it can be found almost everywhere in the world — preserved by part-cooking, tinned, in jars and china pots etc. Unfortunately, certain countries forbid the importation of raw foie gras for health reasons, but it is freely available commercially in a few European countries.

There are numerous ways of cooking and serving raw and preserved, part-cooked foie gras. Our favourite ways of serving it cold are as a terrine, a *ballotine* or in a brioche. If you are preparing foie gras to serve hot, pull the lobes gently apart, but cook them in one piece or cut into 1.5cm (¾in) thick slices. Foie gras may then be baked, grilled, poached, cooked *en papillote* or steamed. It must never be overcooked, but should be pink in the middle.

A little clear gravy, some small 'turned' vegetables, a bed of salad or some fruit segments make a happy accompaniment to foie gras. A few drops of an aromatic vinegar — sherry or raspberry, for instance — added to the gravy will enhance the mellowness of warm foie gras.

BALLOTINE DE FOIE GRAS TRUFFE

(*Ballotine* of foie gras with truffles)

It is not essential to use the truffles in this recipe, but they give the *ballotine* a sublime flavour that is delicious.

1 *Gratinée Normande (page 71)*
2 *Consommé de crustacés (page 68)*
3 *Soupe de moules (page 72)*

INGREDIENTS

1 fresh goose foie gras, weighing about 800g (1lb 12oz)

pinch of caster sugar

50ml (2fl.oz) Armagnac

50ml (2fl.oz) port

2 truffles, preferably raw, each weighing 75g (2½oz)

100g (4oz) pork caul *or* 150g (5oz) very finely sliced back fat

2L (3½pts) Chicken stock (see page 48)

4 tbls fresh tarragon

2½ tsp fine salt

1 tsp freshly ground white pepper

Serves: 8 people
Preparation time: 20 minutes
Cooking time: 20 minutes
Wine: A sweet, but not too heavy, white wine such as a Barsac or Saint Croix du Mont will balance the foie gras.

Picture: page 116

PREPARATION

PREPARING AND DEVEINING THE FOIE GRAS: Soak the foie gras in cold water for 2 to 3 hours to get rid of the impurities. 30 minutes before deveining the foie gras, pour in a little hot water to bring the temperature up to about 40°C (100°F); this makes it easier to handle.

Drain the foie gras, then separate the 2 lobes with your hands. Using a small, sharp knife, gently open up the inner sides of the lobes and cut out the veins; take very great care not to break them. Still using the knife, cut away any greenish parts left by the gall bladder. Lay the lobes, cut sides upwards, on a round dish or plate. Season with salt, sugar and pepper and sprinkle over the Armagnac and port. Cover with greaseproof paper and place in the refrigerator for at least 12 hours, turning the foie gras so that it absorbs the marinade.

COOKING

Peel the truffles with a vegetable peeler and cut into eighths. Stud the insides of the 2 lobes with the truffle pieces. Re-form the lobes by folding them over into roughly their original shape. Wrap them in the pork caul or back fat, then bind up tightly in muslin or cheese-cloth. Tie a knot of kitchen string at either end of the foie gras and fasten the wrapping in 2 places in the middle, not too tightly.

Pour the chicken stock into a saucepan and heat it to not more than 70°C (160°F). Plunge in the foie gras and simmer for 20 minutes. Add the tarragon after 15 minutes. Take the pan off the heat and leave the foie gras to cool in the cooking liquid. When it is cold, chill in the refrigerator for at least 24 hours.

TO SERVE

Remove the string, muslin and pork caul from the *ballotine*. Put it on a small round pastry rack set on a plate and place in the refrigerator. If necessary, clarify the half-set chicken stock with egg whites. Using a spoon, coat the *ballotine* with the half-set jelly. Pour a little jelly over the bottom of a silver dish and chill in the refrigerator until set. Place the *ballotine* on top of the jelly and serve with freshly made toast or grilled White bread (see page 43).

So that the chicken stock is sufficiently gelatinous, you could add a few split calves feet when you prepare it. You can vary the cooking method by preparing the foie gras up to the marinating stage; place in a terrine, cover and set in a bain-marie. Place in the oven preheated to about 200°C/400°F/Gas 6. Immediately turn off the oven and leave the foie gras undisturbed for 35 minutes. Allow it to cool, then place in the refrigerator for at least 24 hours.

FOIE GRAS CHAUD AUX CITRUS

(Hot foie gras with citrus fruits)

Y ou can use goose liver instead of duck liver in this recipe, but it is not as delicate and has less flavour. The contrast of the cold, brightly coloured citrus fruits with the warm foie gras, with its pink interior, makes this a succulent and delicate dish, full of delicious subtleties. If you find the blanched orange and lime zests bitter, candy them in 1 tbls each sugar and water.

PREPARATION

THE ORANGES: Using a vegetable peeler, cut off 8 good slices of orange zest. Cut into fine *julienne*, blanch, refresh, drain and keep in a cool place. Using a supple-bladed knife, cut off all the orange skin and pith. Cut the flesh into segments between the membranes. Squeeze the pulp to extract all the orange juice and pour the juice over the segments.
THE LIME: Prepare the lime in exactly the same way as the oranges, and set aside separately from them.
THE FOIE GRAS: Pull the 2 lobes apart with your hands. Using a small knife, remove the green part left by the gall bladder, as it might be bitter. Cut the small lobe into 4 slices and the larger lobe into 8 slices. If any large blood vessels are showing, cut them out. Lay the slices on a plate or on absorbent paper and place in the refrigerator.

COOKING

Set a sauté pan over fairly high heat. Season the slices of foie gras with salt and pepper and put them in the pan. Cook them lightly for 1 minute, until they are golden; the heat should be neither too fierce nor too gentle. Using a palette knife, carefully turn the slices to cook for 1 minute further. Transfer them from the pan directly onto a serving

INGREDIENTS

1 fresh duck foie gras, weighing about 400g (14oz)

3 oranges

juice of 1 lemon

1 lime

1 passion fruit

60g (2oz) butter

100ml (4fl.oz) Armagnac

300ml (12fl.oz) Veal or Duck stock (see pages 48 or 49)

1 tbls Curaçao

salt

freshly ground black pepper

Serves: 4 people
Preparation time: 35 minutes
Cooking time: about 6 minutes
Wine: This very rich dish needs a very rich wine: Gewürztraminer Vendange Tardive would be a perfect marriage.

dish and keep warm.

THE SAUCE: Pour off the fat from the pan, set it over high heat and deglaze with Armagnac. Flame the Armagnac, pour in the duck or veal stock and passion fruit pulp and reduce until syrupy. Add 4 tbls orange juice and the Curaçao, then the juice of half a lemon. Lower the heat and cook gently for about 4 minutes, then beat in the butter. Correct the seasoning if necessary, then pass through a conical sieve.

TO SERVE

Pour the sauce over the foie gras slices. Arrange rosettes of orange segments around the foie gras and place a lime segment on each slice. Scatter over a little orange and lime *julienne* and serve immediately. The final steps of the cooking, saucing and serving should happen as quickly as possible. Your guests should already be seated and ready to enjoy this deceptively light first course on presentation.

Serves: 12 people
Preparation time: 1 hour 30 minutes
Cooking time: 1 hour 10 minutes
Wine: A soft elegant red wine from the Santenay or Savigny-les-Beaune or a Grand Cru Beaujolais such as Brouilly.

PATE EN CROUTE AU SUPREME DE VOLAILLE

(Pâté *en croute* with breast of chicken)

This pâté will be at its best 2 to 3 days after cooking. It will keep for 1 week in the refrigerator.

If you do not have an *en croûte* mould, you can use a 32 x 12 x 11cm (12½ x 5 x 4½in) terrine instead.

PREPARATION

Cut the lean pork, 210g (7oz) of the fat and 300g (10oz) veal into wide strips. Place them in a bowl, pour over the port and 2 tbls Cognac and leave to marinate for several hours. Infuse the tarragon in the chicken aspic. Cut the chicken breasts into long strips, about 1cm (½in) wide. Heat 30g (1oz) butter in a frying pan and seal the chicken strips on both sides. Set aside.

Cut 50g (2oz) pork fat into small dice and place them in the frying pan set over low heat. Finely chop 2 tbls shallots and add them to the pan. Increase the heat to high and add the chicken livers, thyme and bay-leaf. Cook quickly for 30 seconds. Season with salt and pepper, put in the remaining Cognac and ignite. Remove the pan from the heat and leave the mixture to cool in the refrigerator.

When the mixture is cold, place it in a food processor or blender, add the remaining veal and process for a few minutes. Rub the resulting purée through a fine sieve into a bowl set in crushed ice. Using a wooden spatula, gradually work in the cream, then the egg yolk. Season to taste with salt and pepper.

Pass the marinaded meats through the medium blade of a mincer. Finely chop the remaining shallots and sweat them in 30g (1oz) butter. Leave to cool, then mix the shallots in with the minced meats, together with the whole egg and the chopped parsley.

Season the mixture with 2½ tsp salt per kg (2lb 3oz) meat and add pepper to taste.

ASSEMBLING THE PATE

Preheat the oven to 220°C/450°F/Gas 8.

Generously butter a mould. On a lightly-floured marble or wooden surface, roll out the pastry to a thickness of about ½cm (¼in) and line the mould with the pastry. Reserve the trimmings. Line the pastry with very fine slices of pork fat. Spread a layer of minced meat over the bottom of the mould. Wrap the chicken liver mixture in very fine slices of pork fat to make a sort of sausage and lay it lengthways on top of the minced meat.

Wrap the strips of chicken breast in very fine slices of pork fat and lay them so that they are above, below and on either side of the liver 'sausage' (see illustration on page 66). Fill up the mould with the remaining minced meats.

Roll out a piece of pastry to a thickness of about ½cm (¼in), to use as a lid. Brush the edges with egg wash and place the lid on top of the pâté. Seal the edges and crimp the sides with a pastry crimper.

Brush the pastry lid with egg wash and decorate with the reserved pastry trimmings. Make 3 small holes in the pastry and put a cylinder of paper in each; these 'chimneys' will allow the steam to escape during cooking.

Bake the pâté in the preheated oven for 10 minutes, then lower the temperature to 160°C/300°F/Gas 2 and bake for a further hour. When the pâté is cooked, leave it to cool for 12 hours, then pour in enough half-set tarragon-infused chicken aspic through the 'chimneys' to fill the space between the filling and the pastry crust.

INGREDIENTS

225g (8oz) chicken breast fillet

400g (14oz) shoulder or chine of pork

360g (12oz) fresh pork back fat

500g (1lb 1oz) nut of veal

3 tbls port

3 tbls Cognac

1 tbls tarragon

Chicken aspic (see recipe for Chicken stock, page 48)

90g (3oz) butter

30g (1oz) shallots

100g (4oz) chicken livers

1 sprig thyme

1 bay-leaf

100ml (4fl.oz) double cream)

1 egg yolk

1 whole egg

4 tbls finely chopped parsley

800g (1lb 12oz) Puff pastry trimmings *or* Pâté crust (see pages 248 or 250)

pinch of flour

1 egg yolk, beaten with 1 tbls milk, to glaze

salt

freshly ground black pepper

Picture: page 66

Place the pâté in the refrigerator and leave it to rest for at least 24 hours before serving.

TERRINE DE HOMARD SAUCE VERTE

(Lobster terrine with green sauce)

This terrine will keep in the refrigerator for up to a week and is excellent for a busy hostess, or if you have weekend guests. You can replace the pork fat with Herb pancakes (see page 228).

It is absolutely essential to use live lobsters so that the mousse has a good, firm, moist consistency. You could use half quantities to make a smaller terrine but mousses generally work better if you make them in larger quantities.

PREPARATION

THE LOBSTER MOUSSE: Remove the lobster claws and tails and take out the meat and the corals from the heads, but be sure to discard the gritty sacs from near the corals and the trails from the tail meat. Place the lobster meat, corals and 2 egg whites in a blender or food processor and process until you have a liquid purée (this should only take a few seconds).

Using a pestle, rub the purée through a fine sieve into a bowl set in crushed ice. Using a wooden spatula, work 750ml (1½pts) cream into the mixture, a little at a time, then add 1 tsp salt. The mousse should have a very soft, almost runny consistency. Cover the bowl with buttered paper and place in the refrigerator.

THE SALMON MOUSSE: Using a fish filleting knife, take the salmon flesh from the bone and remove the skin. Cut 5 very thin slices of salmon, total weight about 70g (2½oz), for use in assembling the terrine. Set these aside.

Place the remaining salmon flesh and the remaining egg white in the blender or food processor and process until you have a smooth purée (this should only take a few minutes). Rub the purée through a fine sieve into a bowl set in crushed ice. Using a wooden spatula, gradually work in the rest of the chilled cream, a little at a time, then add ½ tsp salt. This mousse should have a firmer consistency than the lobster

1

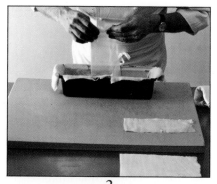

2

1 Lining the terrine
Using a sharp knife, cut several very thin slices from the slab of barding fat and neaten up the edges.
2 Place the slices in the terrine so that they overhang along one edge and both ends. Do not cut them off as they will be needed later.

3

4

3 Assembling the terrine *Mix half the lobster mousse into the salmon mousse, adding the chopped pistachio and diced truffle at the same time.*
4 Half fill the terrine with the mousse mixture and smooth over the surface with the back of a spoon.

5

6

5 Having lightly salted the salmon slices, lay them on top of the mousse in the terrine and gently flatten down with your finger tips.
6 Pour the remaining mousse into the terrine, smoothing over with a palette knife to ensure that every crevice is filled.

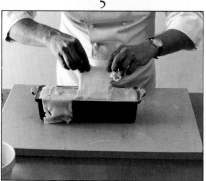

7

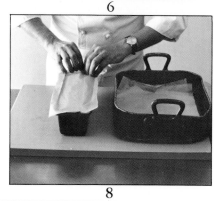

8

7 Fold the barding fat edges over the top of the mousse, trimming off any excess fat so that it does not overlap itself.
8 Cover the terrine with greaseproof paper and fit foil on top to seal. Place in a bain-marie, preferably lined with greaseproof paper in case the water boils.

mousse. Cover the bowl with buttered paper and place in the refrigerator.

ASSEMBLING THE TERRINE: Preheat the oven to 110°C/225°F/Gas ¼. Line the sides of a terrine measuring about 32 x 8 x 7.5cm (12 x 3¼ x 3in) with very thin slices of back fat.

Using a wooden spatula, stir half the lobster mousse into the salmon mousse. Finely dice the truffle and mix it into the mousse. Skin the pistachio nuts, finely chop and add them to the mixture. Using a palette knife, spread the mixture over the bottom of the terrine.

Lightly salt the salmon slices and lay them over the mixed mousse. Fill up the terrine with the remaining lobster mousse and cover with finely sliced back fat.

COOKING

Cover the terrine with greaseproof paper and foil, then place in a bain-marie and cook in the very slow oven for 1 hour 25 minutes. Test whether the terrine is cooked by piercing the centre with a trussing needle; it should come out clean and damp.

TO SERVE

Leave the terrine in a cold place for 24 hours before eating it. To unmould, dip the dish into hot water for several seconds and wipe it dry. Loosen the edges of the terrine with a knife, then turn it onto a serving dish. Remove the back fat, cut the terrine into 1½cm (¾in) slices and serve on individual plates with toast and green sauce.

TERRINE DE LAPEREAU AUX NOISETTES ET PISTACHES

(Terrine of rabbit with hazelnuts and pistachios)

Like all terrines, this one benefits from being left for 2 or 3 days after being cooked. On no account eat it before 24 hours after cooking, as the full flavour will not have developed. Depending on the temperature of your fridge, the terrine will keep for 10 to 15 days, as long as you do not cut into it. A slice of French bread, freshly grilled and served with the terrine, makes a better accompaniment than toast.

PREPARATION

Preheat the oven to 220°C/425°F/Gas 7.

THE RABBIT: Using a sharp knife, cut the meat off the bones. Put the liver and the meat, except the fillets from the saddle, on a plate and sprinkle over the Armagnac. Cover the plate and place in the refrigerator.

Chop up the bones and trimmings and put them in a roasting pan. Roast in the preheated oven until browned. 5 minutes before the bones are ready, add the carrot and onion cut into rounds.

Pour off the excess fat from the pan and tip the contents into a saucepan. Deglaze the roasting pan with 100ml (4fl.oz) white wine and pour the liquid into the saucepan. Pour in enough water to cover, set the pan over high heat and bring to the boil. Skim the surface, lower the heat, add the bouquet garni and simmer gently for 1 hour. Strain the stock through a conical sieve, return it to the saucepan and reduce by half. This stock will be used later for cooking the terrine.

THE MEATS: Cut the lean pork into strips. Finely slice the pork fat. Cut the rabbit fillets lengthways in half and wrap them in the sliced fat. Reserve enough fat slices to line and cover the terrine.

Slice the remaining fat (about 220g/8oz) into strips. Pass the pork, the strips of fat, the rabbit meat and liver through the medium blade of a mincer. Keep in the refrigerator.

THE SHALLOT: Peel, wash and chop. Sweat it with the butter until soft, then keep in a cool place.

THE THYME, BAY-LEAF, MAJORAM, PARSLEY AND GARLIC: Chop very finely. Set aside.

THE PISTACHIOS: Pour over boiling water and skin them. Set aside.

THE HAZELNUTS: Spread them out on a baking sheet and place in a very hot oven (240°C/475°F/Gas 9) or under a hot grill for a few minutes, until the skins begin to blister. Rub the hazelnuts with a cloth to remove the skins. Set aside.

ASSEMBLING THE TERRINE: Using your hands or a wooden spatula, work together the minced meats, eggs, the chopped shallot, herbs, garlic and the remaining white wine. Season to taste.

Line a terrine measuring about 30 x 10 x 8cm (12 x 4 x 3in) with fine strips of pork fat. Divide the mixture into 4 and put in one-quarter of it. Arrange half the pistachios and hazelnuts so that they will look attractive when the terrine is sliced. Add another quarter of the minced meats. Lay the rabbit fillets down the centre of the terrine. Add

INGREDIENTS

1 rabbit, about 2kg (4lb 4oz) skinned weight

50ml (2fl.oz) Armagnac

1 carrot

1 medium onion

200ml (8fl.oz) dry white wine

1 small bouquet garni

500g (1lb 1oz) neck or shoulder of pork

550g (1lb 3oz) pork back fat

1 shallot

15g(½oz) butter

1 sprig thyme

½ bay-leaf

½ tbls marjoram

3 tbls parsley

1 garlic clove

30 pistachio nuts, shelled

50 whole hazelnuts, shelled

2 eggs

salt

freshly ground black pepper

Serves: 14 people
Preparation time: 1 hour 15 minutes
Cooking time: 55 minutes
Wine: A heavier claret like Pomerol which is more like a Burgundy or perhaps a fine Rioja with its lovely oaky taste from northern Spain.
Picture: page 66

another layer of minced meats. Spread over the hazelnuts and pistachios, fill the terrine to the top with the minced meat mixture and cover with fine strips of pork fat.

Place in the refrigerator for 4 to 6 hours.

COOKING

Preheat the oven to 220°C/425°F/Gas 7. Place the terrine in a bain-marie and bake in the preheated oven for 25 minutes. Spoon off any grease which has formed during cooking. Pour over the rabbit stock and reduce the oven temperature to 190°C/375°F/Gas 5. Cook for a further 30 minutes. Remove the terrine from the oven and place a lightly weighted board (maximum weight about 500g/1lb) on top, to compress the terrine.

INGREDIENTS

1 oven-ready chicken, weighing about 1.6kg (3lb 6oz)

100g (3½oz) ham

225g (8oz) fresh breast or shoulder of pork

300g (10oz) veal rump

450g (1lb) pork back fat

500ml (1pt) double cream

1 egg

100ml (4fl.oz) Armagnac

3 tbls parsley

3 tbls chives

2 tbls tarragon

2 shallots

1 tbls butter

1 tbls melted butter

salt

freshly ground black pepper

TERRINE DE POULET AUX HERBES

(Chicken terrine with herbs)

This is a delicious terrine to pack in your picnic hamper for an 'al fresco' meal in the country. It is also an excellent dish for a buffet.

PREPARATION

Remove the chicken flesh from the bones and place the breast fillets in the refrigerator. Thinly slice enough back fat to line and cover a terrine measuring 28 x 16 x 6cm (11 x 6½ x 2½in).Cut all the meats and the remaining back fat into thin strips. Put the meat through the mincer twice, together with the boned chicken legs and the chicken liver. Put the minced meats into a well-chilled bowl and work the mixture with a wooden spatula. Stir in the cream, egg and Armagnac. Add 2½ tsp salt per kg (2lb 3oz) meat and season to taste with pepper. This is the *farce*.

Finely chop all the herbs. Peel and chop the shallots. Heat 1 tbls butter in a small saucepan and sweat the shallots for 2 to 3 minutes. Cool and add the herbs. Slice the chicken breasts into strips 2cm (¾in) wide. Roll the strips in the melted butter, then in the chopped herbs and shallots. Set aside on a plate.

ASSEMBLING THE TERRINE: Line the terrine with fine strips of pork fat. Spread half the *farce* over the bottom of the terrine, then make a layer of sliced chicken breast, fill with the remaining *farce*, then top with thin slices of pork fat. Leave in a cold place for 4 to 6 hours.

COOKING

Preheat the oven to 200°C/400°F/Gas 6.

Place the terrine in a bain-marie and cook in the preheated oven for 1 hour. Remove from the oven and place a weighted board (maximum weight 500g/about 1lb) on the terrine to compress it gently until it has cooled completely.

Serves: 10 people
Preparation time: 45 minutes
Cooking time: 1 hour 30 minutes
Wine: A big powerful red such as the Gigondas or Châteauneuf-du-Pape from the southern end of the Côtes du Rhône.
Picture: page 66

RILLETTES DE CANARD

(*Rillettes* of duck)

R*illettes* are among the great classic dishes of France. They can also be made with pork, but the most famous of all are the *Rillettes de Tours*, which are made from goose meat, pork and foie gras.

You can chop up the carcass and bones of the duckling, freeze them and use them later for gravy or stock. If you can persuade your butcher to bone the duck for you, preparing the *rillettes* will be much simpler. For how to bone a duck, see Dodine of duckling, pages 90 and 91.

PREPARATION

THE DUCKLING: Lay the duckling breast-side down and, using a sharp knife, bone it out through the back. Remove the skin from the flesh. Cut off 150g (5oz) fat from the fattiest parts of the skin. Cut the fat into very small dice and reserve. Discard the skin.

Remove the flesh from the bones and cut out the breast fillets and the flesh from the thighs. Cut into strips about 3 or 4cm (1¼-1½in) long. Keep in a cool place. Do not use the flesh from the lower part of the legs. Discard the sinews.

THE BARDING FAT: Cut into very small dice.

THE ONION AND CARROT: Peel and wash. Cut the carrot in half lengthways and the onion horizontally.

COOKING

Place the barding fat and the duck fat in a casserole. Pour in enough

INGREDIENTS

1 oven-ready duckling, weighing about 2.1kg (4lb 10oz)

400g (14oz) barding fat

1 medium onion

1 medium carrot

125g (5oz) pork fillet, cut into 4 pieces

1 garlic clove

1 medium bouquet garni, containing 10g (⅓oz) sage

1 tsp soft green peppercorns

350ml (14fl.oz) dry white wine

salt

freshly ground black pepper

Serves: 12 people
Preparation time: 45 minutes
Cooking time: 3½ hours
Wine: A big full-bodied wine. A superb red Lirac (famous for its excellent and strong rosés) from southern Côtes du Rhône, north of Avignon.

water barely to cover. Set the casserole over medium heat, cover and cook gently for about 30 minutes, stirring occasionally with a spatula, until all the water has evaporated. At this stage, the fat should have melted. Add the pork fillet and the duck flesh, the unpeeled garlic clove, carrot, onion and bouquet garni. Season with a little salt, pour in two-thirds of the white wine and bring to the boil. Cover the casserole and set it over very gentle, regular heat, so that the mixture is barely trembling. Stir with a spatula from time to time to prevent the mixture sticking to the bottom of the casserole. Leave to cook for 3 hours.

COOLING

Leave the mixture in the casserole, but remove all the vegetables and aromatics. Pour over the remaining white wine, add the green peppercorns and cover the casserole with a damp cloth, which must not touch the meat. Put the casserole in a cool, airy place.

POTTING THE MEAT: When the mixture is lukewarm, work the meats together with your fingertips until all the shredded flesh and the fat are thoroughly mixed together. Correct the seasoning with salt and pepper. Put the *rillettes* into earthenware pots or terrines and cover them with greaseproof paper. They will keep for 3 or 4 weeks in a cold place. Keep them in a refrigerator for at least 1 or 2 days before eating them if you want them to be at their best.

TO SERVE

Serve the *rillettes* with plain or toasted country bread; never serve pickled onions or gherkins with them, or you will ruin the subtle, delicate flavour of this excellent dish.

Picture: page 116

DODINES DE CANETONS TRUFFES

(Dodines of duckling with truffles)

Dodines are a derivative of terrines and pâtés and are the finest and most savoury of all such dishes. They keep very well in the refrigerator for about 10 days. They look quite spectacular when they are served sliced, displaying their hidden treasures. Garnish them with a few salad leaves, flavoured with sherry vinegar and your favourite oil.

PREPARATION

BONING THE DUCKLINGS: Singe the ducks over a gas flame for a few seconds, then use a small knife to remove any remaining hard quills or down. Gently wipe the ducks with a cloth and, using a heavy knife, cut off the feet about 1.5cm (¾in) above the joint. Cut off the wings where they join the wing-tips. Place 1 of the ducklings, breast side down, on a chopping board. Using a boning knife, cut along the backbone, starting in the middle of the neck and ending just before the parson's nose.

Bone the duck by sliding the knife between the flesh and bones of the carcass. The skin should still be attached to the flesh; be careful not to make a hole in it. When the flesh has been eased off the carcass, chop through the neck and remove the head. Cut out the thigh bones. Cut out part of the drumstick bones by lightly sawing through 3cm (2½in) below the joint, then snapping them. Remove the wing bones in exactly the same way, sawing 3cm (2½in) from the joint and snapping as before.

Lay out the boned duck, skin-side down and cut away the largest nerves from the thigh and breast flesh. Sprinkle over a pinch each of saltpetre and sugar, moisten with 70ml (3fl.oz) port and rub in these ingredients with your fingertips, so that they penetrate the flesh. Fold over the duck in the middle, put it on a dish and keep for 12 hours in the refrigerator. Repeat the operation with the second duckling.

THE STUFFING: Slice off 2 thin 3cm (1¼in) squares of pork back fat and reserve. Cut the pork fillet and the remaining fat into large dice. Discard the greenish gall bladder from the duck livers and place these 3 ingredients in a bowl. Sprinkle with salt and pepper and the rest of the saltpetre and moisten with the remaining port. Stir well with a wooden spatula, cover with greaseproof paper and keep in the refrigerator for 12 hours. Pass the mixture through the medium blade of a mincer, pour it into a bowl set in crushed ice, then stir in the eggs with a wooden spatula. Slowly incorporate the cream, a little at a time.

Fry 1 tbls of the stuffing to check the seasoning is correct, but do not taste it until it is completely cold.

THE FOIE GRAS: Prepare it as for *Ballotine* of foie gras, (see page 76). Peel the truffles and cut into wide strips. Stud the foie gras with the truffle strips. Chop the truffle parings and add them to the stuffing. Using a damp tea-towel, roll the foie gras into 2 sausage shapes and set aside until later.

INGREDIENTS

2 ducklings, with their giblets and necks attached, each weighing about 3kg (6lb 6oz)

1 tsp saltpetre

1 tsp caster sugar

250ml (10fl.oz) ruby port

600g (1lb 4oz) pork fillet

1kg (2lb 2oz) pork back fat, rind removed

600g (1lb 4oz) duck livers

4 eggs

400ml (16fl.oz) very cold double cream

2 fresh duck foies gras, each weighing about 350-400g (12-14oz) or equivalent weight of tinned foie gras

2 truffles, each weighing about 60g (2oz), preferably fresh

45g (1½oz) salt

freshly ground white pepper

Serves: 16 people (2 dodines each, for 8 people)
Preparation time: 2 hours 15 minutes
Cooking time: 1 hour 30 minutes to 1 hour 45 minutes
Note: Start preparing this dish 3 to 4 days before you plan to serve it.
Wine: A deceptively delicate dish which would be well suited to a Cru Beaujolais such as a Morgon or a red wine from the Loire — a Touraine or an Anjou.

1 *Lay the plucked duckling onto the board and remove any stubs or hard quills with the blade of a knife against your finger.*
2 *Slice through the wing joints and using a heavy knife, chop off the feet just above the joint.*

1

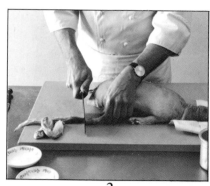

2

3 *Place the duckling breast-side down and slice down the neck and along its backbone to the parson's nose. Ease the meat away from the rib-cage with the point of the knife.*
4 *Once you have freed the flesh from the carcass, cut the head off making the cut halfway down the neck.*

3

4

5 *Scrape away the flesh from the drumsticks before sawing through and snapping them off.*
6 *Lay out the flesh in a baking tray. Scatter on salt and sugar and rub in the port marinade thoroughly, making sure all the crevices are wetted.*

5

6

7 *Fold over the edges of the flesh and leave it to absorb the marinade for 12 hours.*
8 *Once the duck has had time to marinate, take the foie gras and remove the veins with the help of a knife, making a few incisions.*

7

8

9

10

9 *Place the sliced truffle into the cuts. Any truffle scraps can be used in the stuffing.*
10 *Roll the foie gras up in a damp cloth to ensure that it retains its shape and set on one side.*

11

12

11 *Spread most of the stuffing thickly onto the inside of the flesh with a spatula, making sure that every corner is filled.*
12 *Unwrap the foie gras and place lengthways down the centre of the duckling to act as a backbone.*

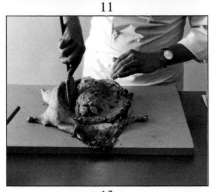

13

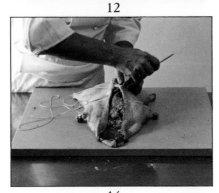

14

13 *Spread the remaining stuffing on the foie gras.*
14 *Fold the skin of the back over the foie gras and sew up with fine string, starting from the parson's nose. Fold back the loose skin at the neck and sew up. Place foil on the bone-ends to prevent burning.*

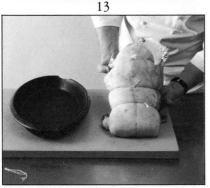

15

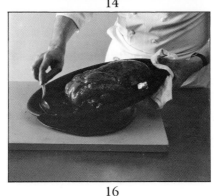

16

15 *Tie 3 pieces of string around the duckling, so that it will retain its shape during cooking, and place in a heatproof dish the size of the duckling.*
16 *Baste the duckling during cooking.*

ASSEMBLING THE DODINES

Lay the 2 ducklings on the chopping board, skin-side down. Line the small hole, made by boning near the parson's nose, with the reserved fat. Spread half the stuffing on each. Then place the foie gras 'sausage' in the middle and lift a little stuffing around the top of each of these. Fold over the duck flesh and sew up, using a trussing needle and fine string, to re-form the ducks into their original shape.

Tie up each duck in 3 places round the middle, but do not pull the string too tightly. Place each of the ducklings, breast-side up, in an oval roasting dish, 35-40cm (14-16in) long. Keep in the refrigerator for 3 to 4 hours.

COOKING

Preheat the oven to 240°C/450°F/Gas 8. Roast the ducklings in the very hot oven for 10 minutes, then reduce the temperature to 180°C/350°F/Gas 4 and bake for a further 1 hour 20 minutes to 1 hour 35 minutes. Every 10 minutes, use a spoon to baste the duckling with the fat which runs during cooking. Pour some off if there seems to be too much. Pierce the centre of the ducklings with a trussing needle to see if they are cooked; the needle should come out hot.

When the *dodines* are cooked, remove the string and leave to cool in the roasting dishes at room temperature for 4 hours. Spoon off all the fat which collects between the *dodines* and the dishes. Place the dishes in the refrigerator for at least 48 hours.

TO SERVE

Serve the *dodines* whole for a buffet, glazed with chicken aspic or left plain. For a dinner party, slice the *dodines* and serve as a terrine on individual plates, accompanied by toasted bread.

PRESERVING AND BOTTLING

Bottling fruit and vegetables conjures up delightful memories of the past and fills us with nostalgia. For our grandparents and later our parents, the preparations for bottling our produce every summer were like a sort of cult and we all took part in the ritual peeling and paring of all kinds of vegetables and fruits.

What a pleasure it was to gather together among all that appetizing and brightly coloured garden produce, which would be held captive in glass jars only a few hours after being harvested. Then the dark shadows of the larder or cellar would welcome those summer foods which we knew would bring a taste of sunshine into our family meals during the winter months.

With a little basic knowledge and a certain amount of practice, you can easily produce perfect bottled fruit and vegetables, with all their many advantages.

BASIC FACTS ABOUT PRESERVING AND BOTTLING

If you have your own vegetable garden or orchard, stagger production so that nothing goes to waste and make the most of your produce throughout the year.

Go into the country and visit market-gardens, smallholdings and farms; buy crates of best quality fresh produce at seasonal prices; this will save you quite a lot of money.

If you have a store-cupboard full of preserved foods, you can always throw together an impromptu meal, without feeling that you have not got the desired ingredients or that the recipe will be humdrum.

You should take pride in serving fresh, natural home-grown foods, prepared entirely by yourself as they always seem to taste better than those bought in shops. Preserved foods will also save preparation time before a meal, so you will have more time to spend with your guests.

PREPARING FOOD FOR BOTTLING

Make sure that all vegetables and fruits are top quality, completely unblemished and absolutely fresh — just picked if possible. Peel and wash them quickly but very carefully. Never leave them to soak in water, or they will lose valuable mineral salts.

Most preserved foods need to be blanched in boiling water, refreshed immediately in cold water and then drained before being packed in jars; this process will clean them and preserve their original colours and shapes. Pack the prepared foods immediately in immaculately clean jars with hermetic seals. Lay the fruit or vegetables in the jars without packing them too tightly. Leave a 2 to 3cm (1in) space between the top of the jar and the fruit or vegetables. Cover vegetables with at least 1L (1¾pts) of water, salted with 1 or 2 tsp salt per litre of water; add 1 tbls of lemon juice to those products which may become discoloured, such as celeriac. Cover fruits with a plain or vanilla-flavoured sugar syrup; use 250 to 500g (10oz to 1lb 2oz) sugar per litre (1¾pts) water. The amount of salt or sugar required for vegetables or fruits will depend upon the variety.

PRESERVING EQUIPMENT

You can use the classic galvanized metal preserving pans, but a large casserole, small boiling copper pressure cooker or automatic cooker will do just as well. It is important to wedge the jars firmly in the sterilizing pan so that they do not rattle against each other and crack; they should all be at about the same height in the sterilizer. It is absolutely essential to add salt in order for the water to reach the required temperature. Use cold water salted with not more than 300g (12oz) salt per litre (1¾pts) of water in the bain-marie. When the water boils, it should reach 108°C (225°F) to ensure complete sterilization. (Boiling point of unsalted water is 100°C/212°F.) The water must never come above the contents of the jars; it should be just level with the contents and the lids must never, ever be submerged.

Preserving takes between 35 minutes and 1 hour after boiling point and we process the food only once. The time taken depends on how well-cooked you like your fruit and vegetables and on their size. If you are using a pressure cooker or automatic cooker, reduce the time by at least one-third and follow the manufacturers instructions *to the letter*. Once cold, store the jars in a cool, shady place away from direct light. The bottled foods will keep for several months provided that they are not subjected to any change of temperature.

If you are bottling foods commercially, we recommend that you sterilize them several times; divide the total sterilizing time between several boilings to be certain that all bacteria spores are positively destroyed. To give you some idea of suitable products for bottling, these are some which we preserve during the year for our clients to enjoy at *Le Gavroche* and *The Waterside Inn*: Wild mushrooms like Pleurotes, mousserons, triconomes, girolles (chanterelles), trompettes de la mort (craterelles), ceps and pieds de mouton. We also bottle truffles, snails, mirabelle plums, raspberries and white peaches.

HORS D'OEUVRES

PETITS FLANS D'ESCARGOTS EN HABITS VERTS

(Little flans with snails in green coats)

This unusual and original first course is one of our latest culinary creations and has proved immensely popular. Try to use fresh snails, as they have a much better flavour than tinned ones. You can preserve several dozen snails at a time. Store them in sterilized jars, so that you do not have to cook them freshly too often.

PREPARATION

THE FLAN CASES: Preheat the oven to 200°C/400°F/Gas 6.

On a lightly floured marble or wooden pastry board, roll out the pastry as thinly as possible. Roll it round a rolling pin, then unroll it over 6 flan tins measuring 8cm (3in) diameter, 1.5cm (1½in) deep. Dip a small piece of pastry into the flour and use it to push the pastry into the flan tins to line them. Roll the rolling pin over the edges of the tins to remove any surplus pastry. Prick the pastry with a fork and then leave to rest in the refrigerator for at least 10 minutes.

BAKING BLIND: Line the pastry cases with a circle of greaseproof paper and fill with dried beans. Bake in the preheated oven for 10 minutes. Remove from the oven, take out the beans and paper, unmould the pastry cases and place on a wire rack.

THE PARSLEY PUREE: Plunge the parsley into boiling water for a few seconds, then drain. Pour the cream into a saucepan and bring to the boil. Add the parsley and boil for a moment. Purée in a blender or food processor for 2 or 3 minutes, then rub through a fine sieve using a pestle or a plastic pastry scraper. Return the mixture to the pan and keep hot. It should have the consistency of a liquid purée; if it seems too thin, reduce over high heat for a few minutes.

THE SOUFFLE MIXTURE: In a small saucepan, make a white roux with 1 heaped tsp butter and 1 heaped tsp flour. Stir in 100ml (4fl.oz) cold milk and bring to the boil. Take the pan off the heat, add the egg yolk, season to taste with salt and pepper and keep warm.

INGREDIENTS

36 snails

80g (2½oz) Puff pastry or trimmings (see page 248)

1 tbls flour, plus 1 pinch flour

70g (2oz) parsley, stalks removed

250ml (10fl.oz) double cream

40g (1½oz) butter

100ml (4fl.oz) milk

1 egg yolk

6 egg whites

¼ tsp Chlorophyll (see page 59)

2 tbls snipped chives

2 tbls snipped tarragon

salt

freshly ground pepper

Serves: 6 people
Preparation time: 1 hour
Cooking time: 13 minutes
Wine: A light, chilled red wine such as a Beaujolais Nouveau would be perfect or from further south in Provence one of the little reds produced near St Tropez.

1 *Bavarois de piments doux (page 98)*; 2 *Cervelas de saumon Curnonsky (page 100)*; 3 *Tourte aux carottes (page 103)*; 4 *Tourte aux trois mousses sauce iodée (page 105)*; 5 *Mousseline de brochet Chloé (page 109)*; 6 *Mousseline de volaille au Roquefort (page 111)*; 7 *Mousseline de homards (page 112)*; 8 *Soufflé Eléonora (page 114)*; 9 *Soufflé Suissesse (page 115)*; **Opposite** *L'oreiller rose Maltaise (page 101)*.

ASSEMBLING AND COOKING THE FLANS

Preheat the oven to 220°C/425°F/Gas 7. Divide the parsley purée between the pastry cases.

In a frying pan, heat 30g (1oz) butter until light nutty brown. Roll the snails in the butter, drain and put 6 in each pastry case. Beat the egg whites until well risen, then fold them into the soufflé mixture, together with the chlorophyll, chives and tarragon. Heap a little soufflé mixture in a dome shape on top of each flan and smooth the surface with a palette knife. Bake in the preheated oven for 3 minutes. Slide each flan onto a plate and serve immediately.

INGREDIENTS

4 medium red peppers

4 medium green peppers

60g (2oz) butter

300ml (12fl.oz) Chicken stock (see page 48)

300ml (12fl.oz) Veal stock (see page 48)

1 medium carrot

1 small leek

1 shallot

6 medium tomatoes

2 egg whites

4 gelatine leaves (about 15g/½oz)

250ml (10fl.oz) double cream

3 tbls snipped fresh basil

salt

freshly ground black pepper

BAVAROIS DE PIMENTS DOUX

(*Bavarois* of sweet peppers)

PREPARATION

THE PEPPERS: Peel with a vegetable peeler. Cut in half and discard the seeds and white parts. Coarsely chop the flesh and reserve 1 tbls of both the red and green peppers to make the jelly. Melt 1 tbls butter each in 2 shallow pans; put the green peppers in 1 pan and the red peppers in the other and sweat until tender. Rub the peppers separately through a fine strainer and keep the 2 purées in separate bowls at room temperature.

THE JELLY: Peel and finely slice the carrot, leek and shallot. Put the chicken and veal stocks into a saucepan, together with the reserved 2 tbls peppers and the sliced vegetables. Add 1 crushed tomato and the egg whites.

Set the pan over high heat and bring to the boil, stirring frequently with a wire whisk, so as to prevent the egg white from sticking to the bottom of the pan and thus not doing its job of clarifying the liquid. As soon as the liquid begins to tremble, lower the heat to not more than 90°C (200°F). Do not stir again, or the jelly will go cloudy. Soak the gelatine leaves in cold water. When the liquid has been simmering for 30 minutes, add 2 of the soaked gelatine leaves, then very carefully strain the liquid through a conical sieve. Keep in a cool place.

PREPARING THE MOULDS: Use moulds measuring 7cm (2¾in) by 5cm (2in) by 3.5cm (1½in). When the jelly is cold, brush the insides of each to a thickness of about 2mm (1/16in). Then refrigerate.

THE *BAVAROIS* MIXTURE: Heat 125ml (5fl.oz) jelly to lukewarm. Stir in 1 gelatine leaf and immediately set the jelly to cool in crushed ice. Whip the double cream until the whisk leaves a trail when lifted. Beat half the cream into the red pepper purée, using a whisk, then carefully fold in half the cold, runny jelly with a spatula. Repeat the operation with the green pepper purée.

FILLING THE MOULDS: When the *bavarois* mixtures are half set, spoon them into 6 small dariole moulds, arrange the pale pink mixture in one side of the mould and the soft green mixture in the other. Place in the refrigerator for at least 2 hours before serving.

THE TOMATO SAUCE: Plunge the remaining 5 tomatoes into boiling water, refresh in cold water, then peel, deseed and dice them. Add the finely snipped basil and stir in the remaining half-set jelly. Season liberally with salt and pepper.

Serves: 6 people
Preparation time: 45 minutes, plus 2 hours setting
Wine: A fruity, medium dry wine with a touch of acidity: a Chenin Blanc from the middle Loire or Beaujolais Blanc.
Picture: page 96

TO SERVE

Turn out the moulds onto well chilled serving plates. If they are difficult to unmould, slide the point of a sharp knife between the mould and the jelly. Pour the tomato sauce around the edge of each *bavarois*. Serve with hot toast.

CASSEROLETTE D'ESCARGOTS POULBOT

(Snails Le Poulbot)

Y ou can simplify the preparation of this dish by using tinned snails, but they will not have the same fine flavour as fresh snails. If you have bottled your own snails (see 'Preserving and Bottling' page 92) these will be just as good as fresh ones.

INGREDIENTS

3 dozen snails

4 shallots

1 small garlic clove

20g (¾oz) parsley

20 hazelnuts, shelled

60g (2oz) butter

1 tbls green Chartreuse

600ml (24 fl.oz) double cream

salt

freshly ground black pepper

PREPARATION

Peel, wash and finely chop the shallots and garlic, keeping them separate. Wash and very finely chop the parsley. Put the hazelnuts in a roasting pan and place them in a very hot oven or under a hot grill for a few minutes until lightly coloured. Tip the hazelnuts onto a cloth, gather up the edges and rub lightly to remove the skins. Finely chop the nuts. Drain the snails, wash them well in cold water and pat dry.

Serves: 6 people
Preparation time: 25 minutes
Cooking time: 10 minutes
Wine: A dry white distinctive Chablis or a Puligny-Montrachet.

COOKING

In a sauté pan set over low heat, sweat the shallots in 30g (1oz) butter until soft. Add the snails, then the chopped hazelnuts. Pour in the Chartreuse and ignite. Stir in the cream, then the garlic, and simmer for 5 minutes. Season to taste and beat in the remaining butter.

TO SERVE

Serve in very hot individual pottery or snail dishes. Decorate each snail with a sprinkling of parsley.

INGREDIENTS

500g (1lb 1oz) boned, skinned salmon

2 egg whites

700ml (28fl.oz) double cream

100g (4oz) fillet of turbot or brill

100g (4oz) fillet of sole

310g (11oz) butter

30g (1oz) cooked lobster or langoustine tails

1 tbls Cognac

10g (½oz) truffle

10g (½oz) soft green peppercorns

25g (¾oz) raw foie gras

10g (½oz) chives

1.2m (4ft approx.) pork sausage casing

400g (14oz) leeks

200g (7oz) breadcrumbs

dill leaves, to garnish

salt

CERVELAS DE SAUMON CURNONSKY

(Cervelas of salmon Curnonsky)

As with all mousse-based recipes, it is hard to achieve good results using only a small quantity of the mixture so do not try to make less than the given quantity.

You can keep the poached sausages in their skins for up to a week before using them; be sure to keep them in the refrigerator.

PREPARATION

THE SALMON MOUSSE: Put 400g (15oz) salmon and the egg whites into a blender or food processor and process for several minutes. Rub through a fine sieve into a bowl set in crushed ice. Using a wooden spoon, stir in 500ml (1pt) cream and 1 tsp salt, a little at a time. Keep in a cool place.

THE GARNISH FOR THE MOUSSE: Cut the turbot or brill, the fillets of sole and the remaining salmon into ½cm (¼in) dice. Heat 15g (½oz) butter in a shallow pan and quickly sear the fish, one variety at a time, adding 15g (½oz) butter for each fish. Remove from the pan and keep cool.

Cut the lobster or langoustine tails into small dice. Roll them in 1 tbls melted butter, pour in the Cognac and ignite. Keep cool. Mash the truffle, green peppercorns and raw foie gras and snip the chives.

FILLING THE SAUSAGES: Stir all the garnish ingredients into the

Serves: 10 people
Preparation time: 1 hour
Cooking time: 22 minutes
Wine: A dry, rich flavoured wine: a light, young Gewürztraminer or a fine Vouvray Demi Sec.
Picture: page 96

salmon mousse. Tie a knot at one end of the sausage casing, then pull the casing up over a large funnel or sausage-maker. Using your thumb, push the mousse mixture through the funnel into the sausage filler, a little at a time. When the sausage casing is full, tie up the end with string. Divide the sausage into 10 equal links, tying off each section with kitchen string.

POACHING: Prick the sausages with a very fine needle to prevent them from bursting during cooking.

Bring a round pan of salted water to the boil, lower the heat, put in the sausages and poach gently for 15 minutes. Immediately lift the sausages out of the casserole and plunge into very cold water.

THE LEEKS: Meanwhile, trim and wash the leeks, discarding the greenest parts. Finely slice them and sweat in a shallow pan with 100g (3½oz) butter until tender but still crisp. Add 500ml (1pt) cream. Simmer gently until reduced to a creamy consistency and season to taste with salt.

COOKING

Preheat the oven to 225°C/110°F/Gas ¼. Using the point of a small, sharp knife, carefully cut off the sausage casing. Melt 100g (3½oz) butter and roll the sausages first in the butter and then in the breadcrumbs. Put the sausages in a sauté pan with 50g (2oz) butter and place in the preheated oven for 7 minutes. Turn the sausages halfway through the cooking time.

TO SERVE

Spread the creamed leeks on a plate and arrange the sausages on top, transferring them from the sauté pan with a palette knife; take very great care, as they are extremely fragile. Serve at once, garnished with sprigs of dill leaves.

L'OREILLER ROSE SAUCE MALTAISE

(Pink pillows with sauce Maltaise)

You can create an extremely pretty effect by garnishing this delicately-coloured dish with blanched samphire. Alternatively scatter some sprigs of chervil over the sauce. This will provide a pleasing colour contrast.

INGREDIENTS

120g (4oz) Puff pastry
(see page 248)

pinch of flour

1 egg yolk, mixed with 1
tbls milk, to glaze

100g (3½oz) red
peppers

120g (4oz) tomatoes

30g (1oz) shallots

1 tbls butter

8 small green asparagus
spears

2 tbls double cream

500ml (1pt) milk

200g (7oz) Salmon
mousse (see page 105)

1 quantity Sauce
Maltaise (see page 58)

zest of ½ orange, cut
into *julienne* and
blanched

salt

freshly ground white
pepper

Serves: 4 people
Preparation time: 35
minutes
Cooking time: 3
minutes
Wine: A sweet wine
from the Coteaux du
Layon such as Quart de
Chaume or its neighbour
from Bonnezeaux.
Picture: page 97

PREPARATION

PREPARING THE PILLOWS: On a lightly-floured marble or wooden board, roll out the pastry to a thickness of about 5mm (¼in). Using a sharp knife, cut out 4 regularly-shaped rectangles, 9cm (3in) long and 5cm (2in) wide. Arrange the rectangles on a baking sheet brushed with cold water. Brush them with beaten egg wash and, using the point of a knife, make a light incision around the perimeter of each rectangle, 5mm (¼in) in from the edge. Mark small criss-cross patterns on the interior rectangles. Leave the pastry to rest in a cool place for at least 10 minutes before baking.

COOKING THE PILLOWS: Preheat the oven to 240°C/475°F/Gas 9 and bake the pillows for about 6 minutes. As soon as you remove them from the oven, run the point of a knife round the incisions in the rectangles. Slide the knife blade underneath the 'lids' and carefully lift them off. Place all the pastry on a wire rack.

THE PEPPERS: Skin them, discard the white parts and seeds and finely dice the flesh.

THE TOMATOES: Plunge into boiling water, peel, deseed and chop.

THE ASPARAGUS: Peel with a vegetable peeler, break off the tips and cook them in boiling, salted water until still crisp. Refresh and drain.

THE PEPPER AND TOMATO *COULIS*: Peel and finely chop the shallots. Heat the butter in a saucepan and gently sweat the shallots until soft. Add the diced peppers then, after 2 or 3 minutes, the chopped tomatoes. Season with a little salt and cook gently for 20 minutes. Stir in the cream, increase the heat and boil for 5 minutes. Season with salt and pepper and then rub the mixture through a fine sieve, or leave it just as it is. Keep hot.

THE SALMON MOUSSELINES: Pour the milk into a shallow pan and add 175ml (7fl.oz) water. Bring the liquid to the boil and salt it lightly. Using 2 teaspoons, form the mousse into 12 small egg shapes. Lower the heat to no more than 80°C (185°F), put the mousseline balls into the pan and poach very gently for 3 minutes, being sure to turn them over after 1½ minutes.

TO SERVE

Preheat the oven to 170°C/325°F/Gas 3.

Drain the mousselines on a tea-towel for a few seconds. Spoon the pepper and tomato *coulis* into the bottom of the pastry pillows which should be lukewarm. Put the pillows onto a heated china dish and place 3 mousseline 'eggs' in each one. Place in the preheated oven for 30 seconds.

Pour the sauce Maltaise over the pillows and arrange 2 asparagus tips on each one. Put the lids on top, garnish with the orange *julienne* and serve immediately.

PAPILLOTES DE SAUMON FUME CLAUDINE

(Smoked salmon parcels Claudine)

PREPARATION

THE MOUSSE: Place the smoked salmon trimmings and the smoked trout in a blender or food processor and process for 1 minute. Rub the resulting purée through a fine sieve into a small bowl set in crushed ice. Using a spatula fold in 2 tbls melted, cooled fish aspic, then gradually stir in the cream adding a very little at a time, particularly at first, to avoid any lumps. Season to taste with salt.

ASSEMBLING THE *PAPILLOTES*: Lay the 6 slices of smoked salmon on a wooden board or work surface. Divide the mousse between the slices, then roll up each one. Fold over the ends to form neat parcels. Arrange the parcels on a round wire rack and place in the refrigerator. When they are very cold, use a spoon to coat the *papillotes* with the half-set fish aspic.

Although the fish aspic is not absolutely essential, it is well worth taking the time to prepare it. It helps to absorb the cream into the mousse, which lightens the mixture. It also gives a beautiful shine to the colour of the smoked salmon. You could decorate the centre of each *papillote* with a pattern of tarragon leaves and truffles, for example — but keep the decoration discreet!

INGREDIENTS

6 slices smoked salmon, each weighing about 45g (1½oz)

100g (4oz) smoked salmon trimmings

25g (1oz) smoked trout fillet

275ml (11fl.oz) double cream

6 tbls fish aspic (see recipe for Fish stock, page 50)

salt

Serves: 6 people
Preparation time: 25 minutes
Wine: A dry wine such as a Pouilly Fumé or a Sancerre. It should be fresh and crisp, but not too thin.

Picture: front cover

TOURTES AUX CAROTTES

(Carrot *tourtes*)

This simple starter was such a favourite with our clientele at *The Waterside Inn* that it has been reappearing regularly on the menu

INGREDIENTS

12 medium carrots

50ml (2fl.oz) double cream

50g (2oz) butter

pinch of sugar

1 sprig lemon thyme

1 sprig parsley

1 garlic clove

350g (12oz) Puff pastry (see page 248)

1 egg yolk, beaten with 1 tbls milk, to glaze

120ml (4fl.oz) Veal stock (see page 48)

juice of 2 oranges

30g (1oz) clarified butter

salt

pepper

Serves: 6 people
Preparation time: 30 minutes
Cooking time: 10 minutes
Wine: A slightly sweet wine such as a Demi Sec Vouvray or even better would be a light, young Moselle such as Bernkasteler.
Picture: page 96

by popular request.

The sweet orange juice combined with the richness of the veal stock makes a perfect marriage with the pastry and carrots.

PREPARATION

THE CARROT PUREE: Peel and wash 6 carrots, cut them into large chunks and steam them or cook in boiling, salted water.

When the carrots are tender, drain them, add the cream and boil for 5 minutes.

Place the carrots in a blender or food processor and process for a few minutes, then rub through a fine sieve. Correct the seasoning and set aside in a cold place.

THE VICHY CARROTS: Finely chop the lemon thyme and parsley. Peel and very finely chop the garlic.

Peel and wash 3 carrots and cannelize them lengthways in 4 or 5 places. Using a mandoline, cut them into rounds approximately 3mm (1/10in) thick.

Place the sliced carrots in a shallow pan with a little water, 25g (1oz) butter, a pinch of sugar and salt and cook until barely tender. Quickly reduce the cooking liquid if necessary, then add the finely chopped thyme, parsley and garlic. Set aside in a cold place.

THE PUFF PASTRY: Preheat the oven to 220°C/425°F/Gas 7.

Roll out the pastry to a thickness of about 3mm (1/10in). Using a 10cm (4in) plain cutter, cut out 6 circles and place on a baking sheet. Arrange a few Vichy carrots on each circle, overlapping them slightly; leave a border of about ½cm (¼in) around the edge of each pastry circle. Spoon 2 tbls carrot purée on top of the Vichy carrots, then top the purée with more overlapping Vichy carrots.

Glaze the borders of the pastry circle with egg wash. Cut out 6 more large circles of pastry and, using a small pastry cutter, cut a 4cm (1½in) hole in the centre of each one and discard.

Lay the pastry circles over the carrots and gently press down onto the glazed borders. Glaze with egg wash and decorate with the tip of a knife. Leave to rest in a cold place for 10 minutes.

TO COOK

Bake the *tourtes* in the preheated oven for 10 minutes. Remove from the oven and brush the tops with a little clarified butter.

Meanwhile, make the following sauce to serve with the *tourtes*. Peel and wash 3 carrots, cut them into chunks and purée in the blender or food processor with the veal stock and orange juice. Pour into a saucepan, set the pan over high heat and reduce the sauce for 10 minutes. Beat in the remaining butter and pass the sauce through a conical sieve, into a sauceboat.

TO SERVE

Place each *tourte* on a warmed serving plate. Pour the sauce around the *tourtes* at the table.

TOURTE AUX TROIS MOUSSES, SAUCE IODEE

(*Tourtes* of 3 fish mousses with sea-scented sauce)

This dish does take an enormous amount of time to prepare, but the result is worth every second.

It is impossible to describe the exquisite subtlety of the three mousses and their sauce without tasting them.

You can make larger *tourtes* if you prefer. Bake them at the lower temperature of 200°C/400°F/Gas 6. The cooking time will depend on the size of the *tourte* (one for 4 people will take about 30 minutes). To check whether the mousse is cooked, insert a larding needle into the centre of the *tourte*; it should come out clean, damp and very warm but not hot to the touch of your lips. This is the perfect method of checking the cooking point of terrines and dodines.

PREPARATION

SALMON	HAKE	SOLE
180g (6½oz) salmon fillet	100g (4oz) hake fillet	100g (4oz) sole fillet
1 egg white (small)	½ egg white	½ egg white
225ml (9fl.oz) double cream	125ml (5fl.oz) double cream	125ml (5fl.oz) double cream
salt, to taste	salt, to taste	salt, to taste

INGREDIENTS

180g (6oz) salmon fillet

100g (4oz) hake fillet

100g (4oz) sole fillet

2 egg whites

975ml (38fl.oz) double cream

50g (2oz) pink shrimps, diced

1 tbls snipped chives

20g (¾oz) truffle, finely chopped

½ tsp Chlorophyll (optional) (see page 59)

440g (14oz) Puff pastry (see page 248)

pinch of flour

3 Herb pancakes 20cm (8in) diameter (see page 228)

2 egg yolks, mixed with 1 tbls milk, to glaze

80g (2½oz) shallots

30g (1oz) clarified butter

90g (3oz) butter

Continued overleaf

6 medium oysters

50ml (2fl.oz) dry white wine

100ml (4fl.oz) fish stock (see page 50)

20g (¾oz) of the following mixed herbs, crushed in equal quantites:

red pepper, citronella, coriander, rose buds, lavender seeds, fennel seeds, lime flowers and juniper, salt, freshly ground white pepper

Serves: 6 people
Preparation time: 1 hour 45 minutes
Cooking time: 12 minutes
Wine: A crisp, dry, but fruity wine, such as Muscadet Sur Lie or an even drier Gros Plant.

1 *Place a 13cm (5in) pastry cutter on a rolled out piece of pastry and cut round the outside.*
2 *After dusting the glass bowl with flour, fit the pastry ring into the bowl, moulding it with your fingertips.*

3 *Cut the 13cm (5in)* crêpes *in half and then into quarters and eighths, making sure not to cut through to the centre, so the sections are still joined together.*
4 *Use these sections to line the pastry already in the bowl keeping the extra pieces for use later.*

Make the 3 mousses in exactly the same way. First, place the skinned fillets and the egg white in a blender or food processor. Process for 2 minutes, until you have a well-blended purée. Rub through a fine sieve into a bowl set in crushed ice. Using a spatula, work in the cream, a little at a time. Season with salt. Finally, add the diced shrimps to the salmon mousse, the chives to the hake mousse, and the truffle and chlorophyll (if you are using it) to the sole mousse. Keep all the mousse in a cool place.

ASSEMBLING THE *TOURTES*: On a lightly floured marble or wooden surface, roll out the puff pastry as thinly as possible (to a thickness of about 2mm/1/12in). Cut out 6 circles with a 13cm (5in) pastry cutter and 6 with an 8cm (3in) cutter.

Flour the insides of 6 Pyrex bowls measuring 10cm (4in) in diameter and 4.5cm (2in) deep. Line them with the larger circles. Cut the pancakes into quarters. Use 2 quarters to line each pastry circle.

Divide the salmon mousse between the bowls and, using the back of a small ladle, make a hollow in the centre. Repeat the operation with the hake mousse and fill up the bowls with the sole mousse.

Cover the tops with pieces of the pancake trimmings and brush the

1

2

3

4

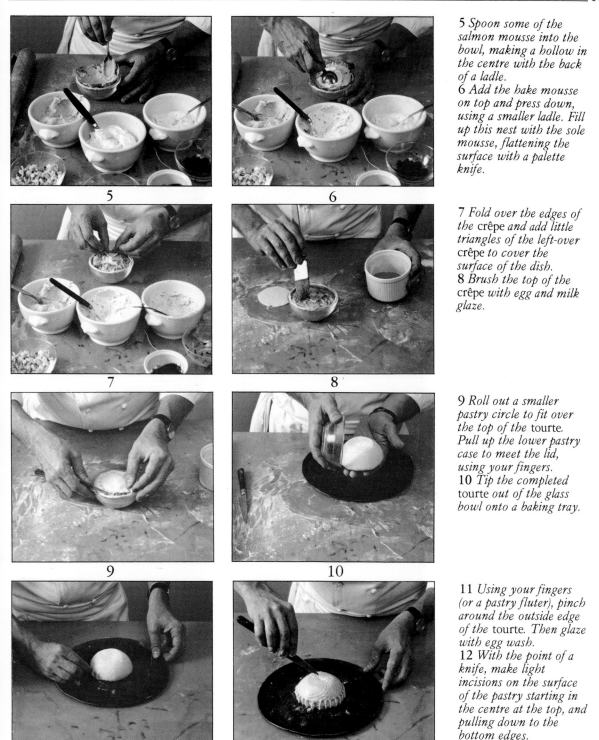

5 *Spoon some of the salmon mousse into the bowl, making a hollow in the centre with the back of a ladle.*
6 *Add the hake mousse on top and press down, using a smaller ladle. Fill up this nest with the sole mousse, flattening the surface with a palette knife.*

7 *Fold over the edges of the* crêpe *and add little triangles of the left-over* crêpe *to cover the surface of the dish.*
8 *Brush the top of the* crêpe *with egg and milk glaze.*

9 *Roll out a smaller pastry circle to fit over the top of the* tourte. *Pull up the lower pastry case to meet the lid, using your fingers.*
10 *Tip the completed* tourte *out of the glass bowl onto a baking tray.*

11 *Using your fingers (or a pastry fluter), pinch around the outside edge of the* tourte. *Then glaze with egg wash.*
12 *With the point of a knife, make light incisions on the surface of the pastry starting in the centre at the top, and pulling down to the bottom edges.*

13 *After cooking for 12 minutes, brush the* tourte *with clarified butter to give it a shine and remove it from the baking tray onto a wire rack or a serving plate.*
14 *The* tourte *looks exquisite when cut in half, revealing the colours of the layers.*

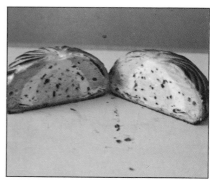

13   14

edges of the pancakes with the egg and milk glaze. Lay the 6 smaller pastry circles over the top and place the *tourtes* in the refrigerator for 10 minutes.

Meanwhile, preheat the oven to 220°C/425°F/Gas 7.

COOKING THE TOURTES

Unmould the *tourtes* from the bowls and place them, wider side down, on a baking sheet.

Pinch up the bottom of each *tourte* with a pastry fluter or between your thumb and forefinger. Glaze with egg wash and, with the point of a knife, mark the tops with lines in the shape of a rosette, as in a Pithiviers gateaux.

Bake in the preheated oven for 12 minutes.

THE SAUCE: Meanwhile, peel and finely slice the shallots and sweat them in a shallow pan with 30g (1oz) butter for 2 minutes. Add the white wine, fish stock and the mixture of herbs and spices. Increase the heat and reduce the liquid by half.

Put in the oysters with their juices and the remaining double cream. Boil for 5 minutes, then pour into the blender and process until smooth. Rub the sauce through a conical sieve back into the pan.

Set over low heat and stir in 60g (2oz) butter, a little at a time. Season to taste, then keep hot in a bain-marie.

TO SERVE

Picture: page 96

Place the very hot *tourtes* in shallow soup plates. Brush with clarified butter to make them shiny. Pour a ribbon of sauce round each one and arrange a few fennel leaves on the sauce. Serve immediately.

MOUSSELINE DE BROCHET CHLOE

(Mousseline of pike Chloé)

Like all mousse recipes, this dish is difficult to make in smaller quantities if you want to obtain good results.

If you prefer, you can use crayfish butter or 200ml (8fl.oz) Sauce Américaine (see page 146) instead of the lobster butter.

PREPARATION

THE PIKE: Place the pike fillets and egg whites in a blender or food processor and process for 2 minutes, until you have a well-blended purée. Rub through a fine sieve into a bowl set in crushed ice. Using a spatula, work in 750ml (1½pts) cream, a little at a time. Finally, season with salt. Cover the mousse with buttered greaseproof paper and place in the refrigerator.

THE LEEKS: Peel, wash, discard the green parts; cut into *julienne*.

THE CARROTS: Peel, wash and cut into *julienne*, using only the bright orange parts.

THE SCALLOPS: Finely dice the white flesh and corals.

Heat 15g (1½oz) butter in a shallow pan and quickly sauté the scallops for 10 seconds. Pour in the green Chartreuse and ignite. Remove from the heat and set aside.

COOKING

THE GARNISH: Heat 15g (1½oz) butter in a shallow pan. Put in the *julienne* of leeks and sweat over medium heat until still crisp. Transfer to a bowl. Cook the carrots in the same way, place in a bowl and keep the vegetables at room temperature.

THE SAUCE: Pour the remaining double cream into a saucepan. Set over high heat and reduce by one-third. Using a small wire whisk, beat in the lobster butter, a little at a time. Let the mixture bubble once, then take the pan off the heat and stir in the Hollandaise sauce. Do not allow the sauce to reboil. Season to taste with salt and pepper and set the pan in a bain-marie.

POACHING THE MOUSSELINES: Fill a shallow pan two-thirds full with

INGREDIENTS

500g (1lb 1oz) skinned pike fillets (ie 1 pike weighing about 1kg (2lb 2oz)

2 egg whites

1.15L (2pts) double cream

600g (1lb 4oz) leeks

500g (1lb 1oz) carrots

9 scallops

45g (1½oz) butter

1½ tbls green Chartreuse

350g (12oz) lobster butter (see recipe for Crayfish butter, page 61)

⅓ quantity Hollandaise sauce (see page 57)

500ml (1pt) milk

salt

freshly ground white pepper

Serves: 6 people
Preparation time: 1 hour
Cooking time: 10 minutes
Wine: This rich dish needs a rich wine such as an Alsace Pinot Gris (Tokay).

Picture: page 96

the milk and some water.

Bring the liquid to the boil and add a little salt. Using two large kitchen spoons, shape the mousse into 6 mousselines the size of an egg.

Reduce the heat to not more than 80°C (185°F) and poach the mousselines for 5 minutes on each side, turning them once with a spatula or slotted spoon.

TO SERVE

Preheat the oven to 170°C/325°F/Gas 3.

Drain the mousselines on a tea-towel for a few seconds. Divide the carrot and leek *julienne* and the scallops between 6 serving plates. Arrange a mousseline on top, cover with buttered greaseproof paper and place in the preheated oven for 1 minute. Pour the sauce generously over the mousselines and serve immediately.

INGREDIENTS

2 chicken breast fillets, total weight 200g (8oz) taken from a 1.3kg (2lb 12oz) chicken

1½ egg whites

500ml (1pt) double cream

1 tsp fine salt

Makes: about 700g (1½lb)
Preparation time: 25 minutes

MOUSSE DE VOLAILLE

(Chicken mousse, basic recipe)

This chicken mousse is used as the basis or as a secondary ingredient in many recipes, including Poussins Françoise (see page 178). It keeps very well in the refrigerator for 48 hours.

Use the chicken legs in another dish, either poached or grilled with a fresh herb or lemon butter or to make a white chicken stock.

Although it is not essential to use breasts from a whole chicken, the flesh will have a better texture and will absorb more cream if they are freshly boned.

PREPARATION

Remove the skin from the breast fillets and cut out the sinews with a small knife.

Place the chicken flesh and the egg whites in a blender or food processor and process for a few minutes until you have a smooth purée. Rub the purée through a fine sieve into a bowl set in crushed ice. Using a spatula, work the cream into the mixture, a little at a time. Finally, season with salt.

Bring a little salted water to the boil to cook a 'tester'. Poach 1 tsp mousse in the boiling water, keeping the temperature at about 80°C

(185°F). After 2 minutes, turn the mousse and poach for a further 2 minutes, then drain.

Cut open the poached mousse with a small knife and taste it to see whether the texture, lightness and seasoning are as they should be. If necessary, add a little more cream or salt to the mousse mixture.

Cover the mixture with buttered or greaseproof paper and place in the refrigerator.

MOUSSELINE DE VOLAILLE AU ROQUEFORT

(Mousselines of chicken with Roquefort)

This light, delicate dish is extremely satisfying to prepare, as well as to eat. Your guests will be pleasantly surprised by these excellent mousselines.

As they are so fragile, you may find it easier to serve the mousselines on individual plates.

PREPARATION

THE WALNUTS: Plunge them into boiling water and remove the skins. Soak 4 halves in the milk and chop the remainder. Using a fork, mix the walnuts thoroughly with the Roquefort, then add the Armagnac. Using 2 teaspoons, form this mixture into 4 small *quenelle* shapes. Place them on a saucer and chill in the refrigerator.

THE APPLE: Peel and core the apple and cut it into 'matchsticks', as evenly-sized as posssible. Melt the butter in a small shallow pan and sweat the apple 'matchsticks', keeping them crunchy.

POACHING THE MOUSSELINES: Using a large kitchen spoon and a palette knife, shape the chicken mousse into 4 mousselines, the size of a large egg. Make a small cavity in each one, using either a small spatula or the back of a teaspoon dipped in the egg white. Place the little Roquefort *quenelles* in the cavities, close up and smooth over the holes with a palette knife.

Bring the chicken stock or 1L (1¾pts) salted water to the boil in a sauté pan. Reduce the heat so that the liquid is barely trembling and poach the mousselines for 5 minutes on each side. Turn them very carefully with a spatula, without lifting them out of the cooking liquid, as they will be extremely fragile.

INGREDIENTS

20g (¾oz) Roquefort cheese

25g (1oz) shelled walnuts

50ml (2fl.oz) milk

1½ tsp Armagnac

1 crisp eating apple, preferably Cox or Reinette

25g (1oz) butter

½ quantity Chicken mousse (see page 110)

½ egg white

1L (1¾pts) Chicken stock (optional) (see page 48)

1 quantity Sauce mousseline (see page 58)

sprigs of chervil, to garnish

salt

Serves: 4 people
Preparation time: 25 minutes
Cooking time: 10 minutes
Wine: This is a difficult dish to find a wine that exactly suits it, but a Monbazillac from western Dordogne would be ideal.

Picture: page 96

TO SERVE

Preheat the oven to 170°C/325°F/Gas 3.

Drain the mousselines on a tea-towel for a few seconds. Strew the apple 'matchsticks' on a shallow dish, bi-metal or silver if possible, and place the mousselines on top. Cover with buttered paper and place in the preheated oven for 2 minutes.

Remove from the oven and pour over the sauce mousseline. Decorate each mousseline with a sprig of chervil and a well-drained walnut half. Serve at once.

INGREDIENTS

2 small live hen lobsters, each weighing about 300g (10oz), with their eggs if possible

1 large live lobster, weighing about 1.3kg (2lb 12oz)

2 egg whites

750ml (1½pts) double cream, well-chilled

150g (5oz) very large, green spinach leaves

300g (10oz) butter, at room temperature

50g (2oz) Beluga caviar

3 medium shallots

200ml (8fl.oz) Champagne

30g (½oz) fine salt

Serves: 6 people
Preparation time: 1 hour 45 minutes
Cooking time: 18 minutes
Wine: This expensive, exotic dish deserves a full fat white wine such as a Grand Cru Meursault or Chablis.
Picture: page 96

MOUSSELINES DE HOMARDS

(Mousselines of lobster)

This is a speciality of *Le Gavroche*; our diners are always lost in wonder at its perfection and delicacy.

Although the mousselines are served as a hot dish, they are never actually more than lukewarm, because of the low cooking temperature. Once served, they go cold very quickly.

PREPARATION

Kill all the lobsters with a needle (see page 35).

THE HEN LOBSTERS: Pour 2L (3½pts) water into a saucepan, add 30g (1oz) salt and bring to the boil. Remove the lobster eggs and keep on a plate in the refrigerator. Rinse the lobsters in cold water, plunge them into the boiling water and cook for 12 minutes, then drain immediately. Do not cook them for longer than this or they will lose their flavour.

Leave to cool, take out the meat from the shells, then slice 6 medallions from each tail and wrap in a damp cloth. Finely dice the remaining lobster meat and keep in a bowl.

THE LARGE LOBSTER: Rinse in very cold water and detach the claws and tail. Using a mallet, crack the claws and take out the meat. Cut open the tail shell with scissors and use a spoon to scrape out the meat. Immediately, discard the gritty sac from near the coral in the head. You should now have about 400g (15oz) lobster meat. Put the meat in a blender or food processor, together with the egg whites and 2 tsp salt and process until well mixed. Rub through a fine sieve into an earthenware or stainless steel bowl set in crushed ice. Work the mixture with a wooden spatula, stirring in the double cream a little at a time. The mixture should be soft, and slightly runny. Place in the refrigerator.

THE SPINACH: Bring a saucepan of water to the boil. Remove the spinach stalks and blanch the leaves in boiling water for 30 seconds. Drain immediately, then plunge into iced water to prevent any further cooking. Dry each leaf by spreading it out flat on a tea-towel.

ASSEMBLING THE MOULDS: Preheat the oven to 200°C/400°F/Gas 6. Using a pastry brush, thickly coat the insides of 12 oval dariole moulds with melted butter. The moulds should be about 6cm (2¼in) long and 6cm (2¼in) deep. Line the bottoms and sides with the spinach leaves. Half-fill the moulds with lobster mousse. Using the handle of a coffee spoon, put a small amount of caviar in the centre and sprinkle over a few lobster eggs and a little diced lobster. Fill the moulds with the remaining lobster mousse, and fold the spinach leaves over to enclose it completely.

COOKING

Place the moulds in a bain-marie and pour in some water heated to 70°C (160°F); make sure that the water temperature is constant. Cover with foil and bake in the preheated oven for 18 minutes; it is important that there is little variation in the water temperature.

THE *BEURRE BLANC* AND CHAMPAGNE SAUCE: Meanwhile, peel and finely chop the shallots and put into a small saucepan with the Champagne. Set over low heat and reduce until slightly syrupy. Take the pan off the heat and beat in a little butter. Set over a low heat again and beat in the remaining butter, a little at a time. When the butter becomes creamy and begins to foam, crush the remaining lobster eggs with the flat of a knife and stir them into the sauce; they will give it a delicate orange tinge. Season to taste and keep in a bain-marie.

TO SERVE

Wrap the lobster medallions in foil and place in the preheated oven to warm through. Very carefully unmould the lobster mousselines onto serving plates; they will be very fragile. Top each one with a lobster medallion and a little caviar. Pour a ribbon of sauce through a conical sieve around each mousseline and serve immediately.

After spending so long on the preparation of this dish, try to find a few minutes to create several tomato roses for the garnish.

INGREDIENTS

500g (1lb 2oz) spinach

200g (7oz) tomatoes

75g (2½oz) butter

40g (1½oz) noodles

180g (6oz) Gruyère cheese

60g (2oz) Bayonne or Parma ham

50g (2oz) plain flour

600ml (24fl.oz) milk

5 egg yolks

pinch of nutmeg

150ml (6fl.oz) double cream

12 egg whites

salt

freshly ground black pepper

Serves: 6 people
Preparation time: 40 minutes
Cooking time: 12 minutes
Wine: A glass of Brut Champagne would go beautifully well with this dish.

Picture: page 96

SOUFFLE ELEONORA

(Soufflés Eléonora)

The marriage of the different ingredients in these soufflés make them creamy, delicate and fresh-tasting. Your guests will be delightfully surprised by them. Lining the bottom of the baking dishes with greaseproof paper or foil prevents the soufflé mixture from being splashed by water if it happens to boil.

PREPARATION

THE SPINACH: Remove the stalks and wash the leaves. Cook in boiling, salted water until barely tender, refresh in cold water, drain and squeeze out the excess moisture with your hands. Set aside.

THE TOMATOES: Plunge into boiling water, peel, deseed and chop. Cook for a few minutes in a frying pan with 1 tsp butter, then keep in a warmish place.

THE NOODLES: Cook them 'al dente' in boiling, salted water, refresh and set aside.

THE GRUYERE: Cut 6 very fine slices to cover the soufflé dishes. These should be 10cm (4in) diameter and 6cm (2¼in) deep. Very finely grate the remaining cheese. Brush the insides of the dishes with melted butter and coat them with grated Gruyère. Reserve the rest.

THE BAYONNE OR PARMA HAM: Slice it very finely, then cut into small strips and set aside.

THE SOUFFLE MIXTURE: Preheat the oven to 220°C/450°F/Gas 8.

Make a white roux by melting 60g (2oz) butter in a saucepan set over a low heat. Whisk in the flour and cook gently for 2 or 3 minutes, stirring continuously. Take the pan off the heat and leave to cool.

Bring the milk to the boil, then pour it over the roux, whisking with a wire whisk. Set the pan over high heat and, stirring continuously, bring the mixture to the boil. Take the pan off the heat and beat in the egg yolks. Season with a pinch of nutmeg and salt to taste. Keep in a warm place.

THE GARNISH: In a shallow pan set over high heat, reduce the cream until it becomes slightly syrupy. Add the cooked noodles, spinach and ham. Bring to the boil, then keep warm.

ASSEMBLING THE SOUFFLES: Beat the egg whites with a pinch of salt until they form soft peaks. Using a whisk, gently incorporate one-third of the egg whites into the soufflé mixture, then using a spatula, fold in the remainder, together with half the remaining grated Gruyère. Correct the seasoning if necessary.

Fill the soufflé dishes one-third full with the soufflé mixture, then sprinkle over the remaining grated Gruyère. Divide the garnish and tomato between the dishes. Pile the remaining soufflé mixture into the dishes, so that it comes about 1cm (½in) above the top of the dishes. Lay a thin slice of Gruyère on each soufflé.

COOKING

Place the soufflé dishes in a deep, ovenproof dish lined with greaseproof paper or foil. Pour in enough very hot water (about 70°C/160°F) to come halfway up the sides of the soufflé dishes and bake in the preheated oven for 12 minutes.

SOUFFLE SUISSESSE

(Soufflés with Swiss cheese)

This is an original way of serving a cheese soufflé; the cheese is not incorporated into the soufflé mixture but is used to glaze it. Nevertheless, it is a light dish with a wonderful aroma, which has delighted diners at *Le Gavroche* since the day we opened. As they cook, the soufflés will absorb the cream and will be very rich and creamy.

PREPARATION

THE SOUFFLE MIXTURE: Preheat the oven to 200°C/400°F/Gas 6.

Melt 65g (2oz) butter in a small saucepan set over low heat. Using a small wire whisk, stir in the flour. Cook gently for 2 or 3 minutes, stirring continuously.

Take the pan off the heat and leave the roux to cool slightly. Bring the milk to the boil, then pour it over the cooled roux, whisking all the time. Set the pan over high heat and, stirring continuously, bring the mixture to the boil and cook for 3 minutes.

Take the pan off the heat and stir in the egg yolks. Season to taste with salt and pepper. Dot the surface with 1 tbls butter, cut into small pieces, to prevent a skin from forming. Set aside at room temperature.

Meanwhile, chill 8 round 8cm (3in) tartlet tins in the refrigerator or

INGREDIENTS

140g (5oz) butter

65g (2oz) flour

700ml (28fl.oz) milk

5 egg yolks

1L (1¾pts) double cream

6 egg whites

200g (7oz) grated Gruyère or Emmental cheese

salt

freshly ground white pepper

Serves: 4 people
Preparation time: 25 minutes
Cooking time: 8 minutes
Wine: With this creamy sauce, serve a light Pouilly Fuissé.

1 *Terrine de homard sauce verte (page 82)*
2 *Dodine de caneton truffes (page 88)*
3 *Foie gras chaud au citrus (page 79)*
4 *Ballotine de foie gras truffée (page 76)*

Top *Oeuf froid Carême (page 122)*
Above *Oeufs brouillés aux oeufs (page 119)*

freezer for a few minutes. Remove and immediately grease them generously with softened butter and arrange on a baking sheet.
ASSEMBLING THE SOUFFLES: Pour the cream into a gratin or bi-metal dish. Lightly salt the cream, then warm it gently without letting it boil. Beat the egg whites with a pinch of salt until they form stiff peaks. Pour the soufflé mixture into a wide-mouthed bowl. Using a whisk, quickly beat in about one-third of the beaten egg whites, then, using a spatula, carefully fold in the remainder. Using a tablespoon, heap up the mixture in the tartlet tins to form 8 large mounds.

TO COOK AND SERVE

Bake the soufflés in the preheated oven for 3 minutes, until the tops begin to turn golden. Remove from the oven and, protecting your hands with a cloth, turn out each soufflé into the dish of warm cream. Sprinkle over the Gruyère or Emmental and return to the oven for 5 minutes.

The soufflés must be taken immediately to the table; serve them with a spoon and fork, taking care not to crush them.

EGGS

Children are fascinated by their shape and form, their different sizes and subtle colours, but these are not the only qualities of eggs. In cooking, they are used for thickening, clarifying and emulsifying. They may be prepared and cooked in a multitude of ways, each more alluring than the last; they are wonderful poached, soft-boiled, hard-boiled, fried, baked or scrambled, not forgetting those delicious omelettes — open or rolled-up, plump and cooked to perfection, an omelette is a marvellous lunch dish, which makes more of eggs than any other recipe.

Without eggs, there would be no patisserie or biscuits. Like butter, flour and sugar, they are an indispensable ingredient. In some delicate recipes, where measurements must be very accurate, the necessary quantity of eggs is generally given by weight rather than number, because the weight of an egg can vary by between 50 and 70g (2 to 2½oz), which could lead to disastrous results!

OEUFS BROUILLES A LA RHUBARBE

(Scrambled eggs with rhubarb)

This is a dish of contrasts with the slightly acid dices and the sweetness of the rhubarb sticks. People often order it in disbelief and then join the long list of the converted!

PREPARATION

THE RHUBARB: Peel it if stringy, otherwise leave on the skin. Dice two-thirds of the rhubarb and sweat it in 30g (1oz) butter until crisp to the bite. Set aside. Cut the remaining rhubarb into 5cm (2in) sticks. Boil the sugar with 100ml (4fl.oz) water. Toss in the rhubarb sticks and take the pan off the heat, leaving the rhubarb in the syrup.
THE ALMONDS: Skin and split in two, then soak them in the milk.
THE BREAD: Cut into 12 triangles. Heat 80g (3oz) clarified butter in a frying pan and fry the bread until golden on both sides. Drain on absorbent paper, or put the triangles directly onto a plate.
THE EGGS: Break into a bowl and beat lightly with a fork. Brush the bottom of a shallow pan with about 20g (½oz) melted butter and pour in the eggs. Set the pan over a low heat, stirring gently with a wooden spatula until the eggs are creamy. Draw the pan off the heat, season to taste, then add the cream and the diced rhubarb.

TO SERVE

Divide the egg and rhubarb mixture between 6 plates. Drain the rhubarb sticks, which should be hot, and place them in the middle of the eggs. Arrange 6 drained almond halves around the rhubarb, then scatter the chives between the almonds. Place 2 bread triangles on each plate.

INGREDIENTS

12 eggs
350g (12oz) rhubarb
130g (4½oz) clarified butter
100g (4oz) sugar
18 whole almonds, fresh if possible
125ml (5fl.oz) milk
1 bunch chives, snipped
3 slices white bread
2 tbls double cream
2 tsp salt
pepper

Serves: 6 people
Preparation time: 20 minutes
Cooking time: 7 minutes

OEUFS BROUILLES AUX OEUFS

(Scrambled eggs with eggs)

A simple, original and very attractive dish; when the poached egg yolk is broken and mingles with the caviar, it is a delight to the eyes and the tastebuds. If red caviar is available, we usually use two-thirds Beluga and one-third red caviar, alternating the two colours.

INGREDIENTS

12 hen's eggs
12 quail's eggs
2 tbls white wine vinegar
2 slices white bread
100g (4oz) clarified butter
20g (1oz) snipped chives
100g (4oz) Beluga or Sevruga caviar
80ml (3fl.oz) double cream
salt
freshly ground black pepper

Serves: 4 people
Preparation time: 15 minutes
Cooking time: 7 minutes
Picture: page 117

PREPARATION

THE HEN'S EGGS: Fill the shallow pan with water, add the vinegar and set over high heat. When the water boils, poach 4 eggs, keeping the yolks soft, then lift them into a bowl of warm (60°C/140°F), lightly salted water.

THE QUAIL'S EGGS: Soft-boil the eggs for 1 minute. Put into cold water, shell and place them in a bowl with the poached eggs.

THE BREAD: Trim off the crusts. Cut the bread into 12 equal-sized triangles. Fry them over high heat in 100g (4oz) clarified butter until golden on both sides. Lay them on absorbent paper.

COOKING

Break the 8 remaining hen's eggs into a large bowl and beat lightly with a fork. Brush the bottom of a shallow pan with about 20g (1½oz) butter and then pour in the eggs. Set them over low heat, (60°-70°C/140°-160°F) stirring gently with a wooden spatula until the eggs are creamy. Take the pan off the heat, add the cream and season to taste with salt and pepper.

TO SERVE

Divide the scrambled eggs between 4 serving plates. Place a poached egg in the centre and arrange 3 quail's eggs around the edge, interspersed with the bread triangles. Cover each poached egg with a spoonful of caviar and arrange the rest on top of the quail's eggs. Sprinkle over the snipped chives and serve immediately.

Serves: 6 people
Preparation time: 30 minutes
Cooking time: 4 minutes

OEUF CAROLINE

(Eggs Caroline)

In this light dish, the taste of the egg marries perfectly with the soft milkiness of the corn.

PREPARATION

THE PASTRY CASES: Roll out the short pastry or puff pastry on a lightly

floured marble or wooden board. If you are using short pastry, it should be 2-3mm (1/10in) thick; if puff pastry, roll it as thinly as possible. Using a plain or fluted 8.5cm (3¼in) pastry cutter, cut out 6 rounds of pastry. Line 6 tartlet tins, 7.5cm (3in) diameter, with the pastry circles and flute the edges by pinching with your fingers. BAKING THE PASTRY CASES BLIND: Preheat the oven to 190°C/375°F/Gas 5. Prick the bottom of the pastry cases with a fork or sharp knife. Place a circle of greaseproof paper in each one and fill with dried beans or cherry stones. Bake in the preheated oven for 10 minutes. When the pastry shells are cooked, remove the baking beans and greaseproof paper. Remove the pastry shells from the tins and set them on a wire rack in a cool place.
THE EGGS: Fill a shallow pan with water, bring to the boil, add the vinegar and poach the eggs. Remove them from the pan with a slotted spoon and put them into a bowl of very cold water. Cut off any ragged edges from the whites and place the eggs on a tea-towel.

INGREDIENTS

6 eggs

130g (5oz) short pastry (see page 250) *or* 100g (4oz) Puff pastry (see page 248)

1 pinch flour

150g (5oz) sweetcorn

1 quantity Hollandaise sauce (see page 57)

40g (1½oz) butter

3 tbls white wine vinegar

1 tbls snipped chives

salt

freshly ground white pepper

ASSEMBLING THE EGGS

Preheat the grill to high. In a saucepan, sweat the sweetcorn with the butter and add the snipped chives. Cover the bottom of each pastry shell with corn and pour over a little Hollandaise sauce. Heat the poached eggs in boiling, salted water for 30 seconds. Drain well, then place an egg in each pastry shell. Pour a generous amount of sauce over and around the eggs. Place under a hot grill for a few seconds until the sauce is a pale nutty brown colour. Heat 6 plates so that they are very hot and then serve the eggs immediately.

OMELETTE A L'OSEILLE

(Sorrel omelette)

A refreshing dish, this tastes just as good cold as hot. If you serve it cold, do not add the cream and Gruyère.

PREPARATION

Preheat the grill to high.
THE SORREL: Remove the stalks, wash the leaves, roll them up like a

INGREDIENTS

6 eggs

70g (2½oz) sorrel

45g (1½oz) butter

100ml (4fl. oz) double cream

1 pinch nutmeg

1 tsp oil

1 tbls Gruyère, grated

salt

freshly ground black pepper

Serves: 2 people
Preparation time: 15 minutes
Cooking time: 2 minutes

cigar and snip them very finely. Sweat in a sauté pan with 1 tbls butter, until all the water from the sorrel has evaporated. Set aside.
THE CREAM: Whip in a bowl until the whisk leaves a trail when lifted. Season with salt and nutmeg. Set aside.
THE EGGS: Break them into a bowl and beat with a fork. Season to taste with salt and pepper.

COOKING

In an omelette pan, heat the oil with 30g (1oz) butter until the fat sizzles. Pour in the eggs, stirring very gently with a fork, and cook until the omelette is set as you like it. Just before folding the omelette, add the sorrel, spreading it across from side to side.

TO SERVE

Roll the omelette onto a silver or flameproof porcelain serving plate. Cover with the cream and sprinkle over the grated Gruyère. Glaze immediately under the hot grill for about 2 to 3 minutes — just long enough for it to turn pale golden.

INGREDIENTS

4 globe artichokes, preferably Breton

juice of ½ lemon

6 tbls white wine vinegar

1 tbls flour

4 eggs

4 medium slices smoked salmon, weighing about 150g (5oz)

50ml (2fl.oz) Fish aspic (optional) (see page 50)

1 small truffle, about 30g (1oz)

⅓ quantity Mayonnaise (see page 60)

1 tbls tomato ketchup

1 tsp Cognac
Continued

OEUF FROID CAREME

(Eggs Carême)

We never tire of preparing or eating this recipe. It has always been served at *Le Gavroche* — a simple, marvellous dish, which is much loved by both of us. Frequently we have been found picnicking on an Oeuf Carême at midnight!

PREPARATION

THE ARTICHOKES: Snap off the stalks and, using a sharp knife, trim off the leaves until only the neatly-shaped hearts are left. Squeeze over a little lemon juice.

Cook the artichoke hearts in a saucepan of boiling, salted water with 3 tbls vinegar, or in a white court bouillon (1 tbls flour, 3 tbls vinegar and salted water). They will take 20-35 minutes, depending on their size. Use the point of a knife to test whether the artichokes are done, then leave them to cool in their cooking liquid.

THE EGGS: Bring a shallow pan of water to the boil, add 3 tbls vinegar and poach the eggs. Lift them out with a slotted spoon and place them in a bowl of very cold water. Trim the ragged edges from the white and place the eggs on a tea-towel.

THE SMOKED SALMON: Use a plain 8cm (3¼in) pastry cutter to cut a neat circle from each slice. Lay them on a round cake rack and coat each with half-set fish aspic. Decorate as you like with a little truffle and place in the refrigerator. Cut the smoked salmon trimmings into small dice and keep them in a bowl.

THE GARNISH: Roughly chop the remaining truffle and add it to the diced salmon. Stir in the mayonnaise, add the ketchup and Cognac and season to taste with salt and pepper. Keep at room temperature.

salt

freshly ground black pepper

Serves: 4 people
Preparation time: 45 minutes
Cooking time: 2½ to 3 minutes

Picture: page 117

TO SERVE

Remove the chokes from the artichoke hearts and pat dry with a cloth. Divide the garnish between the 4 artichoke bottoms, place an egg on each one and top with a round of smoked salmon. Serve on a cold, but not chilled, plate. You could add a sprig of chervil for colour instead of the truffle if you prefer.

SALADS

These are all too often sad, dreary affairs; sometimes they swim limply in the water they were washed in, at other times, they are crunchy with sand and dirt. Ignored or scorned by many a chef, they are relegated to being prepared by the washers-up.

But salads deserve better than this. They can rival any dish for flavour. With their varied, often brilliant colours, whether they be sweet or tart, half-cooked or raw, warm or cold (but never *too* cold), a good salad will tempt you to eat even when you are not hungry.

Seasonings play an important part in the success of a salad; they will vary according to the salad ingredients. The following seasonings are the ones most commonly used in salad dressings: oils (peanut, olive, walnut, hazelnut), vinegars (wine, distilled, cider, sherry, raspberry), mustards (Dijon, Meaux), *crème fraîche*, lemon, egg yolks, onions, salt, pepper and sugar.

SALADE CAPRICE DES REINES

(The Queens' capricious salad)

U se either fresh or tinned truffles for this salad. If you are feeling poor, you can substitute finely sliced button mushrooms and a few sprigs of chervil for the truffles.

INGREDIENTS

375g (13oz) chicory

1 small celery stalk

200g (7oz) crisp eating apples

juice of 1 lemon

½ quantity Mayonnnaise (see page 60)

4 tbls double cream

50g (2oz) truffles (optional)

salt

freshly ground white pepper

Serves: 4 people
Preparation time: 15 minutes

PREPARATION

THE CHICORY AND CELERY: Trim and wash if necessary, pat dry and cut into large sticks about 5cm (2in) long and 1cm (½in) wide.
THE APPLES: Peel, core and cut into small sticks, about half the size of the chicory and celery sticks. Sprinkle with half the lemon juice.

TO SERVE

Pile up the chicory and celery like a dome in the centre of a salad bowl. Arrange the apples in a row round the edge. Stir the cream and the remaining lemon juice into the mayonnaise and season to taste with salt and pepper, then pour the mixture over the chicory and celery. Sprinkle the dome with a *julienne* of truffles.

SALADE DE BETTERAVES MIMOZA

(Beetroot salad Mimosa)

INGREDIENTS

1.25kg (2lb 12oz) raw beetroot

4 eggs

3 tbls olive oil

2 garlic cloves

2 tbls red wine vinegar

3 tbls snipped chives

salt

freshly ground black pepper

Serves: 4 people
Preparation time: 15 minutes
Cooking time: 1 hour 5 minutes

PREPARATION

THE BEETROOT: Preheat the oven to 220°C/425°F/Gas 7. Place the beetroot in a saucepan and cover with lightly salted cold water. Set the pan over high heat and bring to the boil. Cook for 45 minutes. Pierce the centre of the beetroot with a trussing needle or the point of a knife to check that they are tender.

Drain and put in a roasting pan. Place in the preheated oven for 20 minutes; this will eliminate some of the water and bring out the sweetness of the sugar in the beetroot. Remove from the oven and keep cool. Peel the beetroot as soon as it is cold and slice thinly. Set aside.
THE EGGS: Meanwhile, hard-boil and shell the eggs, chop the yolks and set aside. Discard the whites.

THE VINAIGRETTE: Peel and chop the garlic and put it in a frying pan with the oil. Set the pan over low heat (about 40°C/105°F) and heat very gently until the aroma of garlic begins to rise from the oil. Remove from the heat.

In a salad bowl, mix together the pepper, salt and vinegar; pour in the oil and add the beetroot. Mix everything gently.

TO SERVE

Serve this salad on a platter or plate, sprinkled with the chopped egg yolk and snipped chives.

SALADE DE HOMARD A LA MANGUE

(Lobster salad with mangoes)

This is a dish of stunning colours, with a delicate taste and pronounced individual flavours. If the lobster should be carrying eggs, add some to the salad; they will give it a magical note.

Empty out the lobster head; discard the gritty sac, but keep the coral and intestines to use in another recipe — perhaps to enrich a fish sauce, in fish soup or in a Sauce Américaine (see page 146).

PREPARATION

THE COURT BOUILLON: In a saucepan, combine 2.5L (4¼pts) water, the coarse salt, bouquet garni, white wine vinegar and crushed peppercorns. Set over high heat and bring to the boil.

THE LOBSTER: Using the back of a chopping knife lightly crack the claws, then plunge the lobster into the court bouillon and cook for 20 minutes. Using a slotted spoon, lift the lobster out of the pan and put it in a colander. Keep in a cold place for at least 1 hour.

THE SAUCE: Peel one mango; scrape off all the flesh from around the stone, place in a blender or food processor and purée until smooth. Add the basil leaves, olive oil and lemon juice or sherry vinegar; season with salt and pepper and process the mixture again for 1 minute. Transfer to a small bowl and keep at room temperature.

THE SALAD: Trim and wash the radicchio and lettuce. Drain and keep in a cool place.

THE AVOCADO AND THE SECOND MANGO: Peel with a supple-bladed

INGREDIENTS

1 live lobster, weighing about 700g (1lb 8oz)

2 fresh mangoes

60g (2oz) coarse salt

1 small bouquet garni

200ml (8fl.oz) white wine vinegar

1 tsp white peppercorns, coarsely crushed

6 basil leaves

100ml (4fl.oz) olive oil

juice of 1 lemon *or* 1 tbls sherry vinegar

1 radicchio heart

1 lettuce heart

½ avocado

1 small truffle, cut into *julienne*

salt

freshly ground black pepper

sprigs of chervil, to garnish

Serves: 4 people
Preparation time: 35 minutes
Cooking time: 20 minutes
Picture: page 128

knife and cut into small, regular slices. Keep in a cool place.

TO SERVE

Separate the lobster head and tail. Using the tip of a pair of scissors, cut through the rings on the underside of the tail and take out the lobster meat from the shell. Remove the trails. Cut 4 medallions, about 5mm (¼in) thick, from the thickest part of the tail. Finely dice the remaining tail meat.

Put the two types of lettuce into a large salad bowl, together with the avocado and mango slices and the diced lobster meat. Pour over three-quarters of the sauce; gently mix all the ingredients together and divide the salad between 4 serving plates. Pour the remaining sauce over the centre of each salad. Place a lobster medallion on the sauce and top each one with a *julienne* of truffle.

Very delicately, remove the two lobster claws from their shells, taking care not to break them. Cut them in half through the thickest part, pick out the cartilage, then place half a claw on the edge of each plate. Garnish with chervil sprigs. Serve cold but not chilled.

SALADE RUSTIQUE AU XERES

(Country salad with sherry vinegar)

INGREDIENTS

220g (8oz) tender spinach

1 tbls sherry vinegar

3 tbls olive oil

220g (8oz) *Ballotine* of foie gras (see page 76)

1 small truffle, weighing 20g (¾oz)

salt

freshly ground black pepper

Serves: 4 people
Preparation time: 15 minutes

PREPARATION

THE SPINACH: Remove the stalks and wash the leaves. Drain well and gently pat dry with a cloth. Roll up the leaves like a cigar and slice into 1cm (½in) strips.

THE VINAIGRETTE: Combine in a large bowl a pinch of salt, freshly ground pepper, the vinegar and oil; correct the seasoning if necessary. Add the spinach and toss it gently in the dressing. Divide between 4 serving plates.

THE FOIE GRAS: Using a fish filleting knife dipped in hot water, cut into 12 thin slices; dip the knife into hot water between each slicing. Arrange 3 slices of foie gras attractively on each plate.

THE TRUFFLE: Cut into 12 thin rounds and place one on each slice of foie gras.

Make sure that the spinach leaves are small or medium-sized; they will be more tender than large, fleshy leaves. The salad will be simpler to prepare if you use tinned foie gras, but it will not taste quite as exotic. If you like, enhance the presentation of this dish with a small tomato 'rose' on each plate.

SALADE DU VICAIRE

(The curate's salad)

This salad may be used as a first course, in which case serve it on individual plates. It is a version of the dandelion salad which we have adored ever since we were children.

PREPARATION

THE SALADS: Trim, wash and dry them.
THE CROUTONS: Toast the bread under the grill or in the oven until dry and golden brown, then rub with the peeled garlic clove.
THE BACON: Remove the rind and slice the bacon, then cut into even-sized sticks (*lardons*). Place in a saucepan, cover with water, bring to the boil and blanch for 2 minutes. Refresh and drain.
THE VINAIGRETTE: In a salad bowl, mix together the salt, mustard, lemon juice and wine vinegar, then stir in the olive and peanut oil and the pepper.

TO SERVE

Toss the salad in the bowl containing the vinaigrette. In a frying pan set over high heat, sauté the *lardons* until pale golden. Pour the *lardons* and the fat they have rendered onto the salad.

Deglaze the pan with the cider vinegar. Heat for 1 minute to reduce the vinegar by half, then pour it over the salad. Quickly toss everything together, then arrange the croûtons on top and scatter over the hard-boiled egg yolks. Serve immediately.

In France on Sundays, it was customary for families to invite the local curate for lunch. This salad particularly reminds us both of the simple yet gourmet taste of the curates of that epoch which is why we have given the recipe its name.

INGREDIENTS

1 full-hearted lettuce, weighing about 350g (12oz)

½ curly endive, weighing about 250g (8oz)

1 small radicchio, weighing about 100g (4oz)

10 bunches corn-salad, weighing about 100g (4oz)

18 slices French bread, cut from a baguette

1 garlic clove

200g (7oz) smoked bacon, in one piece

⅔ tsp Dijon mustard

juice of ½ lemon

2 tbls wine vinegar

30ml (1fl.oz) olive oil

80ml (3fl.oz) peanut oil

1½ tbls cider vinegar

3 hard-boiled egg yolks, sieved or finely chopped

salt

freshly ground black pepper

Serves: 6 people
Preparation time: 25 minutes
Cooking time: 2 minutes
Picture: page 128

1

2

3

1 *Feuilleté d'huitres tièdes aux framboises (page 135)*
2 *Salade de homard à la mangue (page 125)*
3 *Salade du vicaire (page 127)*
Above *Cassolette d'écrevisses aux tagliatelles sauce
Nantua (page 142)*

CHAPTER SEVEN

CRUSTACEANS AND SHELLFISH

Seafood and shellfish bring a fresh, natural taste to a meal. Their beautiful colours and the tang of the sea add a festive and elegant tone to the table. All crustaceans and shellfish are best prepared as simply as possible. They should be plainly cooked in a court bouillon or *nage* and will taste even better served warm with melted butter or cold with mayonnaise.

The only tedious preparation is the shelling; we suggest that you tie a napkin round your neck, so that you are not drenched by the cooking water which may spurt out of the claws and shell. We have a humane method of killing lobsters just before cooking. Plunge a trussing needle deep between the eyes; death will be instantaneous.

HOMARD A L'ESCARGOT

(Lobsters in snail butter)

This is one of our very favourite recipes, which we have been cooking for over 20 years. You can prepare this dish well in advance of the meal, so as to avoid a frantic rush just before serving. Decorate the serving dish with a bouquet of watercress and a few vegetable 'flowers'. A green or mixed salad perfectly complements this dish, which will scent your kitchen with its wonderful aroma of garlic.

PREPARATION

THE COURT BOUILLON: Fill a saucepan with 2½L (4½pts) water, the

INGREDIENTS

2 small live lobsters, each weighing about 450g (1lb)

360g (12oz) Snail butter (see page 62)

60g (2oz) coarse salt

1 small bouquet garni

200ml (9fl.oz) white wine vinegar

1 tsp peppercorns

½ quantity Béarnaise sauce (see page 55)

Serves: 2 people
Preparation time: 15 minutes
Cooking time: 20 minutes
Wine: This dish would be suitably matched by a Petit Château from Medoc in Bordeaux or a light Chianti.

coarse salt, bouquet garni, white wine vinegar and the crushed peppercorns and bring to the boil over high heat.
THE LOBSTERS: Using the back of a chopping knife, gently crack the claws. Plunge the lobsters into the court bouillon and cook for 20 minutes. Remove them with a slotted spoon, place in a colander and leave in a cool place for at least 1 hour.

TO SERVE

Place the lobsters on a board and, using a chopping knife, bring it down sharply on the point where the tail meets the head. Remove the gritty sac and intestinal vein. Reserve the coral and intestines on one side and reserve for later use.

Pull off the claws and shell them, taking care not to break the flesh. Arrange the claw meat in the heads, where the coral and intestines were. Pull the tail out of its rings, taking care not to detach the head from the body. Rub a generous amount of softened snail butter over the inside of the tail shell. Put the tail flesh back into the shell and smear the whole lobster, including the head, with snail butter. Reserve about a quarter of the butter.

Preheat the oven to 220°C/425°F/Gas 7. 10 minutes before serving, place the lobsters in the preheated oven. Heat the remaining snail butter in a frying pan and, when it is sizzling, pour it over the lobsters. Serve immediately on a silver or china dish. Serve the Béarnaise sauce separately in a sauceboat.

Serves: 4 people
Preparation time: 50 minutes
Cooking time: 15 minutes
Wine: This rich dish needs an Alsace Riesling with its balance of hard and gentle, flowery and strong nose or a white wine from Tuscany.
Picture: page 140

PETITE BLANQUETTE DE HOMARD
(Blanquette of lobster)

This delicate, creamy dish, with its bright colours, can be made equally well with langoustines. Allow 9 langoustines per person and 'turn' the vegetables to the shape of half an olive.

Keep the unused pieces of lobster head in the refrigerator or freezer to use another time in a sauce of lobster butter.

PREPARATION

COOKING THE LOBSTERS: Bring the *nage* to the boil in a large saucepan. Lightly crack the claws, then plunge the lobsters into the boiling *nage* for 15 minutes. Lift them out with a slotted spoon and keep in a cool place. When they are cold, remove the meat from the claws and tails and cut the tail meat into 1.5cm/½in chunks.

THE VEGETABLES: Peel and wash them. Using a sharp knife, 'turn' all the vegetables except the leek and mushrooms into pointed almond shapes. Slice the leek very finely and cut the mushrooms into quarters. Cook each vegetable separately in a little *nage*, but keep them very crunchy. Lay them on a slightly damp tea-towel.

THE SAUCE: Pour 500ml (1pt) of the *nage* in which the vegetables were cooked into a shallow pan. Reduce the liquid by one-third. Add the cream and bring to the boil. Put all the vegetables into the *nage* and cook for 2 minutes before adding the lobster meat. Lower the heat and do not allow the mixture to boil.

INGREDIENTS

4 live lobsters, each weighing about 450g (1lb)

2 quantities *Nage* (see page 47)

160g (6oz) carrots

120g (4oz) turnips

120g (4oz) celeriac

120g (4oz) leek, white part only

160g (6oz) cucumber

100g (3½oz) button mushrooms, tightly closed

200ml (8fl.oz) double cream

25g (1oz) butter

2 egg yolks

2 branches chervil

cayenne pepper

salt

TO SERVE

Stir the sauce with a wooden spatula over low heat. Lightly beat the egg yolks with 1 tbls *nage*. Stir the butter and egg yolks into the sauce. Correct the seasoning with salt if necessary, add a small pinch of cayenne pepper, then tip everything pell-mell into a shallow serving dish or onto plates. Sprinkle over some chervil and serve immediately.

CRABE DES ILES

(Caribbean Crab)

PREPARATION

THE CRABS: Cook for 20 minutes in boiling, salted water. If possible, use sea water. Drain and leave the crabs to cool completely, uncovered, for at least 2 hours.

Use the crackers or mallet to crack the legs and claws. Remove the shell from the body and pick out the white meat with a small knife. Put the meat in a bowl. There should be about 600g (1lb 4oz) white meat.

THE PEPPERS: Skin the peppers by rubbing them with oil and putting them into a very hot oven or under the grill. Turn them until the skin blisters and becomes slightly charred on all sides. Hold the peppers under cold running water, rubbing them slightly with your hand. The skin should then come off easily. Pat the peppers dry with a cloth. Remove the white parts and the seeds and cut the peppers into small

INGREDIENTS

2kg (4lb 4oz) crabs (about 2 or 3)

½ avocado, diced

50g (2oz) red pepper, fresh or tinned

50g (2oz) fresh green pepper

1 tbls peanut oil

1 garlic clove

juice of 2 limes

3 drops Tabasco

300ml (12fl. oz) double cream

6 medium tomatoes

Continued overleaf
Picture: front cover

1 tbls home-made
tomato *concassé* or 1 tsp
tomato paste

2 tbls soft green
peppercorns,
finely chopped

1 lemon

6 parsley sprigs

salt

pepper

tomato or radish roses,
to garnish

Serves: 6 people
Preparation time: 45
minutes
Cooking time: 20
minutes
Wine: A Crozes-
Hermitage with its
delicate full flavour or a
dry Graves Blanc.

diamond shapes, then add them to the crabmeat.

THE GARLIC, LIME JUICE AND TABASCO: Peel, crush and chop the garlic clove. Add it to the crabmeat, together with the lime juice, avocado and Tabasco. Mix well and season to taste.

THE TOMATO MOUSSE: Peel, deseed and roughly chop the tomatoes. Whip the cream until the whisk leaves a trail when lifted and fold in the tomatoes, tomato *concassé* or paste and the chopped green pepper-corns. Season to taste.

TO SERVE

Serve in exotic shells or on crab shells. Divide the tomato mousse between the shells and top with the crabmeat. Decorate each one with a cannelised slice of lemon, a sprig of parsley and finally a tomato or radish rose.

The home-made tomato *concassé* is optional, but it does heighten the flavour of the mousse without adding the acid taste of concentrated tomato paste. The brown crabmeat can be used for hors d'oeuvres or canapés, or you could freeze it for future use.

Serves: 4 people
Preparation time: 45
minutes
Cooking time: 20
minutes
Wine: The sweetness of
this dish needs a
Sauvignon, which is
slightly spicy and
smokey and is
particularly good with
shellfish, or a dry Gros
Plant.

GRATIN DE CRABE JACQUELINE

(Gratin of crab Jacqueline)

This is a delicious, fruity dish which has a subtle sweetness — the flavour of the crab marries harmoniously with the fruit. Served as an hors d'oeuvre, the gratin needs no additional vegetables. If served as a main course, a rice pilaff is the perfect accompaniment and you should not really need to serve it with anything else.

Harissa is a very strong, peppery paste used in Middle Eastern cooking. Use it with caution! If you cannot find harissa, replace it with cayenne pepper.

PREPARATION

THE CRABS: If necessary, scrub them under cold water to remove any silt stuck to the shell. Cook the crabs for 20 minutes, in boiling sea water if possible, otherwise in boiling salted water. Lift them out of the water and keep in a cool place for at least 2 hours.

When they are cold, crack the legs and claws with lobster crackers or a mallet, then remove the body shell. Pick out all the white meat, discarding any cartilage and bits of shell. You should have about 550g/1lb 4oz white meat. Set aside. Using a spoon, scrape out the brown meat to use in the sauce.

THE SAUCE: Peel the shallots, carrots, orange and grapefruit and cut into small dice. Sweat them with the butter in a shallow pan until soft. Add the pineapple skin and the chopped centre core.

Add the bouquet garni, the brown crabmeat and the harissa. Continue to cook for 3 to 4 minutes, then pour in the white wine. Simmer for a further 20 minutes, then rub the sauce through a fine conical sieve. Return the strained sauce to the cleaned pan and reduce by half. Cut the pineapple flesh into *julienne* and keep in a cool place.

TO SERVE

Preheat the grill to high. Stir the cream and the white crabmeat into the sauce and bring to the boil. Add the *julienne* of pineapple and simmer very gently for 2 or 3 minutes. Season to taste with salt and pepper, then stir in the Hollandaise sauce. Do not allow the mixture to boil. Lightly butter a flameproof gratin dish. Tip the crab mixture into the dish and place it under the hot grill until it turns a pale golden colour. Serve immediately.

INGREDIENTS

1 or 2 crabs, total weight about 1.75kg (3lb 10oz)
60g (2oz) shallots
1 carrot
1 orange
1 grapefruit
50g (1½oz) butter
250g (8oz) pineapple
1 medium bouquet garni
⅛ tsp harissa
500ml (1pt) sweet white wine
250ml (10fl.oz) double cream
2 tbls Hollandaise sauce (see page 57)
salt
freshly ground black pepper

FEUILLETES D'HUITRES TIEDES AUX FRAMBOISES

(Warm oyster feuilletés with raspberries)

This is the kind of delectable, exotic dish one dreams about before tasting it . . . and often afterwards, too.

Raspberry vinegar can be bought ready-made if you do not want to make your own.

Serves: 4 people
Preparation time: 40 minutes
Cooking time: 12 minutes
Wine: Only a fruity, slightly sweet wine can match all the distinctive flavours in this dish. From the Rhine Valley comes the most distinguished of all German wine, the Rüdesheim.

PREPARATION

THE PUFF PASTRY: On a lightly floured marble or wooden surface, roll out the pastry to a thickness of about 5mm (¼in). Using a small, sharp knife, cut out 4 oyster shapes. Place the pastry shapes on a flan tin or

INGREDIENTS

24 oysters

280g (10oz) Puff pastry (see page 248)

pinch of flour

1 egg yolk, beaten with 1 tsp milk, to glaze

70g (2½oz) very fine French beans or sea asparagus (samphire)

100g (4oz) beansprouts

30g (1oz) shallots

32 winkles (optional)

1 tsp oil

3 tbls Raspberry vinegar (see page 63)

1 tbls double cream

150g (5oz) butter

100g (4oz) fresh raspberries

salt

Picture: page 128

small baking sheet brushed with a little water. Brush the pastry shapes with a mixture of egg yolk and milk and 'pink' the edges with a knife. Lightly cut a line 2mm (1/10in) in from this edge — this will form the lid after baking. Leave the pastry to rest for at least 20 minutes in the refrigerator or somewhere cool.

Meanwhile, preheat the oven to 220°C/425°F/Gas 7. Bake the pastry 'oysters' in the preheated oven for 12 minutes. When they are cooked, cut round the line you drew beforehand. Slip the knife blade underneath and lift off the 'lids'. Set the pastry cases and lids on a wire rack and keep warm.

THE OYSTERS: Open them over a bowl, so as to catch the juices. Keep the oysters on absorbent paper at room temperature and strain the juices into a shallow pan.

THE BEANS: Top and tail them and cut into 1cm (½in) lengths. Cook them in boiling, salted water until they are tender but still crisp; refresh, slice into *julienne* and set aside.

THE BEANSPROUTS: Plunge into boiling, salted water for 30 seconds, refresh, drain and set aside.

THE SHALLOTS: Peel and finely chop.

THE WINKLES: Add the oil to a pan of boiling, salted water and cook the winkles for 2 minutes. Remove them from their shells with a pin.

THE SAUCE: Add the chopped shallot and the raspberry vinegar to the pan containing the oyster juices. Rub 40g (1½oz) puréed raspberries through a sieve into the pan. Set over high heat and reduce the liquid until syrupy. Add the cream and let the mixture bubble once more. Stir in the butter, a little at a time, correct the seasoning if necessary and keep warm.

TO SERVE

Preheat the oven to 190°C/375°F/Gas 5. Place the pastry 'shells' on serving plates and warm them in the oven for 30 seconds.

Meanwhile, stir the beans, beansprouts, oysters and winkles into the sauce. Set the pan over medium heat and, as soon as the sauce begins to tremble, take the pan off the heat.

Fill each pastry shell with 2 oysters, arrange 4 oysters around each one and pour the sauce into and around the pastry shells. Top each one with its lid. Arrange the remaining 60g (2oz) raspberries on the sauce around the edge of each plate and serve immediately.

MOUCLADE D'AUNIS

Simple to make, this is always a popular dish — the curry flavour is very discreet. Leaf spinach or spinach *'subrics'* (see page 220) or, more simply, steamed rice make the perfect accompaniment.

Bouchot mussels contain no sand and need no de-bearding and very little washing. They are small, plump mussels which are farmed mainly around the coast of Brittany. If you use another variety, they must be de-bearded.

PREPARATION

THE MUSSELS: Scrub and wash them in several changes of water. Put them in a large saucepan with the white wine, cover the pan and cook over high heat, shaking the pan from time to time. As soon as all the mussels are open (after about 8 minutes), drain them through a sieve into a bowl to catch the cooking liquor. Remove the mussels from their shells, cut away the beards and keep at room temperature, covered with a damp cloth.

THE SAUCE: Peel and finely chop the onion and sweat it with the butter in a shallow pan. Stir in the flour and curry powder and cook gently for 3 minutes, stirring continuously with a wooden spatula.

Carefully decant 600ml (24fl.oz) mussel cooking liquor into the pan and bring to the boil, stirring continuously. Lower the heat and simmer gently for 10 minutes, skimming the scum from the surface as often as necessary.

TO SERVE

Add the cream to the sauce, bring to the boil, stir in the mussels and season to taste with salt. Serve at once in a deep dish, with a sprinkling of snipped parsley on top.

INGREDIENTS

6L (10½pts) mussels (preferably Bouchot)

500ml (1pt) dry white wine

1 medium onion

50g (1½oz) butter

2 tsp flour

1 tsp curry powder

100ml (4fl.oz) double cream

salt

finely snipped parsley, to garnish

Serves: 4 people
Preparation time: 40 minutes
Cooking time: 8 minutes
Wine: From Nantes, a minor Muscadet with more acidity such as a Gros Plant or a very dry, young, fresh German wine from Franconia which has the necessary acidity.

PUITS CRESSONNIERES AUX MOULES

(Watercress 'wells' with mussels)

You will be surprised by the delicacy and smoothness of this dish, which is amazingly simple to make. The large quantity of cream needed makes the delicate little 'wells' wonderfully melting and rich.

Serves: 6 people
Preparation time: 40 minutes
Cooking time: 15 minutes
Wine: A traditionally made Vouvray which varies in character vintage by vintage.

Certain years such as the 1970 vintage produced a very dry, but distinguished wine. An alternative would be a lesser known Burgundy which is often overlooked such as Auxey-Duresses.

INGREDIENTS

750g (1½ lb) mussels, preferably Bouchot

50g (2oz) pike, preferably, or whiting fillets

6 egg yolks

800ml (32fl.oz) double cream

½ bunch watercress

50g (2oz) butter

2 tbls Veal stock (optional) (see page 48)

3 tbls snipped chives

salt

freshly ground white pepper

Picture: page 140

The only difficult part of this recipe is unmoulding the 'wells' onto the plates. It is a good idea to make two extra 'wells' in case of accidents. The mousse quantities given are ample for 8 to 10 moulds.

PREPARATION

THE MUSSELS: Scrub, wash and put them in a saucepan. Cover the pan and cook without any liquid over high heat. As soon as all the mussels are open, take the pan off the heat. Remove the mussels from their shells and decant the juices through a fine sieve into a bowl. Set aside. Cover the mussels with a damp cloth and keep in a cool place.

THE PIKE: Rub the pike or whiting through a fine mesh sieve into a bowl. Using a wire whisk, beat in the egg yolks, 450ml (18fl.oz) double cream and 5 tbls of the mussel juices. Season to taste.

THE WATERCRESS: Wash it well and remove the leaves. Sweat these in 1 tsp butter in a small saucepan, add the veal stock and keep warm.

THE SAUCE: Pour 100ml (4fl.oz) mussel juice into a shallow pan and reduce by two-thirds. Stir in 350ml (14fl.oz) double cream and boil until the sauce becomes slightly syrupy. Add 1 tsp butter, season to taste with salt and pepper and keep warm.

COOKING

Preheat the oven to 190°C/375°F/Gas 5. Generously brush the insides of 6 small, savarin moulds 5.8cm (3½in) diameter with melted butter. Pour in the pike or whiting mixture and set the moulds in a bain-marie, with a layer of foil or greaseproof paper between the bottom of the dish and the moulds. Pour in enough hot water to come halfway up the sides of the moulds. Bake in the moderate oven for about 15 minutes. Make sure the mixture is set before you take it out of the oven. It should have the consistency of a crème caramel.

TO SERVE

Invert each mould onto a serving plate, being careful not to split or crush the little crowns of mousse. Arrange the hot watercress leaves in the 'well' in the centre of each crown. Roll the mussels in the piping hot sauce and spoon an equal quantity of mussels and sauce around each 'well'. Sprinkle the mussels with the snipped chives and then serve immediately.

COQUILLES ST. JACQUES GENEVIÈVE

(Scallops Geneviève)

This is a delicate dish which cannot be served too hot, because the scallops must be poached very gently and the delicate sauce must not be boiled. Improve the presentation with a cluster of tiny pastry *fleurons* around the edge of each plate. If you do not want your guest biting on little pieces of shallot, you could rub the sauce through a fine conical sieve.

PREPARATION

THE SHALLOTS: Peel, wash and very finely chop, and place them in a sauté pan.

THE SCALLOPS: Open them and remove the beards. Take out the white flesh (*noix*) and the corals, rinse and pat dry with a cloth. Cut the *noix* horizontally into 2 or 3 slices and put them with the corals in the pan containing the shallots.

COOKING

Pour the fish stock and dry vermouth into the pan and season lightly with salt. Set the pan over high heat. At the first sign of bubbling, lift out the scallops and corals, which should be barely cooked. Place them in the centre of a warm, damp cloth.

THE SAUCE: Reduce the cooking liquid over high heat until it becomes syrupy, then stir in the cream. As soon as it comes to the boil, stir in the butter, a little at a time. Season to taste with salt and pepper. Set the pan in a bain-marie.

TO SERVE

Preheat the oven to 170°C/325°F/Gas 3. Divide the scallops and corals between 4 serving plates. Place in the preheated oven for 1 minute. Coat the scallops generously with the sauce and place a good slice of truffle in the centre of each plate. Brush the truffle slices with clarified butter. Roughly chop the rest of the truffle and scatter over the sauce. Serve immediately.

INGREDIENTS

12 scallops

30g (1oz) shallots

100ml (4fl.oz) Fish stock (see page 50)

200ml (8fl.oz) dry vermouth

2 tbls double cream

90g (3oz) butter

salt

freshly ground white pepper

75g (2½oz) Puff pastry (optional) (see page 248)

1 truffle, about 40g (1½oz)

clarified butter

Serves: 4 people
Preparation time: 20 minutes
Cooking time: 4 minutes
Wine: A fine, crisp Muscadet sur Lie or a light, sometimes slightly tart Sylvaner.

1

2

3

1 *Cuisses de grenouilles aux deux champignons (page 145)*
2 *Petite blanquette de homard (page 132)*
3 *Puits cressonnières aux moules (page 137)*
Opposite *Nouilles aux fruits de mer (page 143)*

INGREDIENTS

48 live freshwater
crayfish or langoustines

2 lobsters, each weighing
about 400g (14oz)

2 quantities *Nage* (see
page 47)

150g (5oz) Chicken
mousse (see page 110)

12 fresh green
peppercorns

200g (7oz) noodles,
preferably fresh (see
page 223)

1 tbls peanut oil

1 medium carrot

2 medium shallots

130g (5oz) butter

4 tbls Cognac

½ bay-leaf

500ml (1pt) double
cream

pinch of cayenne pepper

1 tbls finely chopped
fresh basil

15g (½oz) clarified
butter

salt

Serves: 4 people
Preparation time: 1
hour
Cooking time: 18
minutes
Wine: This rich, creamy
dish needs a wine with a
degree of acidity. Try a
wine made from the
Sauvignon grape such as
a Sancerre. Also suitable
would be a dry, crisp
white from Stellenbosch
in South Africa.

Picture: page 129

CASSOLETTES D'ECREVISSES AUX TAGLIATELLES SAUCE NANTUA

(Cassolettes of crayfish with noodles and sauce Nantua)

This dish may be served as a first course; in which case, halve all the quantities. The chicken mousse adds a more interesting contrasting texture than a fish mousse.

The classic sauce Nantua is a creamy Béchamel, finished with crayfish butter. We prefer the subtlety of our interpretation. Keep the lobster heads in the freezer to use for another recipe, such as lobster butter (see page 60).

PREPARATION

THE SHELLFISH: Bring the *nage* to the boil in a saucepan. Plunge in the lobsters and cook for 15 minutes. Lift them out of the pan with a slotted spoon and set aside.

Remove the intestines from the crayfish (see page 35), plunge them into the boiling *nage* and cook for 3 minutes. Lift them out of the pan with a slotted spoon and set aside.

THE CHICKEN MOUSSE: Heat a pan of boiling, salted water to simmering point (90°C/200°F).

Crush the green peppercorns and stir into the mousse. Using 2 teaspoons, form 8 small *quenelles* the size of pigeons' eggs. Poach them in the simmering water for 2 minutes, then take the pan off the heat and keep the *quenelles* in the poaching liquid.

THE NOODLES: Cook in a pan of boiling, salted water, to which you have added the oil. When they are cooked to your liking, add a little cold water to prevent further cooking and keep in the pan, off the heat.

THE SAUCE NANTUA: Shell 4 crayfish, leaving the heads attached to the tails and reserve.

Separate the heads and tails of the other crayfish, shell the tails and reserve the meat, together with the 4 whole crayfish wrapped in a damp cloth.

Peel, wash and finely slice the carrot and shallots. Place in a shallow pan with 30g (1oz) butter and sweat until tender. Crush the crayfish heads, put them in a sauté pan and set over high heat. Pour in the Cognac and ignite, then add 1L (1¾ pt) *nage*. Add the ½ bay-leaf, lower the heat and reduce the liquid by half.

Add the cream, cook over low heat for 10 minutes, then pour the mixture into a blender or food processor and process for a few seconds. Rub through a conical sieve into a saucepan. Set over high heat and bring to the boil. Lower the heat and cook until the sauce is thick enough to coat the back of a spoon. Stir in 50g (2oz) butter, a little at a time, season to taste with salt and cayenne pepper and set the pan in a bain-marie.

THE LOBSTERS: Separate the heads from the tails. Using scissors, cut off the shells from the tails and slice 4 nice medallions from each tail.

TO SERVE

Pass the remaining *nage* through a conical sieve into a sauté pan. Set over high heat and, as soon as the liquid begins to tremble, put in the crayfish tails, lobster medallions and the 4 whole crayfish. Immediately, take the pan off the heat, leave for 2 minutes, and then drain.

Drain the noodles and heat them in 50g (2oz) butter, seasoned to your taste. Roll them 4 times round a fork and arrange them like little nests in the centre of 4 china scallop shells or small, deep dishes.

Perch 2 chicken *quenelles* on top of each nest and arrange the crayfish tails and lobster medallions around the *quenelles*. Pour a thick ribbon of sauce round the edge and sprinkle over the chopped basil.

Brush the whole crayfish with clarified butter and put one on each dish, with the claws arranged one on either side of the *quenelles*.

NOUILLES AUX FRUITS DE MER

(Noodles with seafood)

Serves: 6 people
Preparation time: 55 minutes
Cooking time: depends on the size of the seafood
Wine: A strong, distinctive, fine Grand Cru Chablis or a Chardonnay from the Napa Valley in California.

This quantity is enough for 6 people as a starter, or for 4 people as a main course. It looks equally good served on individual plates as on a large serving platter. You can substitute any other crustaceans for those suggested in the recipe. If you use Bouchot mussels, you will not need to de-beard them, but you must remember to remove the beards from all other varieties.

PREPARATION

THE MUSSELS: Scrub and wash them in several changes of water. Put

INGREDIENTS

1L (1¾pts) mussels, preferably Bouchot

1 lobster, weighing about 450g (1lb)

6 scallops

6 crayfish tails or 6 Dublin Bay prawns

200ml (8fl.oz) dry white wine

60g (2oz) butter

1 medium shallot

1L (1¾pts) *Nage* (optional) (see page 47)

200ml (8fl.oz) Fish stock (see page 50)

4 medium tomatoes

250g (8oz) fresh noodles (see page 223)

1 tsp oil

200ml (8fl.oz) double cream

pinch of saffron threads

120g (4oz) peeled shrimps (preferably the pink variety)

salt

freshly ground white pepper

Picture: page 141

them in a saucepan with 100ml (4fl.oz) white wine. Cover the pan, set over high heat and cook until all the mussels have opened. Take the pan off the heat and drain the mussels in a colander, straining the cooking liquid into a bowl to use in the sauce. Remove the mussels from their shells, cut off the beards and keep the mussels at room temperature, covered with a damp cloth.

THE LOBSTER: Lightly crack the claws, then plunge the lobster into boiling, salted water or *nage* for 15 minutes. Lift it out of the pan with a slotted spoon. Keep in a cool place. When it is cold, remove the flesh from the claws and tail. Cut the tail flesh into 6 medallions.

THE SCALLOPS: Open them and remove the beards. Take out the white part (*noix*) and the corals, rinse them and pat dry with a cloth. Peel and chop the shallot. Put it in a shallow pan and sweat with 30g (1oz) butter. Add the scallops and pour in the remaining white wine. At the first sign of boiling, immediately drain the scallops, reserving the cooking liquid.

THE CRAYFISH OR PRAWNS: Bring the fish stock to the boil and plunge in the crayfish tails or prawns. Lower the heat and poach very gently for 2 minutes. Remove the pan from the heat, drain the crayfish or prawns and reserve the cooking liquid. If you are using crayfish, shell the tails. In either case, cover the tails with a damp cloth.

THE TOMATOES: Peel, deseed and chop them. Then sweat them with 30g (1oz) butter in a shallow pan, season lightly with salt and pepper and keep warm.

THE NOODLES: Cook 'al dente' in boiling, salted water and the oil. As soon as they are cooked to your taste, add a little cold water to prevent further cooking and drain.

THE SAUCE: Decant the cooking liquid from the mussels, scallops and crayfish or prawns into a shallow pan. Set the pan over high heat and reduce the liquid until it is slightly syrupy. Add the saffron and then the cream, let the sauce bubble for 5 minutes, then strain through a conical sieve.

TO SERVE

Plunge everything except the tomatoes and noodles (not forgetting the shrimps) into the boiling sauce. When the mixture comes to the boil, add the drained noodles. Season to taste with salt and pepper and transfer to a shallow dish. Arrange the chopped tomatoes in the middle and serve at once.

CUISSES DE GRENOUILLES AUX DEUX CHAMPIGNONS

(Frogs' legs with mushroom and truffle)

Frogs' legs are at their most tender and delicate when they are fresh and not too large. The truffle adds a touch of colour, as well as an exquisite flavour. Do not hesitate to double the number of frogs' legs for greedy people!

PREPARATION

THE MUSHROOM AND TRUFFLE: Peel and cut into 'matchsticks'. Keep the peelings for later. Sprinkle the lemon juice over the mushroom

THE SAUCE: Using scissors, cut off both legs from the body of each frog and lightly scrape the points of the feet. The frogs' legs will look like little legs of lamb. Rinse them in very cold water, wrap in a slightly damp cloth and keep in a cool place.

Heat 30g (1oz) butter in the shallow pan, put in the chopped shallot and sweat until soft. Add the frogs' backs, the mushroom and truffle peelings and the thyme and cook over low heat for 3 minutes, stirring continuously with a spatula. Pour in the white wine, reduce by half, add the chicken and fish stocks and cook over low heat for 30 minutes.

Stir in the cream and cook until the mixture is thick enough to coat the back of a spoon. Beat in 30g (1oz) butter, a little at a time, then pass through a conical sieve. Season to taste, add the truffle and mushroom matchsticks and keep the sauce in a bain-marie.

COOKING THE FROGS' LEGS

Do not cook until just before serving. Set a sauté pan over medium heat and put in the butter. Lightly salt the frogs' legs and put them into the pan. Cook until they are done to your liking, about 1½ minutes on each side. Do not allow them to take on any colour. Tip into a small colander and leave for 1 minute, until a little clear juice runs.

TO SERVE

Divide the frogs' legs between 2 deep plates or *cassolettes*. Heat the

INGREDIENTS

1 skewer of 12 frogs' legs weighing about 300g (10oz)

1 large, tightly closed button mushroom

1 truffle weighing about 30g (1oz), fresh and raw if possible

few drops lemon juice

90g (3oz) butter

1 medium shallot, finely chopped

1 sprig thyme

100ml (4fl.oz) dry white wine

150ml (6fl.oz) Chicken stock (see page 48)

100ml (4fl.oz) Fish stock (see page 50)

200ml (8fl.oz) double cream

1 tbls snipped chives

salt

freshly ground white pepper

Serves: 2 people
Preparation time: 30 minutes
Cooking time: 2 to 3 minutes
Wine: A big, round, full-bodied red such as a Nuits St Georges or a Morey St Denis.

Picture: page 140

sauce until it is just coming to the boil; this will poach the mushroom and truffle matchsticks very lightly. Pour the sauce thickly over the frogs' legs, sprinkle with chives and serve at once.

INGREDIENTS

1 live lobster, weighing about 800-900g (1lb 12oz-2lb)

½ onion

3 shallots

1 carrot

3 very ripe tomatoes

4 tbls olive oil

50ml (2fl.oz) Cognac

1 small garlic clove, unpeeled and crushed

1 small bouquet garni, containing 1 stalk tarragon

300ml (12fl.oz) white wine

200ml (8fl.oz) Fish stock (see page 50)

100ml (4fl.oz) Veal stock (optional) (see page 48)

pinch of cayenne pepper

100g (4oz) butter

2 sprigs chopped parsley

salt

freshly ground white pepper

Serves: 2 people
Preparation time: 30 minutes
Cooking time: about 10 minutes
Wine: We feel the only suitable wine would be a fine, rich Gewürztraminer from

HOMARD A L'AMERICAINE

(Lobster à l'Américaine)

This delicious dish is wonderful served only with a plain rice pilaff or steamed rice.

When you want to make only the sauce Américaine, you can use a whole lobster with the addition of a few crushed lobster heads. Keep the lobster meat to use in another recipe.

PREPARATION

THE ONION, SHALLOTS, CARROT AND TOMATOES: Peel and finely chop the onion and shallots. Peel and finely dice the carrot. Plunge the tomatoes into boiling water, refresh, peel, deseed and coarsely chop. CUTTING UP THE LOBSTER: Kill the lobster with a needle (see page 35). Using a heavy knife, cut off the claws where they meet the body and crush lightly with the flat of the knife. Cut the tail into 4 or 5 rings and split the head in half lengthways. Remove the gritty sac from the top of the head and scrape the intestines and coral into a small bowl. All this must be done very quickly. Season the lobster pieces to taste with salt and pepper.

COOKING

Preheat the oven to 220°C/425°F/Gas 7.

Pour the olive oil into a *fait-tout* or a large, shallow round casserole and set over high heat. When the oil is boiling hot, put in the lobster pieces and cook for about 5 minutes, until the meat is lightly coloured and the shells are red. Pour in the Cognac and ignite, then lift out the lobster pieces and transfer to a plate. Keep warm.

Lower the heat, put the shallots, onion, carrot and crushed garlic into the casserole and sweat gently for 3 minutes. Add the tomatoes, bouquet garni, white wine, fish stock, veal stock and a pinch of cayenne pepper. Cook for 20 minutes until the mixture is reduced by one-third. Lay the lobster pieces on this aromatic sauce, cover the casserole and cook in the preheated oven for 5 minutes.

Remove from the oven, extract the lobster meat from the rings and claws and keep warm.

THE SAUCE: Set the casserole over high heat and boil for 5 minutes. Mash the intestines and coral with 50g (2oz) softened butter. Lower the heat and gently stir this mixture into the sauce, taking care that it does not boil.

Rub the sauce through a muslin-lined sieve into a saucepan. Stir in the remaining butter, a little at a time, correct the seasoning and add a touch of Cognac.

Alsace with its fruity perfume and clean, dry finish.

TO SERVE

Arrange the lobster pieces in a vegetable dish, *timbale* or bi-metal dish, coat thickly with sauce and sprinkle with chopped parsley. Garnish the dish with the lobster heads and 'feelers'.

NOTES

Lobster eggs should always be kept and used to sprinkle over fish dishes and salad Gourmand.

If left over at the end of a recipe, any yellow stomach meat from a crab can be worked with butter or cream and a touch of brandy. Spice it well and serve it on toast. This makes an excellent hors d'oeuvre to accompany your aperitif.

All claws and feelers should be saved and used to garnish dishes. The meat inside is especially sweet and succulent and worth all the effort of removing it.

CHAPTER EIGHT

FISH

W hat a variety of fish we serve! They come in many different, luminous colours and every shape and size. Large or small, flat or bulgingly rounded, our fish arrive covered in silt from the cold seas of the north or the warm seas of the south and are often flown in by air. Coming, as they do, from unpolluted waters, they have one thing in common — their purity. Most types of fish feed and grow freely and naturally in the wild, which is not always true of other creatures which we eat, such as meat and poultry.

Fish-lovers sometimes find the preparation rather off-putting; they consider the smell, bones and spatter of dirty water unpleasant, so we have included a number of recipes in this chapter where the preparation is quite simple. However you cook fish, whether poaching, grilling or baking, never overcook it, or the flesh will become rubbery.

If you stuff fish with a mousse, it cannot be served very hot; if it is overheated the mousse will become grainy and dry and may disintegrate. You must serve fish as soon as it is cooked; the serving temperature may vary between 60°C and 80°C (140°F to 185°F) depending on the cooking method. Sauces for fish must always be light, delicate and moist. On no account must they be allowed to overpower the flavour of the fish.

BRESOLLES DE BARBUE SILVANO

(*Bresolles* of brill Silvano)

T his is a light, succulent dish, with a delicate, subtle blend of flavours that taste quite delicious.

Serves: 4 people
Preparation time: 55 minutes
Cooking time: 6 minutes
Wine: A big, light, spicy wine with enough

acidity to combat the vinegar such as an Alsace Riesling Vendange Tardive. A fine, full-flavoured Sancerre would also be ideal.

INGREDIENTS

1 brill, weighing about 1.4kg (3lb)

1 medium shallot

100g (3½oz) button mushrooms

220g (8oz) butter

120g (4oz) white bread, crusts removed

50ml (2fl.oz) milk

120g (4oz) skinned chicken breast

120g (4oz) foie gras, preferably raw

2 egg whites

150ml (6fl.oz) double cream

250g (8oz) carrots

250g (8oz) turnips

150g (5oz) very fine French beans

4 tbls raspberry vinegar (see page 63)

150ml (6fl.oz) Veal stock (see page 48)

salt

freshly ground white pepper

Picture: page 152

PREPARATION

THE BRILL: Fillet the brill and remove the skin. Lightly flatten the fillets with the flat edge of a cook's knife or a mallet. Using a plain, round 10cm (4in) pastry cutter, cut out 8 circles from the fillets and place in the refrigerator. Reserve the trimmings.

THE *DUXELLES*: Peel, wash and finely chop the shallots and the mushrooms separately. In a shallow pan, sweat the shallots with 1 tsp butter; add the mushrooms and cook for about 3 minutes, or until the moisture from the vegetables has evaporated. Keep in a cool place.

THE MOUSSE: Soak the bread in the milk. Put the trimmings from the brill fillets, the chicken breast, foie gras and egg whites in a blender or food processor and process for 2 or 3 minutes. Rub through a fine sieve into a bowl set in crushed ice. Using a spatula, stir in the cream, a little at a time, then the soaked bread. Mix in the *duxelles*, season to taste with salt and pepper and place in the refrigerator.

THE VEGETABLE GARNISH: Peel and wash the carrots and turnips and using a small, sharp knife, 'turn' them into small olive shapes. Cook in boiling, salted water, refresh, drain and wrap in a damp cloth. Top and tail the French beans and cut into 3cm (1¼in) lengths. Cook in boiling, salted water, refresh, drain and put with the carrots and turnips.

ASSEMBLING THE *BRESOLLES*: Place a quarter of the mousse in the centre of 4 of the brill circles. Cover with the remaining circles and press lightly together.

COOKING

Heat 60g (2oz) butter in a sauté pan set over gentle heat. Put in the bresolles and sear for 3 minutes on each side. Transfer to a shallow serving dish and keep hot. Pour off the fat from the pan and deglaze with raspberry vinegar. Pour in the veal stock, increase the heat and reduce the liquid until it is slightly syrupy.

Lower the heat and beat in 150g (6oz) butter, a little at a time. Pass the sauce through a conical sieve, return it to the pan and add the vegetable garnish. Bring the sauce to the boil, season to taste with salt and pepper and keep hot in a bain-marie.

TO SERVE

Pour the sauce thickly over the *bresolles* and serve immediately.

SOLE SOUFFLEE GERMAINE

(Sole soufflé Germaine)

For the presentation of this dish, we suggest that you arrange a few *fleurons* near the head of each sole; they will both look and taste good. To complement the flavour of the delicate fish, serve a *subric* of watercress (see page 221) together with some steamed or boiled potatoes. Boning a sole so that it does not open up at the edges is a very difficult process. If you can produce this recipe successfully, you can consider yourself a skilled cook!

PREPARATION

THE SOLE: Remove the black skins in the following manner. With the point of knife, make a small incision at the end of the tail and gently run the knife backwards and forwards to free the skin. Using a cloth, take hold of a small piece of the skin and pull the whole skin off in one swift movement. Lightly run the back of the knife over the white skin to remove any tiny scales. Trim the edges of the sole very slightly with scissors. Cut off the heads diagonally at the point where they meet the fillets.

Using a filleting knife, make an incision right down the backbone on the skinned side of the sole, leaving 2cm (¾in) uncut at either end. Through this incision, slide the knife blade between the backbone and the fillets to loosen them, stopping about 2cm (¾in) in from the outside edge of the fish. Carefully insert a pair of scissors and cut along the edge of the backbone on one side of the sole, taking great care not to pierce the flesh.

Slide the point of the knife between the underside of the backbone and the fillets on the opposite side of the sole. Using the scissors, cut the backbone in the same way as before and remove it. There should now be a small pocket in each sole. Very carefully trim the sides to remove as many bones as possible and to leave a clean edge. On no account must the fish have an opening on the outside edges. Rinse the sole in cold water and carefully pat dry inside and out with a cloth. Keep in the refrigerator.

THE SHRIMPS: Remove the intestines. Cut off the heads and ends of the tails of 18 and reserve the round backs for the garnish. Finely dice the rest of the shrimps. Sweat in a shallow pan with 1 tbls butter. Pour in the Cognac and ignite. Add 1 tbls double cream, bring to the boil, then

INGREDIENTS

6 sole, each weighing about 300g (10oz)

250g (9oz) shrimps, preferably pink

80g (2½oz) butter

1 tbls Cognac

500ml (1pt) double cream

1 egg, separated

430g (14oz) (about ⅓ quantity) Mousseline of pike Chloé (see page 109)

2 medium shallots, finely sliced

400ml (16fl.oz) dry white wine

250ml (10fl.oz) Fish stock (see page 50)

100g (4oz) Lobster butter (see page 61)

salt

freshly ground white pepper

Serves: 6 people
Preparation time: 1 hour 10 minutes
Cooking time: 15 minutes
Wine: This superb, rich dish deserves a truly superb wine such as Musigny Blanc from Côte de Nuits or the very rare Château Grillet from northern Rhône.

1

2

3

1 *Filets de sole Mazarin (page 158)*
2 *Bresolles de barbue Silvano (page 149)*
3 *Sole soufflée Germaine (page 151)*
Above *Tresse de saumon et*
barbue au gingembre (page 161)

1 *Having loosened the skin of the sole with the point of a knife, strip it away from the flesh with your fingers.*
2 *Trim the edges with a pair of scissors and cut off the head.*

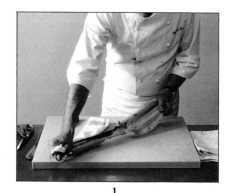

1

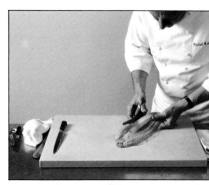

2

3 **De-boning the sole**
Make an incision down the back of the fish and slide the blade of the knife between the backbone and the flesh to ease away the fillet.
4 *With a pair of scissors cut along both outside edges of the backbone.*

3

4

5 *After you have slid the knife blade along the underside of the bone, gently lift out the backbone, leaving the shape of the fish intact.*
6 *Fill the pocket left by the removed backbone with the mousse.*

5

6

7 *Press the edges of the flesh together with your fingers.*
8 *Once you have flattened the mousse down into the pocket with a palette knife, garnish with peeled shrimps and place the fish in the buttered gratin dish and scatter with chopped shallots.*

7

8

whisk in the egg yolk to thicken the mixture and immediately take the pan off the heat and chill the mixture.

ASSEMBLING THE SOLE: Preheat the oven to 220°C/425°F/Gas 7. When the shrimp mixture is completely cold, mix it with the pike mousseline. Sprinkle the insides of the sole with salt and fill the pockets with the mousse. Brush the open edges with egg white. Draw the edges of the fillets together; there should be a gap of about 3cm (1¼in) in the middle and 1cm (½in) at either end. Using a palette knife, smooth down the mousse which spills out between the fillets. Brush the reserved shrimps with egg white and place 3 on each mousse.

COOKING THE SOLE

Butter a fish or gratin dish and strew over the finely sliced shallots. Put in the sole being careful not to spoil the shape. Pour in the white wine and fish stock and add a little salt. Set the dish over high heat and, as soon as the liquid trembles, remove from the heat and cover with well-buttered greaseproof paper. Bake in the preheated oven for 15 minutes. When you take them out of the oven, the fish should have risen slightly like soufflés, because the mousse will have expanded during cooking.

THE SAUCE: Using a fish slice, carefully transfer the sole to a silver or china serving dish. Cover with buttered greaseproof paper and keep hot. Set the gratin dish over high heat and reduce the cooking liquid by two-thirds. Add the cream and boil for several minutes. Remove from the heat and stir in the lobster butter, a little at a time, then season to taste with salt and pepper. Heat the sole in the oven for 1 minute at 170°C/325°F/Gas 3, then pass the boiling hot sauce through a conical sieve directly over the sole.

FRICASSEE DE TURBOTIN

(Fricassée of chicken turbot with spinach parcels)

Serves: 8 people
Preparation time: 1 hour 10 minutes
Cooking time: 2 minutes
Wine: A chilled red wine like a Chinon from the Loire or a Beaujolais Village.

PREPARATION

PREPARING THE TURBOT: Trim the fish and cut off the heads with the scissors. With a sharp knife, make an incision down either side of the backbone. Using a cleaver, split them in two down the middle, starting

INGREDIENTS

2 chicken turbot, each weighing about 1.4kg (3lb)

100g (3oz) button mushrooms

350g (12oz) butter

500g (1lb 2oz) spinach

1 bottle red wine (Gamay-style)

120g (4oz) shallots

1 sprig thyme

½ bay-leaf

½ tsp black peppercorns, coarsely crushed

300g (10oz) Puff pastry (see page 248)

pinch of flour

1 egg yolk, mixed with 1 tbls milk, to glaze

2 tbls peanut oil

300ml (12fl.oz) Fish stock (see page 50)

400ml (16fl.oz) double cream

salt

freshly ground white pepper

at the tail end. Slide the blade of a fish filleting knife between the flesh and the black skin and remove the skin. Using a chopping knife, cut the turbot crossways, in the direction of the bones, into small slices about 1cm (½in) thick. You should have about 32 slices (ie 4 per person). Pat dry with a damp cloth and keep in a cool place.

THE MUSHROOMS: Wash them if necessary and cut off the stalks level with the caps. Keep the stalks and trimmings to use in the sauce. Cut the caps into small, even-sized batons and sweat them in 1 tbls butter. Keep at room temperature.

THE SPINACH: Remove the stalks, wash the leaves and cook in boiling, salted water. Refresh in cold water, drain and use your hands to squeeze out the excess water. Chop the spinach with a knife. Heat 40g (1½oz) butter in a sauté pan until it is nutty brown. Put in the spinach and heat for 1 minute, then add the mushroom batons. Season with salt and pepper and keep in a cool place.

THE RED WINE: Pour into a saucepan. Peel and finely chop the shallots and add them to the pan, together with the thyme, bay-leaf, mushroom stalks and trimmings, the crushed peppercorns and a pinch of salt. Set over high heat and reduce the wine by two-thirds. Keep hot.

THE SPINACH PARCELS: Preheat the oven to 240°C/475°F/Gas 9. On a lightly floured wooden or marble surface, roll out the pastry into a long strip about 3mm (1/10in) thick. Arrange the spinach on the pastry in 8 evenly spaced piles. Season the egg wash with a pinch of salt and brush it round the edges of the spinach. Fold over the pastry so that it completely encloses the spinach and seal the edges by pressing lightly with your fingertips. Use a 9cm (3½in) pastry cutter to cut out each 'parcel'. Place them on a baking sheet, glaze with egg wash and pink the edges with a knife. Score a design on each parcel with the point of a knife, leave to rest for a few minutes, then bake in the preheated oven for 12 minutes. Keep hot.

COOKING THE TURBOT

Heat the oil with 100g (4oz) butter in the sauté pan set over high heat. Lightly salt the turbot slices, but do not flour them. Put in as many as will fit comfortably into the pan and sauté quickly until golden. Cook for 1 minute on each side.

Transfer the cooked turbot to a plate and repeat the operation as often as necessary, depending on the size of your pan. Make sure that the turbot is only half-cooked at the thickest part near the backbone.

THE SAUCE: Pour off the excess fat from the pan, deglaze with the fish stock and reduce by three-quarters. Add the reduced wine and reduce again until the mixture is slightly syrupy. Stir in the cream and bring to the boil. Immediately take the pan off the heat and stir in the remaining butter, a little at a time. Correct the seasoning with salt and pepper and strain the sauce through a conical sieve. Keep hot in a bain-marie.

TO SERVE

Arrange the turbot slices on a serving platter, overlapping in the shape of a crown. Place in the oven at 170°C/325°F/Gas 3 for 1 minute. Pour the boiling hot sauce over the fish and into the centre of the platter and arrange the hot spinach parcels around the edge.

For fewer guests, you can use a smaller chicken turbot and reduce the quantities of the other ingredients accordingly. As preparing the turbot alone takes at least 25 minutes, it is well worth begging the help of your fishmonger, if he is in a good mood!

ESCALOPES DE SAUMON CRESSONNIERE

(Escalopes of salmon with watercress)

Steamed potatoes make a good accompaniment to this dish. It is not essential to use the chlorophyll, although it does add extra flavour and colour to the sauce. Otherwise, the watercress alone is fine.

PREPARATION

THE SALMON: Bone out the salmon from the back. Using a filleting knife with a supple blade, remove the skin. Cut the salmon flesh into 4 good escalopes, each weighing about 200g (8oz). Lay them on a tea-towel and salt them lightly.

COOKING

Heat the clarified butter in a sauté pan set over medium heat. Put in the salmon escalopes and cook for 1 minute on each side. Transfer to a serving dish and keep warm.

INGREDIENTS

1kg (2lb 2oz) middle cut salmon

50g (2oz) clarified butter

250ml (10fl.oz) Fish stock (see page 50)

300g (10oz) watercress, stalks removed

250ml (10fl.oz) double cream

1 tsp chlorophyll (optional) (see page 59)

salt

Serves: 4 people
Preparation time: 20 minutes
Cooking time: 2 minutes
Wine: A dry, round, rich-in-flavour white such as a Chablis Premier Cru or

Meursault from Côtes de Beaune.

Pour off the excess fat from the pan and deglaze with the fish stock. As soon as the liquid bubbles, toss in the watercress leaves and simmer for 2 minutes, then add the cream. Bring to the boil, lower the heat, cover the pan and cook gently for 5 minutes. Add the chlorophyll and season. Pour the sauce onto a plate and lay the escalopes on top.

INGREDIENTS

3 sole, each weighing about 400g (14oz)

260g (9oz) courgettes

220g (7oz) tomatoes

210g (7oz) butter

600ml (24fl.oz) Veal stock (see page 48)

2 sprigs parsley, finely chopped

2½ lemons

20g (¾oz) truffle, finely chopped

2 eggs

50ml (2fl.oz) peanut oil

50ml (2fl.oz) milk

100g (4oz) flour

210g (7oz) breadcrumbs, preferably fresh

salt

freshly ground black pepper

Serves: 4 people
Preparation time: 40 minutes
Cooking time: 4 minutes
Wine: A delicate, pale, refreshing wine from Mâconnais such as Pouilly Fuissé or its neighbour Montagny.

Picture: page 152

FILETS DE SOLE MAZARIN

(Fillets of sole Mazarin)

Leaf spinach makes the perfect accompaniment to this fresh-tasting, simple dish. The recipe can be prepared up to 2 hours in advance, but not more, or the breadcrumbs will become soggy.

PREPARATION

THE SOLE: Remove the skins in the following manner: using the point of a knife, make a small incision at the end of the tail and gently run the knife backwards and forwards to free the skin. Using a cloth, take hold of a small piece of skin and pull it off swiftly in one movement. Remove the white skin in the same way. Using a fish filleting knife, make an incision along the backbone. Ease the knife between the fillet and the bone, making sure that you do not leave any flesh on the backbone, and remove the fillets.

With the point of a knife, trim the outer edges of the fillets. Flatten them lightly with the flat edge of a large cook's knife or with a mallet. Rinse in cold water or wipe with a damp cloth, pat dry and keep in a cool place. Reserve the bones to use in a fish stock.

THE GARNISH: Top and tail the courgettes. Using a cannelizing knife, cannelize them lengthways, then cut into very fine slices, about 2mm (1/12in) thick. Skin, deseed and finely dice the tomatoes.

In a shallow pan set over high heat, melt 40g (1½oz) butter, put in the courgettes and sauté quickly until crisp to the bite. Add the tomatoes and, as soon as the mixture comes to the boil, transfer to a dish and keep at room temperature.

THE SAUCE: Pour the veal stock into a sauté pan and reduce until slightly syrupy. Make a *maître d'hôtel* butter by placing 50g (2oz) butter in a bowl and working with a spatula until soft, mix in the chopped parsley and the juice of half a lemon. Add the courgette and tomato mixture to the reduced veal stock. Set the pan over high heat and bring to the boil. Lower the heat and stir in the *maître d'hôtel* butter, a little at a time. Add the truffle, season with salt and pepper and keep hot.

PREPARING AND COOKING THE SOLE

Combine the eggs, oil and milk in a deep dish or plate and beat with a fork. Add a little salt. Put the flour on one plate and the breadcrumbs on another. Dip each sole fillet first into the flour, shaking off the excess, and then into the egg mixture. Finally, slip them between 2 fingers without pressing them and roll them in breadcrumbs.

Beat out the fillets very lightly with the flat side of a cook's knife or a mallet, then arrange them side by side on a dish. Heat 120g (4½oz) butter in 1 or 2 oval frying pans. Put in the fillets and cook over high heat for 2 minutes on each side, until they turn golden brown.

TO SERVE

Pour the very hot sauce onto the bottom of a silver or china serving dish. Arrange the sole fillets attractively on the sauce. Place 4 canellized lemon halves around the edge of the dish and serve at once.

GOUJONNETTES DE SOLE AU SAUTERNE

(*Goujonnettes* of sole with Sauternes)

This simple, light dish has great delicacy of flavour and colour. The blending of the Sauternes and pistachios is very subtle. This is an easy recipe to prepare, which only needs 10 minutes attention just before serving. If you like, you can enhance the 'greenness' of the dish by adding ½ tsp of chlorophyll (see page 59).

PREPARATION

THE SOLE: Using a fish filleting knife, fillet the sole and remove the skins. Cut each fillet into 3 strips, or *goujonnettes*, rinse in cold water or wipe with a damp cloth and pat dry. Place in the refrigerator.
THE POTATOES: Peel, wash and cut each one lengthways into 4 slices or *pavés*, about 1cm (½in) thick. Wrap in a tea-towel.
THE CARROTS: Peel and wash them. Using a small, sharp knife, 'turn'

Serves: 4 people
Preparation time: 40 minutes
Cooking time: 4 minutes
Wine: The sweetness of the Sauternes used in this dish is just noticeable so we think a suitable white wine should also be slightly sweet. A Vouvray made from Chenin Blanc or its neighbour, Montlouis across the Loire, would be ideal.

Picture: front cover

INGREDIENTS

2 sole, each weighing about 600g (1lb 4oz)

2 large potatoes

2 good-sized carrots

100g (3oz) butter

pinch of sugar

4 large, tightly closed mushrooms

70g (2½oz) shelled pistachio nuts

4 shallots

200ml (8fl.oz) Fish stock (see page 50)

300ml (12fl.oz) Sauternes-style wine

250ml (10fl.oz) double cream

salt

freshly ground white pepper

them the shape of 24 small garlic cloves. Put them into a shallow pan with a little water, 1 tbls butter and a pinch each of sugar and salt and cook until tender. Set aside.

THE MUSHROOMS: Remove and discard the stalks. Wash the caps or wipe with a damp cloth and pat dry. Using a small knife, 'turn' them like the carrots or finely dice them. Sweat in a little butter.

THE PISTACHIO BUTTER: Pour boiling water over the pistachios and skin them. Place in a blender or food processor with 70g (2½oz) softened butter and purée. Rub through a fine sieve and reserve.

COOKING

Preheat the oven to 190°C/375°F/Gas 5. Twist up each *goujonnette* and insert a cocktail stick through each end to hold the shape. Stick 3 along the length of each *pavé*. Butter a sauté pan or gratin dish. Peel and finely chop the shallots and strew them over the dish. Put in the potato *pavés*, the fish stock and Sauternes. Season with salt.

Set the pan over high heat until the liquid begins to tremble. Cover with buttered greaseproof paper and cook in the preheated oven for 4 minutes. When the sole is cooked, remove the cocktail sticks and arrange the *goujonnettes* on a serving dish. Discard the potatoes. Set the pan over high heat and reduce the cooking liquid by two-thirds. Add the cream and cook for a few more minutes. Beat in the pistachio butter and correct the seasoning if necessary.

TO SERVE

Pass the sauce through a sieve directly onto the *goujonnettes*. Sprinkle over the hot 'turned' carrots and mushrooms and serve immediately.

Serves: 4 people
Preparation time: 35 minutes
Cooking time: depends on the ingredients
Wine: A dry, full-bodied Burgundy of great quality and finesse: a Puligny Montrachet or a Grand Cru Meursault which is equally fine.

SYMPHONIE DE LA MER

(Sea symphony)

Each fish has its own distinct taste and though simple, this dish is very delicate. It is essential to serve this dish in deep plates and to give everyone a spoon to sup up the sauce. You can replace the samphire with a sprinkling of fresh, mild-flavoured herbs, such as snipped chives or fresh chervil or a *julienne* of blanched French beans.

PREPARATION

THE FISH: Fillet all the fish and remove the skins except from the red mullet. Rinse for a few seconds in very cold water or wipe with a damp cloth, then carefully pat dry. Leave the red mullet fillets whole, but cut all the rest into long strips, the thickness of your thumb.
THE SCALLOPS: Open them, de-beard and take out the corals and the white *noix*. Rinse and pat dry. Slice the *noix* in half horizontally.

COOKING

Pour the white wine into a sauté pan, set over high heat and reduce by half. Add the fish stock, lower the heat and simmer for 5 minutes.

In the following order and at 1 minute intervals, plunge in the turbot, the monkfish, the sole, the sea bass and the red mullet.

Poach all the fish until the red mullet fillets are cooked; they will take about 1 minute. Using a slotted spoon, transfer the fish to a shallow bi-metal or china serving dish. Cover the dish with a damp cloth and keep in a slightly warm place.
THE SAUCE: Pour the cooking liquid into a saucepan and add the saffron. Set over high heat and reduce by one-third. Take the pan off the heat and, using a small wire whisk, beat in the butter, a little at a time. Season to taste with salt and pepper.

TO SERVE

Arrange the raw scallop slices on top of the fish, then strain the boiling hot sauce through a conical sieve onto the whole dish. Sprinkle with blanched samphire and serve immediately.

INGREDIENTS

1 sole, weighing about 600g (1lb 4oz)

2 red mullet

1 sea bass, weighing about 300g (10oz)

250g (9oz) turbot fillets

300g (10oz) monkfish fillets

4 scallops

1 bottle dry white wine

500ml (1pt) Fish stock (see page 50)

pinch of saffron

60g (2oz) butter

100g (4oz) samphire (optional)

salt

freshly ground white pepper

TRESSE DE SAUMON ET BARBUE AU GINGEMBRE

(Salmon and brill plait with ginger)

The colours of this dish are so dainty and lustrous that you should serve it with only a delicate vegetable purée in a pastry boat.

If you prefer, you can use turbot instead of brill. Keep the fish trimmings to use in a fish mousse or terrine. This recipe works perfectly well for only 4 people if you halve the quantities.

INGREDIENTS

1 brill, weighing about 2.2kg (4lb 11oz)

1 salmon tail, weighing about 1.6kg (3lb 6oz)

550ml (22fl.oz) Fish stock (see page 50)

160g (5½oz) butter

Continued overleaf

2 very ripe tomatoes

2 medium courgettes

30g (1oz) fresh ginger root

3 tbls cognac

3 tbls dry white wine

50ml (2fl.oz) Veal stock (see page 48)

500ml (1pt) double cream

50g (2oz) clarified butter

salt

Serves: 8 people
Preparation time: 1 hour 30 minutes
Cooking time: 3 to 4 minutes
Wine: Salmon is a particularly rich flavoured fish and needs a wine of character and weight. The perfect

1 *Using a fish filleting knife, remove the salmon fillets by slicing upwards from the tail along the edge of the skin.*
2 *It is best to use the middle cut of the fish for this recipe, so laying the prepared square of card against the fish, slice a piece the width of the card.*

3 *Remove the skin from the brill in exactly the same way and again slice off a square.*
4 *Having neatened up the edges of both the fillet squares, cut them into even strips. These should measure 1cm (½in) thick, by 10cm (4in) long.*

PREPARATION

THE BRILL AND SALMON: Using a filleting knife, cut off the 2 brill fillets, starting in the middle of the back and following the line of the backbone. Lift off first one side and then the other. Remove the black and white skins from the fillets. Cut off the salmon fillets and remove the skin. Wipe all the fish fillets with a damp cloth. Trim the thicker parts of the brill, if necessary. Slice the fillets into escalopes, about 1cm (½in) thick. Cut each escalope into large, regular strips, like *goujonnettes*, 1cm (½in) wide and 10cm (4in) long. You should be able to cut 32 strips from each kind of fish.

Make 8 plaits, using 4 strips of each kind of fish per plait. Cover 8 10cm (4in) squares of cardboard with foil. Butter the foil and slide a plait onto each. Arrange in a roasting pan or in 2 sauté dishes and pour over 500ml (1pt) fish stock. Cover with lightly-buttered greaseproof paper and set aside. Preheat the oven to 240°C/475°F/Gas 9.
THE TOMATOES: Plunge into boiling water, then into cold water, peel and deseed. Finely dice the flesh and set aside.
THE COURGETTES: Rinse and cut into 'matchsticks'. Blanch in boiling water for 10 seconds, drain and set aside.

1

2

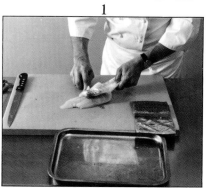

3

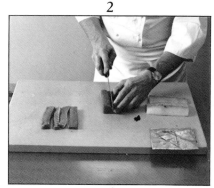

4

THE GINGER: Peel and reserve the peelings. Cut the root into fine *julienne* and set aside.

THE SAUCE: Combine the ginger peelings, Cognac, dry white wine, the remaining fish stock and the veal stock in a shallow pan. Set over high heat and reduce the liquid by half. Add the cream, lower the heat and cook gently for 20 minutes. Stir in the remaining butter, then pass through a conical sieve. Correct the seasoning, add the *julienne* of ginger and place in a bain-marie.

partner to salmon is a Savennières with a honey and flowers smell and a surprising dryness. An alternative would be a Meursault.

Picture: page 153

COOKING

Cook the plaited fish in the preheated oven for 3 to 4 minutes, basting with the fish stock to ensure that they are cooked right through.

TO SERVE

Coat 8 plates thickly with sauce and slide a plait diagonally onto each plate. Place a little warmed diced tomato at one point of the diagonal. Arrange a few warmed courgette 'matchsticks' on either side of the point. Brush very lightly with clarified butter and serve immediately.

5

6

5 Brush the foil-covered square with clarified butter.
6 Place 4 of the salmon strips, side by side, onto the card, making sure that they are equally spaced from each other. Then interweave 1 of the brill strips through the 4 salmon ones.

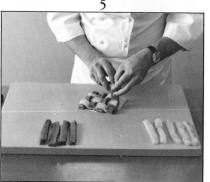

7

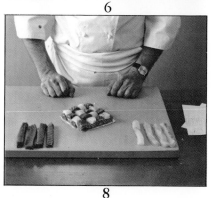

8

7 Repeat the process with another 3 brill strips.
8 The end result will be an extremely professional looking, plaited pattern or tresse.

1

2

1 *Noisettes de chevreuil aux airelles (page 167)*
2 *Poulet fermier aux escargots bread sauce*
(page 181)
3 *Emincé de volaille Andrée (page 182)*
4 *Pavé de dindonneau en blanquette (page 183)*
Right *Suprême de faisan voilé au porto*
(page 169)

3

4

CHAPTER NINE

GAME AND POULTRY

Happy are those who live in the country, who still possess a hen-coop and so can enjoy a plain roast fowl. The taste of a really fresh chicken is only a distant childhood memory for the city-dweller in today's consumer society. Avoid battery-farmed poultry at all costs and choose only guaranteed free-range farm chickens. Some game, of course, still comes from the wild, and so our preference is for hare, snipe, woodcock, grouse and duck.

Reared game, such as pheasant and partridge, can often have a disappointing flavour; Britain, however, produces some of the best game birds in Europe. Although the game season is short, lasting only about 3 to 4 months, it offers a truly splendid gastronomic choice, which fires the imagination of chefs and gourmets. Make sauces from game giblets, carcasses and trimmings; the rich stock gives off the most wonderful aromas which scent every corner of your kitchen. Never hang game for too long or it will lose some of its special flavour.

Finally, before you decide to serve any game, make sure that your guests like it. There are some people who have never even tasted game, but are afraid to try eating this wonderful food, which is definitely an acquired taste.

NOISETTES DE CHEVREUIL AUX AIRELLES

(Noisettes of venison with cranberries)

This is an uncomplicated dish, except for the preparation of the pepper sauce. Like all basic stocks, you should always have this

Serves: 6 people
Preparation time: 30 minutes, plus 2 to 3 hours marinating
Cooking time: 4 minutes
Wine: The sauce *poivrade* needs a heavy weighted, almost

aggressive, dark coloured Burgundy from the Côte de Nuits like the Gevrey-Chambertin or the Griotte-Chambertin.

INGREDIENTS

1 saddle of roe deer, weighing about 3kg (6½lb) on the bone

200g (7oz) cranberries

1 tsp thyme flowers

3 tsp black peppercorns, crushed

100ml (4fl.oz) olive oil

100ml (4fl.oz) port

30g (1oz) caster sugar

½ an orange

½ a lemon

2 medium carrots

1 large onion

1 stick celery

2 garlic cloves

50g (2oz) flour

50ml (2fl.oz) Cognac

150ml (6fl.oz) red wine vinegar

1L (1¾pts) red wine, preferably Gamay-style

1L (1¾pts) Veal stock (see page 48)

1 sprig thyme

100g (4oz) foie gras, preferably raw

50g (2oz) butter

salt

Picture: page 164

sauce to hand, especially during the game season. It keeps very well in the freezer. If you can use blood for the liaison it will taste even better.

For a pretty colour contrast and a complementary taste, serve this dish with a pastry *barquette* filled with a purée of pickled beetroot and some braised celeriac.

PREPARATION

THE SADDLE: Cut out the 2 fillets from the bone. Trim off the skin, nerves and sinews and reserve them. Remove the 2 filets mignons from underneath the saddle. Cut the large fillets into 12 or 18 noisettes and place them in a shallow dish with the 2 filets mignons. Sprinkle over the thyme flowers, 1 tsp crushed peppercorns and the olive oil. Set aside in a cool place for 2 to 3 hours.

THE CRANBERRIES: Put the port, sugar and the zests from the orange and lemon halves into a shallow pan and bring to the boil. Lower the heat, add the cranberries and let the liquid tremble for 30 seconds. Keep at room temperature.

THE SAUCE *POIVRADE*: Preheat the oven to 220°C/425°F/Gas 7. Break up the bones from the saddle and put them into a roasting pan with the venison trimmings. Brown in the hot oven, stirring occasionally so that the bones are browned on all sides.

Slice the carrot and onion into rings and finely chop the celery. Add the vegetables to the roasting pan, together with the unpeeled garlic clove. Then, after a few minutes, sprinkle over the flour and roast for a further 5 or 10 minutes. Remove the pan from the oven and tip the contents into a large saucepan.

Deglaze the roasting pan with the Cognac and vinegar. Set it over high heat, pour in the wine and ignite. Simmer for 5 minutes, then pour the liquid over the bones in the saucepan. Add the veal stock, the remaining crushed peppercorns and the thyme, and simmer very gently for 2½ hours, skimming the surface as often as necessary.

Pass through a conical sieve, rubbing the mixture through with the back of a spoon in order to extract all the juices from the venison trimmings and vegetables. Return the sauce to the pan and keep warm.

COOKING THE NOISETTES: Set a sauté pan over high heat and, without adding any fat, brown the venison noisettes and the filets mignons for 1 minute on each side. Make sure that they are still pink in the middle. Keep warm.

Drain off the fat from the pan, deglaze with the juice from the cranberries, then add the pepper sauce. Rub the foie gras through a fine sieve and add it to the sauce as a liaison. Stir in the butter, a little at a time. Do not allow the mixture to boil. Add the cranberries and correct the seasoning with salt and pepper if necessary.

TO SERVE

Lay the 2 filets mignons in the centre of a shallow dish and arrange the noisettes around the edge. Pour over the boiling hot sauce and serve immediately.

SUPREME DE FAISAN VOILE AU PORTO

(Breast of pheasant veiled in port)

This is a simple, light dish, which even people who are not game enthusiasts will enjoy. It is especially popular with those who hate being presented with half a pheasant on the bone.

PREPARATION

THE PHEASANTS: Using a sharp knife, make an incision in the neck of each pheasant. Oil your fingers and work them between the skin and the flesh, then pull off the skin. Cut off the legs and wing tips and keep them for another use. Lift off the breast leaving 2.5cm (1in) of the wing bone attached to each one. Interlard each one with 6 strips of back fat, about 4cm (1½in) long and 3mm (1/10in) wide. Draw the pheasants, reserving the livers. Make a Game stock with the carcasses (see page 49).

COOKING

In a sauté pan, gently fry the pheasant breasts in 60g (2oz) butter until golden. Cook for a further 5 minutes on each side, making sure they are still pink in the middle. Keep warm.

THE SAUCE: Deglaze the pan with the port, set it over high heat and reduce by two-thirds. Add the game stock and reduce until the liquid becomes syrupy. Incorporate 90g (3oz) butter, a little at a time, pass the sauce through a sieve and correct the seasoning if necessary.

INGREDIENTS

4 pheasants (preferably young hen birds)

150g (5oz) pork back fat

240g (8oz) butter

1 tbls wild rice

1 tsp finely chopped onion

4 large mushrooms

4 baked choux rings 5cm (2in) diameter (see page 249)

4 tbls Leek purée (see page 222)

400ml (16fl.oz) Game stock (see page 49)

400ml (16fl.oz) red port

salt

pepper

Serves: 4 people
Cooking time: 40 minutes
Preparation time: 15 minutes
Wine: A red wine with not too much acidity which is soft, rich and ripe to the nose. A Pomerol or a light Burgundy from the Côte de Beaune.

THE RICE PILAFF: Sauté the wild rice and onions in 30g (1oz) butter, then add water or stock, as in an ordinary rice pilaff. Finely dice the pheasant livers, fry quickly in 30g (1oz) butter and mix into the rice.

THE MUSHROOMS: Cut off the stalks. Fry the caps in the remaining butter for 2 minutes on each side. Fill them with the wild rice mixture, heaping it up into a dome.

THE CHOUX RINGS: Preheat the oven to 170°C/325°F/Gas 3. Cut off the tops of the rings with a serrated or very sharp knife. Warm them in the preheated oven for 1 minute, then fill with the leek purée. Arrange a stuffed mushroom in the centre.

TO SERVE

Picture: page 164

Arrange 2 breast fillets on each plate in a heart shape and place a choux ring at the top of each 'heart'. Pour the sauce over the pheasant.

Serves: 6 people
Preparation time: about 2 hours
Cooking time: 12 minutes
Wine: A strong, gamey taste enveloped in pastry needs a mellow red wine which is soft but rich in flavour and body. A Hermitage from the north of the Rhône Valley or a Châteauneuf-du-Pape from further south.

INGREDIENTS

6 grouse, each weighing about 400g (14oz)

1 medium carrot

1 medium onion

200ml (8fl.oz) red wine, claret-style

1 bouquet garni

6 coriander seeds

50g (2oz) butter

Continued

SUPREMES DE GROUSE AMOUREUSE

(Suprêmes of grouse in love hearts)

This dish can be prepared well in advance of the meal, which leaves very little to do before serving. It is fairly simple to make and will be much enjoyed by game-lovers.

PREPARATION

THE VEGETABLES: Peel, wash and dice. Preheat the oven to 190°C/375°F/Gas 5.

THE GROUSE: Pluck them and, using a medium knife, cut off the legs. Separate the thighs from the drumsticks and remove the thigh bones. Cut off the breast fillets and place them in the refrigerator, together with the thigh meat.

THE SAUCE: Clean the carcasses and roughly chop them, together with the drumsticks and thigh bones. Place in a roasting pan and brown in the preheated oven for 20 minutes. Add the diced carrot and onion and brown for a further 5 minutes.

Transfer the contents of the roasting pan to a saucepan. Deglaze the roasting pan with the red wine. Pour it into the saucepan, add the bouqet garni and coriander and enough water to cover the bones. Bring to the boil, then lower the heat and simmer. Cook for 1½ hours.

Strain through a conical sieve. Return the stock to the saucepan and reduce over high heat until it becomes slightly syrupy. Just before serving, whisk in 50g/2oz butter. Season to taste.

COOKING THE BREASTS: Heat the clarified butter in a sauté pan and, over high heat, sauté the breast fillets for 2 minutes on each side. They should still be rare. Pour in half the Armagnac and ignite. Keep the breast fillets in a cool place.

THE GROUSE MOUSSE: Purée the thigh meat in a blender or food processor for a few minutes, then rub through a fine sieve into a bowl set in crushed ice. Using a wooden spatula, stir in the egg white, then incorporate the double cream, a little at a time. Work in the remaining Armagnac and mix thoroughly. Correct the seasoning with salt.

ASSEMBLING THE HEARTS: Preheat the oven to 220°C/425°F/Gas 7. On a lightly floured marble or wooden surface, roll out the puff pastry to a thickness of about 2mm (1/12in). Lay a pair of breast fillets in the shape of a heart on the pastry, leaving a 3cm (1¼in) space between each heart. Using a palette knife, coat each side of the fillets with grouse mousse. Brush a little beaten egg around the edge of each heart, then cover completely with the remaining puff pastry.

Using a small knife, cut out the pastry round the fillets, leaving a border of about 1cm (½in).

Ingredients
30g (1oz) clarified butter
100ml (4fl.oz) Armagnac
1kg (2lb 2oz) Puff pastry (see page 248)
1 egg, beaten
½ egg white
350ml (14fl.oz) double cream
salt
freshly ground black pepper

COOKING

Lay the hearts on a baking sheet brushed with water. Glaze with beaten egg, 'pink' the edges and decorate the top with knife markings. Bake in a hot oven for about 12 minutes.

TO SERVE

Arrange the hearts on a silver platter. Serve the sauce separately.

BECASSES FLAMBEES SUR CROUTONS

(Flambéed woodcock on croûtons)

PREPARATION

THE WOODCOCK: Singe over a gas flame for 30 seconds, then wipe

Serves: 2 people
Preparation time: 40 minutes
Cooking time: 16 minutes
Wine: A simple, roasted woodcock deserves a wine of gracious fruitiness and a softness developed from age. A

Pommard or even the softer, more delicate Volnay would be well suited.

INGREDIENTS

2 woodcock, plucked but not drawn, with the heads and necks attached

2 fine slices of pork back fat

60g (2oz) clarified butter

30g (1oz) butter

2 round croûtons of white bread, 7cm (2¾in) diameter 1cm (½in) thick

30g (1oz) fresh foie gras, preferably raw

2 medium shallots, finely chopped

4 tbls port

5 tbls green Chartreuse

½ bottle full-bodied red Burgundy

zest of ½ lemon

2 small bunches watercress

salt

freshly ground black pepper

Picture: page 177

gently with a cloth. Using a small, sharp knife, take out the eyes, but leave on the heads, necks and feet. Interlace the feet.

Draw the heads round and run the long beaks right through both the thighs and the body like a skewer; there will then be no need to truss the woodcock. Season with salt and pepper, cover the breasts with the back fat and tie loosely with string.

COOKING

Preheat the oven to 240°C/475°F/Gas 9. Heat 30g (1oz) clarified butter in a roasting pan set over high heat. Put in the woodcock and sear until golden on all sides.

Roast in the preheated oven for 16 minutes, basting with the cooking juices every 3 minutes; the birds should still be very pink. Remove from the pan and set aside.

THE CROUTONS: Add the remaining clarified butter to the cooking butter in the roasting pan. Set over high heat, put in the croûtons and fry until golden on both sides. Drain on absorbent paper.

THE SAUCE: Remove the trussing string and back fat from the woodcock. Carve off the thighs and place them together with the breast fillets in a small shallow pan.

Using a spoon, remove the entrails. Discard the gizzard and rub the entrails and the foie gras through a fine sieve into a bowl. Mix well with a whisk, season to taste and set aside.

Put the chopped shallots into the roasting pan; crush the woodcock carcasses and add them to the pan. Set over high heat and brown for 3 to 4 minutes. Pour in the port, 2 tbls green Chartreuse and the red wine. Add the lemon zest and reduce by two-thirds.

Pass through a conical sieve into a small shallow pan, set over low heat and beat in the remaining butter and the entrail and foie gras mixture, a little at a time. Do not allow the sauce to boil. Season to taste with salt and pepper and keep in a bain-marie.

TO SERVE

Set the pan containing the thighs and breast fillets over gentle heat. Pour in the remaining Chartreuse and ignite. Put a croûton in the centre of the plates and arrange the two thighs and breasts from each woodcock on the croûtons, with the breasts and thighs facing opposite each other. Strain the hot, but not boiling sauce through a conical sieve over the woodcock and serve at once. Garnish both plates with a bunch of watercress.

Serve the woodcock with Darphin potatoes (see page 218) and a green salad. You could also split the heads in two and stick them into the croûtons; this will improve the presentation and delight lovers of woodcock, who can then enjoy the brains.

Unlike other game birds, woodcock need not to be drawn before cooking, since it excretes every time it flies, leaving the intestines clean. Woodcock is one of the least known game birds yet it is the most delicate and most loved by connoisseurs of game.

CANETON POELE GRANDE CHARTREUSE

(Braised duckling Grande Chartreuse)

In this dish, the green Chartreuse caramelizes the shallots and harmonizes sublimely well with the duck meat. It is a simple dish to make; you can do a lot of the pre-cooking and preparation several hours in advance. Serve the duckling with mange-tout or buttered spinach.

PREPARATION

Preheat the oven to 240°C/475°F/Gas 9.

THE CARROTS AND SHALLOTS: Peel and wash; finely slice the shallots and cut the carrots into small dice. Set aside.

PRE-COOKING: Heat the clarified butter in a casserole. Add the ducklings and fry over high heat until they are golden on all sides. Add half the shallots and all the diced carrots, then 30ml (1½fl.oz) Chartreuse. Cover the pan at once and put it in the hot oven for 15 minutes. Remove from the oven and leave the ducklings to 'rest' for 10 minutes before carving. Carve off the legs and breast fillets and keep warm.

THE STOCK: Pour off some of the fat from the casserole. Chop up the carcasses and return them to the casserole. Cook over high heat for 2 or 3 minutes, stirring with a wooden spatula. Deglaze the casserole with the white wine, reduce the liquid by half, add the bouquet garni and pour in just enough water to cover the bones. Bring to the boil, then lower the heat and simmer for 1 hour, skimming the surface.

INGREDIENTS

2 oven-ready ducklings, each weighing about 1.7kg (3lb 7oz)

100g (4oz) carrots

300g (10oz) shallots

60g (2oz) clarified butter

60g (2oz) butter

80ml (3fl.oz) green Chartreuse

100ml (4fl.oz) dry white wine

1 small bouquet garni

2 tbls snipped chives

½ bunch watercress

salt

freshly ground black pepper

Serves: 4 people
Preparation time: 30 minutes
Cooking time: 40 minutes
Wine: All duck dishes tend to be rather heavy. This one, however, is quite light, so, serve a Châteauneuf-du-Pape or a Cornas.

Strain the stock through a muslin-lined sieve into a bowl, then pour it back into a saucepan and reduce until it becomes slightly syrupy. Keep hot.

THE SAUCE: Sweat the remaining shallots in a shallow pan with 30g (1oz) butter. Do not allow them to colour. Sprinkle in 20ml (1fl.oz) Chartreuse and cook until all the moisture has evaporated. Pour in the duck stock, add the rest of the Chartreuse and bring to the boil. Stir in 30g (1oz) butter, season to taste with salt and pepper and keep hot.

TO SERVE

20 minutes before serving, finish cooking the legs either in the oven or under the grill. Separate the thighs from the drumsticks. Using poultry shears or a cleaver, cut off the ends of the drumsticks.

Remove and discard the skin from the breast fillets. Using a ham knife, carve each fillet diagonally into 4 slices, keeping the slices as slanted as possible.

Re-form the 4 breasts and arrange 1 round the edge of each serving plate. Place the legs in the centre. Cover with greaseproof paper or foil and place in a moderate oven (190°C/375°F/Gas 5) for 3 minutes — just long enough to reheat the breasts, which should still be pink. Coat the breasts with the boiling hot sauce, arrange a few watercress leaves around the legs and sprinkle the chives over the breasts.

Serves: 4 people
Preparation time: 35 minutes
Cooking time: 40 minutes
Wine: This elegant dish deserves a particularly fine wine such as the finest of Burgundy — Romanée Conti or Richbourg. An alternative would be a splendid old Rioja from Spain.

CANETON JULIETTE

(Duckling Juliette)

PREPARATION

PRE-COOKING: Preheat the oven to 240°C/475°F/Gas 9. Lay the ducklings on their backs in a roasting pan and roast in the preheated oven without any fat for 20 minutes. Remove from the oven and allow the ducklings to 'rest' for 10 minutes, then carve off the legs and breast fillets (these are called *suprêmes*). Keep the legs and *suprêmes* separately.

THE STOCK: Chop up the carcasses, put them in a roasting pan and brown in the oven for a few minutes. Meanwhile, peel and dice 100g (4oz) carrots and the shallots, add them to the pan and cook for a few more minutes. Remove the roasting pan from the oven and tip the contents into a saucepan.

Pour off the fat from the roasting pan and deglaze it with the white wine. Set over high heat and reduce the liquid by half, then pour it into the saucepan containing the carcasses. Pour in just enough water to cover the bones and add the bouquet garni. Bring to the boil over high heat, lower the heat and simmer gently for 1 hour, skimming the surface from time to time.

Strain the stock through a muslin-lined sieve into a bowl, then return it to the saucepan. Reduce over high heat until the stock has the consistency of a light syrup. Add the Curaçao and pour the stock into a bowl set in a bain-marie.

THE CARROTS AND LEEKS: Peel and wash the remaining carrots and leeks. Cut into *julienne*, using a chopping knife or a mandoline, if you prefer. Sweat the vegetables in a shallow pan with 30g (1oz) butter, cover the pan and cook until they are tender but still crisp. Pour in the duck stock and simmer very gently for 5 minutes, then beat in 60g (2oz) butter. Correct the seasoning if necessary. The sauce is now ready to serve.

TO SERVE

Finish cooking the duck legs 20 minutes before serving, either in the oven or under a hot grill. Separate the thighs from the drumsticks. Using poultry shears or a cleaver, cut off the ends of the drumsticks. Remove and discard the skin from the *suprêmes*. Using a ham knife, carve each *suprême* diagonally into 4 slices, keeping the slices as slanted as possible. Re-form the *suprêmes* and place them on a serving dish. Arrange the legs around the *suprêmes*.

Cover the dish with greaseproof paper and place in a moderate oven (190°C/375°F/Gas 5) for 3 minutes—just long enough to reheat the *suprêmes*, which should still be very pink.

Remove from the oven and coat the *suprêmes* (not the legs) with a generous amount of very hot sauce. Arrange a bouquet of watercress and perhaps a vegetable 'flower' on the dish to make it look cheerful. Serve the port-glazed potatoes separately so that they remain crisp and are not drowned by the sauce.

You can do the pre-cooking and prepare the sauce for this dish several hours before the meal, which avoids a last-minute panic. No vegetable accompaniment is necessary, other than the port-glazed potatoes,

INGREDIENTS

2 oven-ready ducklings, each weighing about 1.7kg (3lb 10oz)

300g (10oz) carrots

150g (5oz) shallots

100ml (4fl.oz) dry white wine

1 bouquet garni

100ml (4fl. oz) Curaçao

200g (7oz) leeks, white parts only

100g (4oz) butter

1 bunch watercress

4 Potatoes glazed in port (see page 219)

salt

freshly ground black pepper

Far left *Pigeonneau au coulis de pêches (page 186)*
Below *Filets de lapereau grillés aux marrons glacés (page 187)*
Right *Bécasse flambée sur croûtons (page 171)*

since the sauce already contains a *julienne* of vegetables. Improve the presentation with a border of puff pastry ducks, cut out with a duck-shaped pastry cutter and baked in a very hot oven. This is only a suggestion and can easily be omitted if it means making a special batch of pastry.

This dish has been served at *The Waterside Inn* ever since we opened in 1973 and is still a firm favourite.

POUSSINS FRANCOISE

Serves: 6 people
Preparation time: 50 minutes
Cooking time: 10 minutes
Wine: This dish needs a distinctive flavoured wine which is mature, round and elegant such as a St Julien or another claret close in flavour to a Burgundy such as a St Emilion.

INGREDIENTS

6 poussins, each weighing about 400g (14oz)

30g (1oz) red peppers

250g (9oz) Chicken mousse (see page 110)

60g (2oz) sweetcorn kernels

1.5L (2½pts) Chicken stock (see page 48)

40g (1½oz) butter

30g (1oz) flour

2 tbls snipped chives

2 tbls double cream

salt

freshly ground black pepper

Serve the poussins with a rice pilaff with *beurre noisette* (butter cooked to a light, hazelnut colour) or buttered leaf spinach.

Boning the poussins is a very fiddly job which requires some dexterity. For illustrated instructions on how to bone poultry see page 90 . If you have a friendly butcher you might persuade him to do it for you!

PREPARATION

THE POUSSINS: Singe them over a gas flame to get rid of any hard quills. Cut off the leg bones at the first joint and wipe the poussins gently with a cloth. Lay them breast-side down on the work surface. Using a small, pointed knife, make an incision down the entire length of the backbone and bone the poussins, being very careful not to pierce the skin. Take out the thigh bones, leaving only the lower leg bones and the wing bones on the poussins.
THE STUFFING: Skin the red peppers and cut into *brunoise*. Mix them with the chicken mousse, together with half the sweetcorn.

Lay the poussins, skin-side down, on a wooden board or work surface. Divide the mousse equally between them. Pull up the skin on both sides and re-form the birds into their original shape. Tie each poussin in three places with kitchen string; keep the string loose enough for expansion during cooking.

COOKING

Bring 1L (1¾pts) chicken stock to the boil in a large saucepan. Lower the heat to simmering and put in the poussins. Cover with greaseproof paper and poach gently for 10 minutes.
THE SAUCE: Meanwhile, melt 30g (1oz) butter in a saucepan. Stir in

the flour and cook for 2 to 3 minutes, stirring constantly. Pour in 500ml (1pt) cold chicken stock, bring to the boil, stirring continuously and skim the surface. Add the snipped chives, the remaining sweetcorn and the cream. Purée the mixture in a blender or food processor, then rub through a conical sieve. Season to taste and beat in the remaining butter.

TO SERVE

Lift out the poussins from the chicken stock. Drain them on a cloth for a few seconds, then trim the leg bones with scissors. Cut off the string and arrange the poussins on a serving dish or individual plates.

Coat each poussin thickly with sauce and serve the remainder separately in a sauceboat.

POULET BOIS BOUDRAN

(Chicken Bois Boudran)

This is an excellent recipe for an alfresco meal with friends. Celery hearts, cooked in chicken stock, then halved or quartered and served cold make a very good vegetable accompaniment.

It was a favourite dish of the Rothschild family for their luncheons, buffets and picnics.

PREPARATION

Preheat the oven to 200°C/400°F/Gas 6. Clean and singe the chicken to remove any hard quills. Stuff it with the stalks from the herbs, salt and truss it. Put the chicken in a large sauté pan or a roasting pan and smear with softened butter. Set over high heat for 2 minutes, then place the pan in the preheated oven.

Roast the chicken for 35 minutes, basting with the cooking juices every 10 minutes. Remove from the oven and keep at room temperature. Pour off the fat from the pan and deglaze it with water.

THE SAUCE: Peel and finely chop the shallots. Finely chop the herbs. In a large bowl, mix together the oil and vinegar, a pinch of salt and 3 turns of the pepper mill. Beat with a small wire whisk, then add the tomato ketchup, Worcestershire sauce, Tabasco, the chopped shallots and finally the chopped herbs. Season to taste with salt and pepper.

INGREDIENTS

1 chicken, weighing about 1.6kg (3lb 6oz)
1 tbls snipped chervil
1 tbls snipped chives
2 tbls snipped tarragon
100g (4oz) butter
150ml (6fl.oz) peanut oil
50ml (2fl.oz) wine vinegar
85g (3oz) tomato ketchup
1 tsp Worcestershire sauce
5 drops Tabasco
100g (4oz) shallots
salt
freshly ground black pepper

Serves: 4 people
Preparation time: 25 minutes, plus 2 or 3 hours, marinating time.
Cooking: 35 minutes
Wine: From Marsannay

in the Côte de Dijon comes a lively, fruity rosé which has the depth to withstand this sauce. This pale rosé is perhaps the best rosé produced in Burgundy or any fine rosé will serve as a substitute.

MACERATING THE CHICKEN: Take the chicken off the carcass and cut into 8 serving pieces while it is still hot or lukewarm; submerge the pieces in the sauce. Chop up the carcass containing the herb stalks into small pieces. Return it to the roasting pan and set over low heat. Reduce the cooking liquid by two-thirds.

Pass through a conical sieve into the bowl containing the chicken pieces. Stir gently with a spatula, cover the bowl with greaseproof paper and leave to macerate for 2 or 3 hours — on no account do this for longer than 6 hours or the marinade will overpower the chicken. Keep at room temperature, not in the refrigerator.

TO SERVE

Serve in a shallow dish, thickly coated with all the sauce.

INGREDIENTS

1 *poulet de Bresse*, weighing about 1.6kg (3lb 6oz)

50g (2oz) dried morels, soaked in lukewarm water for several hours

225g (8oz) butter

3 shallots, (about 80g/3oz) finely chopped

3 tbls Cognac

200ml (8fl.oz) Chicken stock (see page 48)

2 ripe pears

300ml (12fl.oz) double cream

salt

freshly ground black pepper

Serves: 4 people
Preparation time: 35 minutes
Cooking time: 20 minutes
Wine: This dish requires a light wine so the subtleties of the sauce

POULET DE BRESSE AUX MORILLES

(Poulet de Bresse with morels)

Bresse, to the northeast of Lyons, is famous for its free–range chickens. With their white feathers, blue-grey feet and bright red coxcombs, they evoke memories of the finest farmhouse poultry as they strut through the green fields. They have very white flesh and firm skin and are exported all over Europe, where they are highly priz-ed. You can use a free-range chicken instead of a *poulet de Bresse*, but it may not always taste as good.

Use fresh morels in season; you will need three times the weight of dried morels. Some buttered French beans will add a little colour and freshness to this rather neutral-looking dish.

PREPARATION

THE CHICKEN: Clean and singe the chicken. Using a medium knife, cut off the legs. With the point of the knife, cut out the thigh bones. Fold the flesh from the thighs down along the drumsticks; wrap it round the lower leg bones and tie up with kitchen string. Do not tie too tightly, or the string will cut into the chicken.

With the knife, remove the breast fillets, leaving the wing bones at-tached to the carcass. Fold over the narrow ends of the breast fillets to meet the wider ends and tie up with string.

THE MORELS: Wash the morels in several changes of water to remove any grit. If necessary, split them down the middle, rinse and drain.

COOKING THE CHICKEN: Heat 120g (4oz) butter in a sauté pan. Lightly salt the chicken pieces and add them to the pan. Turn them in the butter until they are barely coloured, then cover the pan and simmer gently; cook the breast fillets for 10 minutes and the thighs for 20 minutes. Lift the chicken pieces out of the pan and keep at room temperature.

COOKING THE MORELS: Pour off half the fat from the pan. Over gentle heat, sweat the chopped shallots without colouring them, then add the morels and sweat for a few more minutes. Pour in the Cognac and ignite. Add half the chicken stock and simmer gently for 10 minutes. Transfer to a bowl and set aside.

THE SAUCE: Peel and finely chop the pears. Sweat them in a little butter in the same pan you used for the morels. Pour in the remaining chicken stock, increase the heat and reduce the stock by two-thirds. Stir in the cream and let the mixture bubble for 3 minutes. Purée it in a blender or food processor, then rub through a conical sieve, back into the sauté pan.

Add the morels, increase the heat and let the mixture bubble once. Correct the seasoning with salt and pepper, then stir in the rest of the butter, a little at a time.

are not masked. Try an Auxey-Duresses or Monthélie from the neighbouring village of the Côte de Beaune.

TO SERVE

Put the chicken pieces in the sauce for 3 or 4 minutes — just long enough to heat through. It is important not to let the sauce boil, so keep the heat at no more than 90°C (200°F). Serve in a shallow silver or china dish.

POULET FERMIER AUX ESCARGOTS BREAD SAUCE

(Free-range chicken with snails and bread sauce)

This rustic dish 'like granny made' will delight your guests and fill your kitchen with good smells. The sweet, bland bread sauce goes very well with the chicken, but is not essential. A green salad, corn-salad or curly endive will underline the 'country' character of this dish, which needs no vegetable accompaniment.

Serves: 4 people
Preparation time: 25 minutes
Cooking time: 40 minutes
Wine: A young, fresh, fruity Beaujolais Villages, which we feel would be improved by chilling, or a Sancerre Rouge.

INGREDIENTS

1 oven-ready chicken, weighing about 1.6kg (3lb 6oz)

200g (7oz) small button onions

500g (1lb 1oz) small new potatoes

1 branch thyme, finely chopped

½ bay-leaf, finely chopped

60g (2oz) butter

2 tbls olive oil

12 very fat Burgundy snails

100ml (4fl.oz) Chicken stock (see page 48)

100ml (4fl.oz) Veal stock (see page 48)

salt

freshly ground black pepper

Bread sauce (optional) (see page 54)

Picture: page 164

PREPARATION

THE ONIONS: Peel, wash and set aside.
THE POTATOES: Peel them and, using a sharp vegetable knife, 'turn' them into large olive shapes. Keep in a bowl of cold water to prevent them from discolouring.

COOKING

Preheat the oven to 220°C/425°F/Gas 7. Heat the butter and olive oil in a saucepan or casserole set over medium heat. Put in the chicken turned onto one side and cook for 10 minutes; turn onto the other side and cook for a further 10 minutes.

Turn the chicken onto its back. Arrange the potatoes and herbs around it. After 5 minutes cooking, add the onions. Transfer the uncovered casserole to the preheated oven and roast for 20 minutes, basting the chicken with the cooking butter every 5 or 10 minutes. Cut the snails in half and add them to the casserole. Cover and cook for a further 5 minutes. Remove the casserole from the oven and transfer the chicken, vegetables and snails to a serving dish. Keep warm.
THE GRAVY: Pour off half the fat from the casserole. Deglaze the pan with the chicken stock, then add the veal stock. Reduce the liquid by two-thirds, season to taste with salt and pepper and keep hot.

TO SERVE

Cut the chicken into 8 serving pieces (ie 2 thighs, 2 drumsticks and 4 breast fillets). Arrange the chicken pieces on a silver or china serving dish, scatter over the vegetables and snails at random and pour over the boiling hot gravy. Serve the bread sauce separately in a sauceboat.

Serves: 4 people
Preparation time: 55 minutes, plus 2 hours marinating
Cooking time: 15 minutes
Wine: This light, creamy dish which uses Riesling as an ingredient would be suited to a not too sweet Mosel from Bernkastel. If you prefer

EMINCE DE VOLAILLE ANDREE

(Escalopes of chicken Andrée)

It is not necessary to serve a vegetable with this dish, whose mellow flavour and lustrous colour will tempt you even if you are not hungry. A green salad is all that is needed to complement the chicken. Keep the chicken legs and carcasses in the refrigerator or freezer for another use.

PREPARATION

THE CHICKEN: With a sharp knife, cut off the 4 breast fillets and remove the skin. Slice the breasts into very thin escalopes and lay them in a gratin dish or platter. Sprinkle over the snipped basil and olive oil. Leave to marinate for at least 2 hours before using, then place in the refrigerator.

THE TOMATOES: Peel, deseed and cut into 6. Set aside. Cook the noodles 'al dente' in boiling, salted water with 1 tsp oil. Run a little cold water into the saucepan; this will prevent the noodles from cooking any further, while keeping them hot.

THE GRAPES: Peel and deseed them, using a small knife. Be careful not to damage them. Set aside.

COOKING

Heat the sauté pan without adding any oil. Place the chicken escalopes in the pan and cook them for 1 minute on each side; do not allow them to take on any colour. Remove from the pan and keep warm.

Pour off the fat from the pan and deglaze with half the wine, then add the chicken stock. Reduce until the liquid becomes very thick and syrupy. Add the cream, boil for 2 minutes and season to taste with salt and pepper. Add the tomates, grapes and then the drained noodles. Finally, pour in the rest of the wine, increase the heat to high and incorporate the butter in small pieces.

TO SERVE

Pour the noodle mixture into a warmed deep serving dish and arrange the escalopes on top. Serve immediately.

a drier but equally fruity wine, an Alsace Riesling would also do.

INGREDIENTS

2 oven-ready chickens, each weighing about 1.5kg (3lb 4oz)

3 tbls snipped basil

4 tbls olive oil

4 medium tomatoes

180g (6oz) fresh noodles (see page 223)

1 tsp oil

250g (9oz) black grapes

100ml (4fl.oz) Riesling-style wine

100ml (4fl.oz) Chicken stock (see page 48)

400ml (16fl.oz) double cream

50g (1½oz) butter

salt

freshly ground black pepper

Picture: page 165

PAVE DE DINDONNEAU EN BLANQUETTE

(Turkey *pavés* in cream sauce)

Even the most experienced gourmet will be surprised by turkey served in this original way. A mellow, delicate dish, it is very easy to prepare. Spinach *subrics* (see page 221) or spinach purée make excellent vegetable accompaniments.

Serves: 4 people
Preparation time: 45 minutes
Cooking time: 15 minutes
Wine: Needs a Bordeaux heavier than a Médoc so a Pomerol would be ideal. It is the biggest of all wines from Bordeaux. Should this not be available, a wine from

the Côte de Beaune will substitute.

INGREDIENTS

1 boned turkey breast, weighing about 750g (1lb 9oz)

16 dried prunes

½ orange

1 tsp port

500ml (1pt) Chicken stock (see page 48)

4 medium button mushrooms

100g (4oz) butter

juice of ½ lemon

2 leeks

1 tsp Armagnac

300ml (12fl.oz) double cream

salt

freshly ground white pepper

Picture: page 165

If you serve the *pavés* on a large dish, be careful that the mushrooms and leeks do not fall off; they can be very elusive when you try to transfer them onto serving plates!

PREPARATION

THE TURKEY BREAST: Remove the skin and cut 4 even-sized slices from the thickest part of the breast. They should each weigh about 160g (5oz). Use the thinner pieces and trimmings to make a turkey mousse — prepare a half quantity of Chicken mousse (see page 110). Reserve the trimmings in the refrigerator until you make the mousse.
THE PRUNES: Soak in cold water for 1 hour; if they are very moist, use them without pre-soaking.

Cut the orange zest into fine *julienne*, blanch, refresh, drain and mix with 2 tbls turkey mousse and the port.

Using a sharp knife, cut out the prune stones. Fill the cavities with the turkey mousse mixture. Reserve 8 prunes in the refrigerator. Poach the remaining 8 prunes in 100ml (4fl.oz) chicken stock for 5 minutes. Keep them warm in the stock.
THE MUSHROOMS: Wipe clean and discard the stalks. Using a small, sharp knife, 'turn' the mushroom caps. Poach them for 1 minute in 1 tbls water, 1 tsp butter and the lemon juice. Keep in the cooking liquid at room temperature.
THE LEEKS: Peel and wash them and discard the greenest parts. Cook them in 300ml (12fl.oz) chicken stock. Keep warm in the stock.
FILLING THE *PAVÉS*: Using a long, pointed knife, make an incision in the thickest part of the turkey fillets, to form a pocket. Fill each pocket with the remaining turkey mousse and two unpoached prunes. The stuffed turkey fillets will be similar in shape to *pavés* (see Braised *pavés* of beef a l'ancienne, page 198).

Cut out 4 squares of foil or greaseproof paper, each about twice the size of the turkey *pavés*. Preheat the oven to 220°C/425°F/Gas 7.

COOKING

Melt 50g (2oz) butter in a sauté pan set over medium heat. Sear the *pavés* for 2 minutes on each side. Lift them out of the pan and wrap each one in a square of foil or greaseproof paper. Place the 'parcels' in the preheated oven and bake for 10 minutes.
THE SAUCE: Pour off the fat from the pan. Deglaze with Armagnac and

1

2

1 *Lay out the whole turkey breast on a board.*
2 *Using your fingers, ease up the edges of the skin and tear it away from the meat.*

3

4

3 *Cut several thick slices from the skinned turkey breast.*
4 *With a sharp knife, make a deep incision in the fillet to form a pocket.*

5

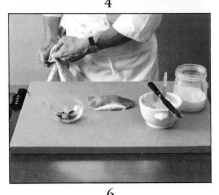

6

5 *Before stuffing the pockets, throw in a little salt. Taking a palette knife, coat the inside wall of the pocket with the mousse. Place 2 stuffed prunes into the corners of the pocket and fill up with more mousse.*
6 *Close up the mouth of the pocket by pressing the edges gently together.*

pour in the remaining chicken stock. Reduce over high heat until the liquid becomes syrupy. Stir in the cream, bring to the boil, then add the remaining butter. Season to taste with salt and freshly ground white pepper and keep the sauce warm.

TO SERVE

Remove the foil or paper from the *pavés* and arrange them in a shallow serving dish or on individual plates. Arrange the poached prunes around the *pavés*, covered with greaseproof paper so they do not dry out and heat in the oven at 170°C/325°F/Gas 3 for 2 minutes.

Remove from the oven, take off the greaseproof paper and coat the *pavés* thickly with the sauce. Decorate each one with half a leek and a mushroom cap and serve at once.

INGREDIENTS

4 pigeons, Bresse if possible

5 peaches, preferably white

140g (5oz) butter

1 tbls oil

icing sugar

2 shallots

pinch of caster sugar

3 tbls Cognac

3 tbls Grand Marnier

200ml (8fl.oz) Veal stock (see page 48)

200ml (8fl.oz) Chicken stock (see page 48)

salt

freshly ground black pepper

Serves: 4 people
Preparation time: 30 minutes
Cooking time: 20 minutes
Wine: A particularly delicious dish which deserves an elegant wine from St Emilion. Nothing so grand as a Cheval Blanc, but one of the Grand Crus would be perfect.

Picture: page 176

PIGEONNEAUX AU COULIS DE PECHES

(Pigeons with peaches)

PREPARATION

THE PIGEONS: Preheat the oven to 240°C/475°F/Gas 9. Salt the insides of the pigeons and smear the outside with 30g (1oz) melted butter. Heat the oil in a sauté pan set over high heat and lightly brown the pigeons on all sides. Roast them in the very hot oven for 12 minutes, then transfer them to a plate and keep warm. The breasts should still be pink in the middle.

THE PEACHES: Preheat the grill to high. Peel them; if necessary, plunge them into boiling water first. Cut in half and remove the stones very carefully, so that the peach halves are not damaged. Reserve the skins and stones.

Melt 50g (2oz) butter in a sauté pan and sweat 8 of the peach halves for 1 minute; they should still be crisp. Sprinkle over a little icing sugar and glaze the peaches under the hot grill. Keep at room temperature.

THE SAUCE: Cut off the pigeon legs and remove the thigh bones. Return the pigeons to the oven for 3 minutes. Carve off the breast fillets and keep at room temperature. Chop the carcasses. Then peel and finely slice the shallots.

Pour off the fat from the pan in which the pigeons were cooked. Set the pan over high heat, add a pinch of caster sugar, and brown the shallots, pigeon carcasses, peach skins and stones and the two remaining peach halves. Deglaze the pan with the Cognac and the Grand Marnier, reduce the liquid by two-thirds and pour in the chicken and veal stock. Simmer over gentle heat for 20 minutes, skimming the surface as often as necessary.

Strain through a conical sieve, return the sauce to the pan and reduce until it becomes slightly syrupy. Correct the seasoning with salt and pepper and stir in 60g (2oz) butter, a little at a time. Keep warm.

TO SERVE

Arrange 2 breast fillets in the centre of each serving plate. Place a leg on either side and put 2 peach halves near the thicker part of the breasts. Heat in a slow oven (120°C/230°F/Gas ¼) for 4 minutes, then pour the very hot sauce over the pigeons.

Although it is not essential, a drop of Angostura Bitters in the sauce will add an extra 'something' to this delicate, subtle and many-flavoured dish.

You can use pineapple instead of the peaches, but it should be grilled rather than sweated in butter. Serve the pigeons with Port-glazed potatoes (page 219) or Savoyard potatoes (page 219).

FILETS DE LAPEREAU GRILLES AUX MARRONS GLACES

(Grilled rabbit fillets with marrons glacés)

A succulent dish, this makes the most of the texture and flavour of the rabbit. When celeriac is out of season, use potatoes prepared in the same way; these are called *pommes de terre fondantes*. You can use the celeriac trimmings in a purée or soup.

The chicken stock is not essential, although it does add body to the sauce. If you do not use the stock, replace it with water.

Vichy carrots or a simple green salad go very well with this dish. The rabbit shapes will stand upright on the plate if you place them on little rounds of mashed potatoes.

Serves: 4 people
Preparation time: 1 hour 10 minutes, plus 4 hours marinating
Cooking time: 3 to 5 minutes
Wine: The quality of wine from the south of France has improved out of all recognition over the last 5 to 10 years. Two wines from this area which would suit the rabbit would be a Minervois or one of the individual properties from the Corbières region.

PREPARATION

THE RABBITS: Using a boning knife, cut off the fillets from the saddles. Cut off the hindlegs and remove the sinews. Place the rabbit pieces on a gratin dish and sprinkle over the olive oil. Finely chop half the thyme and crush the peppercorns. Sprinkle over the rabbit pieces. Cover with greaseproof paper and leave to marinate in the refrigerator for at least 4

Left *Queues de boeuf enrubannées à l'échalote (page 203)*
Above *Côtelettes d'agneau Germaine (page 194)*
Right *Noisettes d'agneau fondantes aux deux poivrons (page 193)*

INGREDIENTS

2 young rabbits, skinned, each weighing about 1.2kg (2lb 10oz)

50ml (2fl.oz) olive oil

2 branches thyme

1 tsp black peppercorns

2 carrots

1 large onion

1 garlic clove

100ml (4fl.oz) Armagnac

1L (1¾pts) Chicken stock (optional) (see page 48) or water

180g (6oz) marrons glacés

130g (4oz) butter

100g (3½oz) clarified butter

200g (7oz) small button onions

pinch of sugar

1 root celeriac

4 thick slices white bread

1 bouquet garni

salt

freshly ground black pepper

Picture: page 176

hours. Turn the fillets after 2 hours.

THE SAUCE: Preheat the oven to 240°C/475°F/Gas 9. Remove the liver, heart and lungs from the rabbits. Chop the shoulders and carcasses. Place them in a roasting pan in the very hot oven and stir with a slotted spoon, so that the bones are well browned on all sides. Peel and coarsely chop the carrots and the large onions. 5 minutes before removing the roasting pan from the oven, add the carrots and onion, together with the crushed garlic clove.

Tip the contents of the roasting pan into a saucepan and pour in the chicken stock and 500ml (1pt) water or 3 pts water. Set over low heat and simmer for about 1 hour, then strain through a muslin-lined sieve. In a shallow pan set over high heat, reduce the Armagnac by half. Add the strained rabbit stock and reduce until it becomes syrupy. Crumble in the marrons glacés and stir in 60g (2oz) butter, a little at a time. Season to taste with salt and pepper.

THE BUTTON ONIONS: Peel and wash them. Glaze in a sauté pan with 20g (¾oz) butter and a pinch of sugar. When they are golden, add just a little water if necessary, cover the pan and simmer gently until tender. Keep warm.

THE CELERIAC: Peel and cut 4 slices, 1.5cm (¾in) thick. Trim into neat oval shapes. Place them in a sauté pan large enough to take all the slices in one layer, cover with water and add 50g (2oz) butter and a pinch of salt. Set the pan over high heat and cook until all the water has evaporated. The celeriac should be a lovely golden colour. Turn the slices with a palette knife and keep warm.

Cut out a rabbit shape from each slice of bread. Heat the remaining butter in a frying pan and fry the rabbit croûtons until golden on both sides. Drain on absorbent paper. Just before serving, grill the rabbit pieces in a ridged grilling pan for 3 to 5 minutes, making sure they are attractively marked with a lattice pattern.

TO SERVE

Place the celeriac ovals on a serving dish or individual plates, then arrange the rabbit fillets in a criss-cross pattern on top. Next, make little piles of button onions and pour the sauce round the celeriac ovals. Lastly, set out the rabbit croûtons, with sprigs of thyme between their paws. As always, the presentation of the dish is extremely important. Thyme is not essential but the green provides a good colour contrast with the rabbit croûtons.

SALMIS DE SARCELLE

(Salmis of Teal)

PREPARATION

THE TEAL: Cut off the breast fillets and set aside. Make a Game stock (see page 49) with the carcasses and legs.

THE ARTICHOKES: Snap off the stalks. Trim them to obtain neat, even-sized hearts. Rub them with a little lemon juice. Cook until tender in a pan of boiling, salted water, to which you have added 3 tbls white wine vinegar and leave to cool in the liquid.

THE BUTTON ONIONS: Peel, wash and dry them. Then cook them gently in a shallow pan with 50g (2oz) butter and a pinch of sugar until they begin to colour. Add a little water if necessary and cook until the onions are tender. Keep warm.

THE BACON: Remove the rind and cut the bacon into 3mm (¼in) dice. Blanch, drain, and then fry in the shallow pan for 2 to 3 minutes, until golden brown. Keep at room temperature.

COOKING

Heat 100g (4oz) clarified butter in a sauté pan set over high heat. Lightly salt the teal breasts and quickly sauté them for a few minutes on each side; they should still be pink in the middle. Remove from the pan and keep at room temperature.

Pour off the fat from the pan, deglaze with the Cognac, then pour in the game stock, which should have a syrupy consistency. Add the redcurrant jelly and raspberry vinegar and cook for 5 minutes. Rub the foie gras through a sieve with the remaining butter and stir into the sauce. Season to taste and do not allow the sauce to boil.

Remove the chokes from the artichoke hearts and cut the hearts into quarters. Place in a saucepan with the button onions and diced bacon. Strain over the sauce.

TO SERVE

Divide the boiling sauce and garnish between 6 piping hot serving plates. Carve the breast fillets into very fine slices. Arrange in a fan shape on each plate and serve immediately.

INGREDIENTS

6 teal

4 medium artichokes

juice of ½ a lemon

3 tbls white wine vinegar

1 tbls flour

500g (1lb 1oz) small button onions

80g (3oz) butter

pinch of sugar

575g (1lb 4oz) smoked bacon, in one piece

100g (4oz) clarified butter

2 tbls Cognac

1 tbls redcurrant jelly

3 tbls raspberry vinegar

100g (4oz) foie gras, preferably raw

salt

freshly ground black pepper

Serves: 6 people
Preparation time: 45 minutes
Cooking time: 10 minutes
Wine: A perfumed, full flavoured, subtle wine with an aftertaste of raspberries like the Côte Rôtie or St Joseph from the Côtes du Rhône.

CHAPTER TEN

MEAT

Generally speaking, our methods of cooking meat vary with the seasons. In spring and summer, we prefer to grill, bake or roast, while autumn and winter are the seasons for braising and stewing.

If you are serving eight or more people, it is always best to serve one large joint of meat. The dining room will be filled with the sublime, mouth-watering aroma of the meat as you carve — a scent to delight every gourmet. Sauces are indispensable to meat and must be prepared with care; they should never be overpowering, but clear gravies should not be too thin. Pass round piping hot sauce in a sauceboat.

In winter, we indulge our greed with *ragoûts* or sautés made with lamb, veal or beef. They do take a great deal longer to prepare than a roast, but they leave you more time to spend with your guests, since they require no carving or last-minute finishing touches.

NOISETTES D'AGNEAU FONDANTES AUX DEUX POIVRONS

(Melting noisettes of lamb with red and green peppers)

PREPARATION

THE MARINADE: 2 hours before cooking, whisk together in a bowl the baking powder, cornflour, chicken stock, thyme and bay-leaf. Put in the lamb noisettes and place in the refrigerator, turning every 20 minutes, until the noisettes have absorbed all the marinade.

Serves: 4 people
Preparation time: 40 minutes + 2 hours marinating
Cooking time: 3 to 4 minutes
Wine: A fruity, lively rosé from Marsannay in the Côtes de Dijon has the depth to withstand the powerful peppers used as a garnish in this dish. An alternative would be a red wine from Côte Chalonnaise.

INGREDIENTS

12 noisettes of lamb, cut from the saddle, each weighing about 70g (2½oz)

1 red pepper

1 green pepper

1 tsp baking powder

20g (¾oz) cornflour

200ml (8fl.oz) Chicken stock (see page 48)

1 sprig thyme

½ bay-leaf

1 tbls peanut oil

150g (5oz) butter

½ medium onion

⅔ tsp paprika

3 tbls Madeira

400ml (16fl.oz) Veal stock (see page 48)

250ml (10fl.oz) double cream

180g (6oz) clarified butter

12 round croûtons of white bread, 4cm (1½in) diameter, 1cm (½in) thick

salt

freshly ground white pepper

Picture: page 189

THE PEPPERS: Smear with the peanut oil and place in a very hot oven or under a hot grill, turning them until the skins blister and the peppers are lightly coloured on all sides. Hold under cold running water and rub lightly with your hand to remove the skins. Pat dry with a cloth. Cut the skinned peppers in half, remove the white parts and the seeds, then cut into *julienne* and keep the trimmings for the sauce.

Heat 60g (2oz) butter in a shallow pan, put in the red pepper *julienne* and cook until crisp to the bite. Set aside. Cook the green pepper in the same way and set aside.

THE SAUCE: Heat 30g (1oz) butter in the shallow pan. Peel and chop the onion and add it to the pan, together with the pepper trimmings and sweat for 2 minutes. Sprinkle with paprika, stir with a wooden spatula, pour in the Madeira and reduce by two-thirds.

Add the veal stock and, over low heat, reduce to a slightly syrupy consistency. Pour in the cream and cook gently for 5 minutes. Stir in 60g (2oz) butter, a little at a time, season to taste, then pass through a conical sieve into a saucepan and keep in a bain-marie.

THE CROUTONS: Heat 120g (4oz) clarified butter in a sauté dish set over high heat. Put in the croûtons and fry until golden on both sides. Drain on absorbent paper.

THE NOISETTES OF LAMB: Heat the remaining clarified butter in a sauté dish set over high heat. Lightly season the noisettes with salt and pepper and add them to the pan. Cook for 1 to 2 minutes on each side, depending on how you like them done, then transfer to a plate.

TO SERVE

Arrange 3 croûtons on each plate and place a noisette on each. Warm the pepper *julienne* and arrange it on top of the noisettes. Pour a ribbon of sauce around each serving and pass the rest separately.

The baking powder in the marinade enhances the flavour of the lamb. It also gives the meat a softer texture.

Serves: 4 people
Preparation time: 20 minutes
Cooking time: 15 minutes
Wine: The sorrel gives the sauce a slight

COTELETTES D'AGNEAU GERMAINE

(Lamb cutlets Germaine)

This dish is very easy to make; it is particularly good with green vegetables, especially French beans or spinach and with grilled tomatoes. The veal stock adds body to the sauce, but it does take the edge off the pleasant tartness of the sorrel.

PREPARATION

THE CUTLETS: Trim off all the fat, leaving only the *noisette* of meat attached to the bones. Scrape clean the ends of the bones with a small knife. Keep the cutlets in a cool place.

THE SORREL: Remove the stalks and wash and drain the leaves. Roll up 5 or 6 leaves together, like a cigar, and, using a sharp knife, shred the roll into very fine strips. Do this with all the sorrel leaves. Set aside.

THE MINT: Wash, pat dry with a cloth, then finely shred the leaves and set aside.

COOKING

Heat 30g (1oz) butter in the pan. Put in the lamb cutlets and brown them on both sides; when they are pink in the middle, or well done, depending on how you like them, transfer to a serving dish.

THE SAUCE: Pour off the fat from the pan, and set over low heat. Put in 1 tbls butter and the sorrel and sweat gently for a few minutes. Add the white wine, reduce it by half, then pour in the veal stock, if you are using it, and the cream. Cook for 4 or 5 minutes, then stir in the remaining butter, a little at a time, and add a few drops of lemon juice. Season to taste with salt and pepper. Pour the sauce over the lamb cutlets and sprinkle on the mint. Serve some sauce in a sauceboat if you prefer.

sour/fresh taste. From Médoc you could choose from a Petit Châteaux or Cru Bourgeois. Another possibility would be a young wine from the Côtes de Bourg.

INGREDIENTS

12 lamb cutlets, about 800g (1lb 12oz)

120g (4oz) sorrel

8 fresh mint leaves

100g (3oz) butter

100ml (4fl.oz) dry white wine

400ml (16fl.oz) double cream

100ml (4fl.oz) Veal stock (optional) (see page 48)

juice of ½ lemon

freshly ground black pepper

salt

Picture: page 189

DAUBE DE BOEUF A LA BEAUJOLAISE

(Beef en daube with Beaujolais)

Plain, steamed potatoes, served separately, are the ideal accompaniment for this comforting winter dish, which will delight both the gourmet and the gourmand.

PREPARATION

THE BEEF: Bone the meat, trim the fat and remove the sinews. Cut into 5cm (2in) cubes. Put the meat into an earthenware or pottery bowl.

Serves: 8 people
Preparation time: 1 hour and 12 hours marinating
Cooking time: 1 hour 45 minutes
Wine: What else but a wine from Beaujolais. We would prefer a Grand Cru Beaujolais, which has more depth and fruit, such as a Morgon or a Moulin à Vent.

INGREDIENTS

3.5kg (7½lb) middle rib of beef on the bone or 2kg (4lb 6oz) boned, trimmed weight

400g (14oz) large onions

350g (12oz) carrots

50g (2oz) garlic

1 bouquet garni

350g (12oz) tightly-closed button mushrooms

1 tsp black peppercorns, crushed

4 tbls olive oil

1L (1¾pts) Beaujolais, preferably Moulin à Vent

210g (7oz) butter

50ml (2fl.oz) Cognac

70g (2½oz) flour

1L (1¾pts) Veal stock (see page 48)

8 thick slices white bread

240g (8oz) clarified butter

350g (12oz) small button onions

pinch of sugar

400g (14oz) smoked bacon, in one piece

2 sprigs parsley

salt

THE MARINADE: Peel and wash the large onions and the carrots and cut into large dice. Mix them with the beef cubes. Lightly crush the unpeeled garlic cloves and add them to the beef, together with the bouquet garni and crushed peppercorns. Remove and wash the mushroom stalks and stir them into the beef. Pour over the olive oil and wine, cover with greaseproof paper and leave to marinate in the refrigerator for 12 hours.

COOKING

Preheat the oven to 180°C/350°F/Gas 4. Drain all the marinade ingredients in a large colander set over a bowl, so as to catch the wine. Pat the beef cubes dry with a tea-towel and lightly salt them. Put 60g (2oz) butter in a cast iron cocotte or a heatproof casserole with a lid and set over high heat. Put in all the vegetables and aromatics from the marinade and lightly brown them for 6 to 8 minutes.

Heat 120g (4oz) clarified butter in a sauté pan, quickly brown the beef cubes on all sides, then arrange them on the bed of aromatics in the cocotte or casserole. Pour in the Cognac and ignite. Deglaze the sauté pan with the wine from the marinade and reduce by one-third. Dust the baking tray with flour and roast in the preheated oven until it is nutty brown. Sprinkle the browned flour over the beef cubes and stir with a wooden spatula.

Pour into the casserole the wine from the sauté pan and the veal stock and add a little water if necessary. All the ingredients should be well covered with liquid. Set the casserole over high heat and cover. The lid must be very tight-fitting, so that the casserole is completely sealed. Place in the moderate oven for about 1 hour 45 minutes. Using the point of a sharp knife, check to see whether the meat is cooked; the length of time this will take varies according to the quality and texture of the meat.

THE CROUTONS: Meanwhile, using a sharp knife, cut out 8 pretty heart shapes from the bread. Heat the remaining clarified butter in a frying pan and fry the bread hearts until golden on both sides. Drain on absorbent paper.

THE BUTTON ONIONS: Peel, wash and pat dry. In a shallow pan, heat 60g (2oz) butter with a pinch of sugar and gently fry the onions until pale golden. Add a drop of water if necessary, cover the pan and cook gently until the onions are tender. Keep warm.

THE MUSHROOMS: Wipe with a damp cloth. Heat 60g (2oz) butter in the frying pan and fry the mushrooms for 2 minutes. Keep at room temperature.

THE BACON: Bring a small saucepan of water to the boil. Remove the bacon rind and cut the bacon into 5mm (¼in) dice. Blanch for 2 or 3 minutes, drain, then fry until pale golden. Keep at room temperature.

TO SERVE

Using a slotted spoon, carefully lift out the meat from the casserole and transfer it to a deep serving dish. Cover the dish and keep warm. Strain the cooking liquid first through the colander and then through a sieve into a shallow pan. Skim off the fat from the surface. Set the pan over high heat and reduce the liquid by one-third, skimming the surface as often as necessary. Stir in the remaining butter, add the button onions, mushrooms and bacon and correct the seasoning. As soon as the mixture comes to the boil, pour it over the beef cubes. Arrange the bread hearts around the edge of the dish, sprinkle with finely chopped parsley and serve at once.

ENTRECOTES CANAILLES
(Scoundrels' sirloins)

PREPARATION

Peel, wash and finely chop the shallots. Set aside. Wash the tarragon, strip off the leaves and snip them. Set aside.

COOKING

Heat the clarified butter in a sauté pan set over high heat. Sprinkle the steaks with salt and cook for a few minutes on each side, until they are done to your liking.

Place the steaks on an upturned plate set in a larger serving dish; this will catch the juices and prevent the steaks from drowning in them, which would spoil the texture of the meat. Pour off the fat from the pan. Sweat the shallots, then the tarragon for 2 minutes. Remove them from the pan.

Deglaze the pan with the vinegar and white wine and reduce until the liquid is very thick and syrupy. Add the cream and let the mixture

INGREDIENTS

4 sirloin steaks, each weighing about 220g (8oz)

80g (3oz) shallots

20g (¾oz) tarragon

1 tbls snipped chives

125g (4oz) clarified butter

50g (2oz) butter

4 tbls tarragon vinegar

100ml (4fl.oz) dry white wine

300ml (12fl.oz) double cream

salt

freshly ground black pepper

Serves: 4 people
Preparation time: 15 minutes

Cooking time: about 15 minutes
Wine: With the tarragon, shallots and cream, the sauce calls for a spicy wine from Alsace. Either a Gewürztraminer with its fruity perfume and clean, dry finish or the Pinot Gris (Tokay) which is rather more heavy and full-bodied.

bubble for 2 or 3 minutes. Still over high heat, beat in the remaining butter and the meat juices from the dish.

TO SERVE

Arrange the steaks on a silver or china serving dish, then pour over all the sauce and sprinkle with chives.

It is not essential to use tarragon vinegar, but it does add extra flavour to the sauce. You can make the sauce more full-bodied by stirring in 50ml (2fl.oz) meat *demi-glace* (see page 48) before adding the cream, but this is only a refinement and is not essential. The accompanying vegetables should be very simple — plain, steamed broccoli or French beans would be our choice.

Serves: 4 people
Preparation time: 1 hour
Cooking time: 1 hour 30 minutes.
Wine: This beautiful deep, velvety sauce needs a marvellous wine. The Chambolle-Musigny possess and exquisite bouquet, soft fruitiness and nobility of flavour. A Vosne-Romanée would also suit.

PAVE DE BOEUF A L'ANCIENNE

(Braised *pavés* of beef à l'ancienne)

Steamed potatoes, braised celeriac and Vichy carrots go very well with this dish. Its light, feminine, sensual sauce will titillate the taste-buds of your guests.

You can prepare and cook this recipe in advance. When you are ready to serve, cover the meat and heat in the oven. Reheat the sauce, add the garnish and pour the mixture over the *pavés*.

Pavé means 'paving stone' in French; the meat takes its name from the thick, rectangular shape of the cut. It is not a classical culinary term, but a rudimentary cut very similar to the paving stones themselves.

PREPARATION

THE BUTTON ONIONS: Peel and wash them. In a sauté pan, heat the butter with a pinch of sugar and fry the onions until they begin to colour. Add 1 or 2 tbls water if necessary and cook gently until the onions are pale golden on the outside and soft inside. Set aside.
THE CEPS AND SHALLOTS: Peel, wash and finely slice the ceps. Peel and finely chop the shallots and put them in a frying pan with 50ml (2fl.oz) olive oil. Cook for 2 minutes, then add the ceps. Increase the heat to high and sauté for 5 minutes, stirring occasionally. Set aside.

THE BACON: Remove the rind and then cut the bacon into large 'matchsticks'. Blanch for 5 minutes, drain and set aside.

THE CARROT, ONION AND CELERY: Peel and wash them all. Then cut into *mirepoix*.

THE MEAT: Cut the meat from the bone, remove the sinews and trim off as much fat as possible. Then cut it into 4 even-sized steaks (these are the *pavés*).

COOKING

Preheat the oven to 190°C/375°F/Gas 5. Lightly salt the *pavés*. Set a cocotte or casserole over high heat. Pour in 100ml (4fl.oz) olive oil and, when it is hot, put in the 4 *pavés* and quickly brown them on both sides. As soon as they are browned, remove them from the casserole. Lower the heat, add the chopped vegetables and cook gently. Add the flour and fry, stirring with a wooden spatula, until the mixture is golden brown. Pour in the Beaujolais and veal stock, stir, bring to the boil and cook for 10 minutes, skimming the surface frequently. Add the crushed peppercorns and the bouquet garni and return the *pavés* to the casserole. Add a very little salt. Cover the casserole and cook in the preheated oven for 1½ hours.

TO SERVE

Lift out the *pavés* from the casserole and arrange them in a deep pottery, china or bi-metal dish. Keep warm. Strain the sauce through a conical sieve into a shallow pan. Strain off any fat or scum from the surface if necessary. Put the small onions, carrots, ceps and the bacon 'matchsticks' into the sauce and heat gently for 5 minutes. Correct the seasoning and pour the sauce and garnish over the *pavés*.

INGREDIENTS

1 piece of rib of beef, weighing about 3.2kg (6lb 12oz) or 1.2kg (2lb 9oz) boned, trimmed weight

32 button onions

1 tbls butter

pinch of sugar

250g (9oz) ceps

50g (2oz) shallots

150ml (6fl.oz) olive oil

400g (14oz) smoked bacon, in one piece

1 medium carrot

1 medium onion

1 celery stalk

60g (2oz) flour

1 bottle Beaujolais, or a light Burgundy-style red wine

1.5L (2½pts) Veal stock (see page 48)

1 tsp black peppercorns, crushed

1 bouquet garni

salt

POT AU FEU SAUCE ALBERT

(Pot au feu with sauce Albert)

Serves: 4 people
Preparation time: 40 minutes
Cooking time: 3 hours

This succulent winter dish must be served piping hot. Serve a purée of Jerusalem artichokes separately; their slightly sweet taste goes wonderfully well with the recipe. Pot au Feu is traditionally served with Dijon mustard, but the sauce Albert creates a subtle, delicate variation. For real connoisseurs put coarse sea salt on the table.

Pot au feu sauce Albert (page 199)

INGREDIENTS

500g (1lb 2oz) oxtail, cut from the middle

600g (1lb 4oz) shin of beef, boned weight

1 ox tongue

5L (9pts) Chicken stock (see page 48)

8 white peppercorns

coarse and fine salt

2 large onions

2 cloves

¼ head celery, cut from the root

1 small garlic bulb

1 small bouquet garni

8 small carrots

4 small leeks

8 small turnips

½ small full-hearted green cabbage

4 small potatoes

2 marrow bones

juice of ½ lemon

8 slices French bread, from a baguette, if possible

15g (½ oz) butter

1 quantity Sauce Albert (see page 58)

Serves: 4 people
Preparation time: 40 minutes
Cooking time: 3 hours
Wine: It is difficult to find a companion to boiled beef and vegetables, but we recommend a Bordeaux wine from either St Emilion or Médoc.

The remaining bouillon can be served plain, as a rich soup, at another meal. When the oxtail is cold, remove the bones and serve the meat with the reserved tongue as an hors d'oeuvre with a vinaigrette, to which you have added a finely chopped shallot and some fresh herbs.

PREPARATION

THE OXTAIL: Cut into 4 serving pieces, through the joints.
THE SHIN OF BEEF: Roughly devein the meat and tie up with string.
THE OX TONGUE: Trim it and remove any gristle if necessary. Put the three meats in an earthenware *fait-tout* or a copper casserole, place under cold running water and leave to soak for about 1 hour. Blanch for a few minutes, then refresh in cold water.

COOKING

THE MEATS: Pour the chicken stock into the casserole or *fait-tout* and add a little salt and the peppercorns. Set over high heat and, as soon as it comes to the boil, put in the oxtail, tongue and shin of beef.

Lower the heat to below boiling point (about 90°C/200°F) and simmer, skimming the surface as necessary.

Meanwhile, cut 1 onion into 3, but do not peel it. Roast in the oven or grill it until brown. Peel the second onion and stud it with the cloves. Set aside. When the meats have been cooking for half an hour, add the browned onion, the clove-studded onion, then the celery root, the unpeeled garlic bulb and the bouquet garni. Simmer for 2½ hours.
THE VEGETABLES: Peel and wash them. Leave the cabbage in one piece and split the leeks down the middle.

Wrap the carrots and turnip in separate pieces of muslin. Tie the leeks and cabbage into bundles. When the meats have been cooking for 2½ hours, add all the vegetables except the potatoes to the casserole and cook for 30 minutes. Put the potatoes into a small saucepan with a little of the cooking liquid (bouillon) and cook for 15 minutes.
THE MARROW BONES: Place in a saucepan, cover with a little bouillon and add the lemon juice. Simmer gently for 20 minutes.
THE BREAD: Lightly butter the slices and grill until golden .

TO SERVE

Skin the tongue and cut off 4 good slices reserving the rest. Slice the shin of beef. Lay the slices in a deep earthenware or china dish and arrange the vegetables in attractive bunches around the edge. Serve the potatoes separately in a vegetable dish. Pour some of the piping hot bouillon over the meat and vegetables.

Remove the marrow from the bones and season lightly with salt and pepper. Spread the marrow on the grilled bread and serve separately on a plate. Serve the sauce Albert in a sauceboat.

Picture: page 200

QUEUES DE BOEUF ENRUBANNEES A L'ECHALOTE

(Oxtail beribboned with vegetables and shallots)

Although this dish takes a long time to prepare, it is actually very simple to make. The combination of the different vegetables mingled with the oxtail gives a very pretty ribbon effect. It may be prepared and cooked up to 2 days in advance. When you want to serve the oxtail, reheat the meat in the strained cooking liquid, beat in the butter, a little at a time, then add the vegetable garnish.

This dish has been a great favourite with our faithful diners over many years.

PREPARATION

THE DAY BEFORE: Soak the oxtails in cold water for several hours. Drain and, using a sharp knife, cut off any excess fat if necessary. Cut the oxtails at each joint and place in an earthenware or pottery bowl. THE MARINADE: Peel and wash the onions, one-third of the carrots and the celery. Cut into large dice. Mix them into the oxtails, together with the orange peel, cloves, crushed peppercorns, bouquet garni and the unpeeled garlic. Remove the mushroom stalks, wash and stir into the oxtails. Reserve the mushroom caps.

Pour over the red wine and 4 tbls olive oil. Cover with greaseproof paper and leave to marinate in the refrigerator for 24 hours.

COOKING THE OXTAILS

Preheat the oven to 190°C/375°F/Gas 5. Drain all the marinade ingredients in a large colander set over a saucepan so as to catch the wine. Set the pan over high heat and boil the wine for several minutes.

INGREDIENTS

2.4kg (5lb 2oz) large oxtails

700g (1lb 12oz) large onions

150g (5oz) celery

1kg (2lb 2oz) medium carrots

2 dried orange peels (optional)

3 cloves

1 tbls black peppercorns, crushed

1 medium bouquet garni

8 large button mushrooms, tightly closed

70g (2½oz) garlic cloves

2L (3½pts) red wine, preferably Burgundy-style

200ml (8fl.oz) olive oil

2 tbls flour

500ml (1pt) Veal stock (see page 48)

2 or 3 pieces of pork rind (optional)

40 medium shallots

200g (7oz) coarse salt

300g (10oz) medium courgettes

Continued overleaf

100g (4oz) butter

parsley sprigs, to garnish

fine salt

Serves: 8 people
Preparation time: 1 hour 30 minutes, plus 24 hours marinating
Cooking time: 2 hours 30 minutes
Wine: A light, stylish, fragrant, young red wine from Monthélie or Aloxe-Corton.

Picture: page 188

Keep warm. Pat the oxtail pieces dry with a cloth and salt lightly. Heat 4 tbls olive oil in a cocotte, casserole or Dutch oven set over high heat. Put in all the vegetables and aromatics from the marinade and brown for 6 to 8 minutes, stirring occasionally.

Heat the remaining olive oil in a sauté pan set over high heat, put in the oxtail pieces and brown them quickly on all sides. Lay them on the bed of vegetables and aromatics in the casserole. Sprinkle the flour on-to a baking tray and roast in the hot oven until it is nutty brown. Sprinkle it over the oxtail at once and stir in with a wooden spatula.

Pour the wine from the marinade and the veal stock over the oxtail. Add about 1L (1¾pts) water; all the ingredients should be well covered with liquid. Lay the pork rind on top and bring to the boil. Cover the casserole very tightly. Cook in the oven for 2½ hours.

PREPARING THE VEGETABLE GARNISH: Increase the oven temperature to 200°C/400°F/Gas 6.

THE SHALLOTS: Arrange the unpeeled shallots on a bed of coarse salt in a roasting pan, making sure that they are not touching. Place in the preheated oven for about 14 minutes.

When the shallots are tender, (check with the point of a knife) remove from the oven, peel and keep at room temperature.

THE CARROTS: Peel and cut lengthways into slices 3mm (1/10in) thick. Bring a pan of salted water to the boil, put in the carrots and cook for 3 minutes. Refresh, drain and lay the carrots on a tea-towel.

THE COURGETTES: Cut off the ends and cut the courgettes lengthways into slices 3mm (1/10in) thick. Cook in boiling, salted water for 30 seconds, refresh in cold water, drain and lay them on the tea-towel with the carrots.

THE MUSHROOM CAPS: Wash them and cut slantways into slices 3mm (1/10in) thick. Put them with the carrots and courgettes.

TO SERVE

When the oxtail is cooked, carefully lift the pieces out of the casserole with a slotted spoon and put them in a deep serving dish. Cover with foil or a lid and keep warm.

Strain the liquid first through a colander and then through a sieve into a shallow pan. Set the pan over high heat and reduce the liquid by two-thirds, skimming the surface as often as necessary. The liquid should be slightly syrupy. Incorporate the butter, a little at a time.

Add all the vegetable garnish and correct the seasoning with salt and pepper. As soon as the sauce comes to the boil, pour it over the oxtail. Sprinkle with finely chopped parsley and serve at once.

TOURNEDOS EN MELI-MELO

(Tournedos with a hotch-potch of mushrooms)

This is a happy departure from the classic and often rather dreary tournedos recipes. It is delicious served with a light potato purée. If you enjoy marrow bone as much as we do, you can top each tournedos with a slice of poached bone marrow. The availability of wild mushrooms varies from season to season and from area to area. It doesn't really matter which varieties you use, as long as the colours and textures of the different mushrooms marry well together.

PREPARATION

THE MUSHROOMS: Peel them all. Wipe the pleurotes with a damp cloth, wash the others if necessary, then pat dry. Heat the olive oil in a cast iron frying pan and fry the mushrooms, one variety at a time — first the ceps, then the chanterelles, the pleurotes and finally the mousserons. Season each variety to taste with salt and pepper. Keep warm. Preheat the oven to 170°C/325°F/Gas 3.
THE TOURNEDOS: Heat the clarified butter in a sauté pan set over high heat. Sauté the tournedos on both sides until they are cooked to your liking. Transfer to a dish and keep warm.
THE SAUCE: Pour off the excess fat from the pan, put in the chopped shallots and sweat them for 1 minute. Deglaze the pan with the white wine and reduce by two-thirds. Pour in the veal stock and reduce by half. Bring to the boil for a few minutes, season to taste with salt and pepper, then stir in the butter a little at a time.

TO SERVE

Scatter the wild mushrooms over the bottom of a silver or china serving dish. Arrange the tournedos on top and place the dish in the preheated oven for 1 minute. Pour on all the sauce and sprinkle over some freshly chopped parsley. Serve immediately.

INGREDIENTS

4 tournedos, trimmed, each weighing about 200g (7oz)

600g (1lb 4oz) mixed, wild mushrooms (chanterelles, pleurotes, ceps, mousserons)

2 tbls olive oil

60g (2oz) clarified butter

60g (2oz) shallots, finely chopped

200ml (8fl.oz) dry white wine

300ml (12fl.oz) Veal stock (see page 48)

80g (2½oz) butter

parsley sprigs

salt

freshly ground black pepper

Serves: 4 people
Preparation time: 35 minutes
Cooking time: about 10 minutes
Wine: With this light, Bercy-style sauce, a claret would be our choice; a Margaux for its finesse or the slightly more acidic St Estèphe.

INGREDIENTS

2 veal kidneys, fat, veins and membranes removed, weighing about 500g (1lb 1oz) after trimming

1 orange

2 lemons

4 tbls port

40g (1½oz) caster sugar

100g (4oz) cranberries

1 tbls white wine vinegar

200ml (8fl.oz) Veal stock (see page 48)

1 tbls butter

1 tbls clarified butter

1 tsp English mustard powder dissolved in ½ tsp water

salt

freshly ground black pepper

Serves: 4 people
Preparation time: 25 minutes
Cooking time: 5 minutes
Wine: Both these wines are from the Côte de Nuits. The Clos de Vougeot is a lush, highly developed wine with plenty of stamina to cope with the sweet and sour sauce. Our other suggestion is a Charmes-Chambertin.

ROGNONS DE VEAU A L'AIGRE DOUX

(Sweet and sour veal kidneys)

Buttered noodles or puréed potatoes are excellent with these kidneys. The cranberries, which may be fresh or frozen, add a hint of tartness to this light, fruity dish, which takes very little time to prepare and is quite delicious. For those with a sweet tooth, the orange and lemon zests can be candied; dissolve 1 tbls sugar in 1 tbls water, add the blanched zests and cook until all the moisture has evaporated.

PREPARATION

THE ORANGE: Finely pare off the rind and cut into *julienne*. Blanch, refresh, drain and keep in a cool place. Using a sharp knife, peel the orange, removing all the pith, cut into segments and keep in a cool place.

THE LEMON: Finely pare the rinds and cut into *julienne*. Blanch, refresh, drain and keep cool. Cut the lemons in half. Squeeze them and reserve the juice.

THE CRANBERRIES: In a small saucepan, heat the port with a quarter of the sugar. When it comes to the boil, add the cranberries and poach for 1 minute. Keep at room temperature.

THE SAUCE: Put the vinegar and the remaining sugar in a shallow pan and set over high heat. When the mixture caramelizes, add the lemon juice to prevent it from cooking any further. Stir in the orange segments and veal stock. Lower the heat and cook gently for about 15 minutes, until the liquid has a syrupy consistency. Strain through a sieve and keep warm.

THE KIDNEYS: Slice thinly. Heat the clarified butter in a shallow pan and, when it is very hot, sauté the kidneys for no more than 1 minute; they should be seared and lightly browned, but still bloody. Transfer to a colander and discard the cooking liquid.

COOKING

Pour off the fat from the pan and deglaze with the port in which the cranberries were cooked. Set over high heat and reduce by half. Pour in the sauce and bring to the boil. Add the kidneys and cranberries, then the mustard. Season to taste with salt and pepper and stir in 1 tbls butter. Take the pan off the heat and serve immediately.

TO SERVE

Tip the kidneys and sauce into a shallow silver or china dish and sprinkle over the orange and lemon zests.

RIS DE VEAU TON SUR TON

(Sweetbreads 'Tone on Tone')

This is a most original recipe with its 'tone on tone' colours and its blending of different tastes. It is a quick and easy dish which should be served with buttered noodles.

If you prefer, you can use lamb sweetbreads, in which case reduce the cooking time to 6 minutes. Also, reduce the quantity of red peppers by one-third, so that the sauce does not overpower the more delicate flavour of the lamb. The soaking time given for the sweetbreads is only a rough guide; the time they will need depends upon their quality and how clean they are; they may need anything between 1 and 12 hours' soaking.

PREPARATION

THE SWEETBREADS: Put them in a saucepan, cover with cold water and soak until they are very white (about 2 to 3 hours). Blanch in boiling water for 5 minutes, refresh, drain and remove the skin and outer membrane. Place the sweetbreads between 2 tea-towels. Press them lightly under a weighted board (the weight should be no heavier than 750g/1lb 12oz). Leave in a cool place.

THE PEPPERS: Smear them with oil and place under a hot grill or over a gas flame. Turn them until the skin blisters. Hold the peppers under cold running water and skin them by rubbing lightly with your hand. Cut in half and remove the white pith and seeds. Cut the flesh into small dice and keep at room temperature.

THE ONION: Peel and wash it and cut into very small dice.

THE TOMATO: Plunge into boiling water and peel. Cut in half, scoop out the seeds and dice the flesh.

THE GARLIC: Peel and crush the clove.

INGREDIENTS

4 veal sweetbreads, untrimmed (about 900g/2lb)

450g (1lb) red peppers

1 medium onion, about 150g (5oz)

1 medium tomato, about 80g (3oz)

1 medium garlic clove

4 tbls olive oil

500ml (1pt) Chicken stock (see page 48)

350ml (14fl.oz) double cream

2 tsp Chlorophyll (see page 59)

2 tbls snipped chives

salt

freshly ground black pepper

Serves: 4 people
Preparation time: 40 minutes
Cooking time: 15 minutes
Wine: This dish needs a straightforward wine big enough to cope with the peppers in the sauce. Two such wines are Côtes du Rhône Village or a red wine from Provence.

Picture: page 212

COOKING

Heat 2 tbls olive oil in a sauté pan. Put in the onion and cook until pale golden. Add the peppers, tomato and garlic and cook until all the moisture from the vegetables has evaporated. Put in the sweetbreads and cook them lightly on both sides, but do not allow them to colour. Bring 400ml (16fl.oz) chicken stock to the boil, then pour it into the sauté pan. Cover the pan and simmer over very low heat for 10 minutes. Lift out the sweetbreads with a spoon, cover and keep warm.

THE SAUCES

RED PEPPER SAUCE: Strain the cooking liquid from the sweetbreads through a conical sieve into a saucepan, rubbing the vegetables with the back of a small ladle. Set over high heat and reduce by two-thirds, then add 200ml (8fl.oz) cream and let the sauce bubble once. Season with salt and pepper and keep warm.
GREEN SAUCE: Pour the remaining chicken stock into a small shallow pan and reduce to a syrupy consistency. Add the rest of the cream and bring to the boil. Using a small wire whisk, beat in the chlorophyll. Season to taste with salt and pepper and keep warm.

TO SERVE

Arrange the sweetbreads, either whole or sliced, on individual plates. Coat each one with red pepper sauce and pour a ribbon of green sauce around the edge. Using the point of a knife, draw wavy zig-zags in the sauce, like the icing on a mille-feuille. Sprinkle with snipped chives.

Serves: 4 people
Preparation time: 20 minutes
Cooking time: 5 minutes
Wine: Although the curry is mild in flavour it offers difficulties in choosing a wine. The Sauvignon grape in Pouilly Fumé which is slightly spicy, green and smoky, would be perfect. Another wine

VEAU A L'ANANAS

(Veal with pineapple)

PREPARATION

THE PINEAPPLE: Using a serrated knife, remove the skin and finely slice the flesh. Cut out the core with a knife or an apple corer. Cut the flesh into large *julienne* and set aside.
THE ALMONDS: Scatter them over a baking tray and place in a hot oven (220°C/425°F/Gas 7) until pale golden. Set aside.

THE VEAL: Cut the fillet into very small, thin escalopes and salt lightly.

would be a Tokay (Pinot Gris) from Alsace.

COOKING

Heat the butter in a shallow pan set over low heat. Put in the veal escalopes and cook for 1 minute on each side; do not allow them to colour. Remove from the pan.

Pour off the fat from the pan and add the curry sauce. When it boils, add the veal and pineapple and bring back to the boil. Immediately, take the pan off the heat and blend in the Hollandaise sauce, either by swirling the pan with a circular motion or by stirring with a wooden spatula. The sauce should then be rather creamy and slightly runny. If it is too thick, add 1 to 2 tsp chicken stock or lukewarm water.

TO SERVE

Tip the contents of the pan into a shallow bi-metal or silver dish. Sprinkle over the toasted flaked almonds.

Once you have added the Hollandaise sauce to the curry sauce, on no account let the sauce boil or it will curdle. This marvellous dish needs no accompaniment other than steamed rice or a rice pilaff. You can use the noisette or saddle from a best end of veal instead of the fillet. As both these cuts are larger than the fillet, slice them into escalopes approximately 4cm (1½in) square.

INGREDIENTS

500g (1lb 2oz) veal fillet, trimmed

250g (9oz) pineapple, unpeeled

150g (5oz) flaked almonds

75g (2½oz) butter

200ml (8fl.oz) Curry sauce (see page 56)

200ml (8fl.oz) Hollandaise sauce (see page 57)

salt

freshly ground black pepper

COTE DE VEAU BOUCANIERE

(Buccaneer's veal chops)

The subtle blend of ginger and raspberry vinegar gives a novel and sophisticated taste to this dish, which is enriched by the veal stock. Serve it with Savoyard potatoes (page 219), or perhaps a purée of parsnips. You can buy raspberry vinegar in delicatessens if you do not want to make your own.

PREPARATION

THE SWEETCORN PANCAKES: Put the flour, eggs and milk in a bowl and mix together thoroughly with a spatula. Add a pinch of salt and

Serves: 4 people
Preparation time: 30 minutes and 1 hour 'resting' for the pancake mixture
Cooking time: 6 minutes
Wine: This is a slightly difficult sauce to complement with the raspberry vinegar and a touch of ginger. Try a wine from St Julien or from St Emilion which has a very light bitterness, but is velvety and full of body after about 10 years bottling.

INGREDIENTS

4 veal chops, trimmed, each weighing about 200g (7oz)

50g (2oz) flour

1 egg

125ml (5fl.oz) milk

120g (4oz) butter

60g (2oz) tinned sweetcorn

3 bananas

pinch of icing sugar

20g (¾oz) fresh ginger root

3 tbls Raspberry vinegar (see page 63)

200ml (8fl.oz) Veal stock (see page 48)

25g (1oz) desiccated coconut

salt

freshly ground black pepper

leave the batter to stand in a cool place for at least 1 hour.

Heat ½ tsp butter in a 15cm (6in) pancake pan. Pour in one quarter of the batter and scatter over a quarter of the sweetcorn. Cook until golden, then turn the pancake with a palette knife and cook until the second side is done. Transfer the pancake to a plate. Cook another 3 pancakes in the same way.

THE BANANAS: Preheat the grill to high. Peel the bananas and cut into 1cm (½in) slices. Lay them on a lightly buttered flan tin or baking sheet. Sprinkle with icing sugar and glaze under the hot grill. Put the banana slices with the pancakes.

THE GINGER: Peel, grate finely and set aside.

COOKING

Heat 30g (1oz) butter in a sauté pan set over high heat. Put in the veal chops and cook for 2 or 3 minutes on each side. When they are done to your taste, remove from the pan; they are best left slightly pink in the middle. Keep warm. Preheat the oven to 170°C/325°F/Gas 3.

THE SAUCE: Pour off the fat from the pan. Put in the ginger and brown over high heat for 1 minute. Deglaze with the vinegar and reduce until very thick and syrupy. Pour in the veal stock and reduce by one-third until slightly syrupy. Stir in 40g (1½oz) butter, a little at a time. Season to taste with salt and pepper, pass through a sieve and keep hot.

TO SERVE

Place a sweetcorn pancake on each serving plate and sprinkle with coconut. Lay a veal chop on each pancake and put the plates in the preheated oven for 2 minutes.

Arrange the glazed bananas around the edge of the plates and pour the boiling hot sauce thickly over the chops. Serve immediately.

TOURNEDOS ARLETTE

Y ou can use small button mushrooms instead of the ceps, but they will not have the same delicacy and mellowness of flavour.

Serve the tournedos with Potatoes Darphin (page 218) or Savoyard potatoes (page 219).

PREPARATION

Preheat the oven to 200°C/400°F/Gas 6.

THE TARTLETS: On a lightly floured marble or wooden surface, roll out the puff pastry as thinly as possible. Cut out 4 circles with a fluted round pastry cutter, 6.5cm (2½in) diameter, and line 4 tartlet tins. Prick with a fork. Line the bottoms with greaseproof paper and fill with dried beans. Leave to rest in a cool place for 10 to 15 minutes, then bake blind in the preheated oven for 10 minutes. Remove from the oven, take out the greaseproof paper and dried beans and keep warm. The pastry cases will be filled with hot watercress purée at the last minute.

THE TOMATOES: Plunge into boiling water and peel. Cut off a little 'hat' from the top and, using a coffee spoon, scoop out the insides.

THE CEPS: Peel, wash and pat dry. Finely chop the ceps and the peeled garlic clove, season with salt and pepper, put in a frying pan and sauté in a little butter for a few minutes. Fill the tomatoes with this mixture and set aside. 5 minutes before serving, heat the tomatoes through in a hot oven.

COOKING

Cut the fillet of beef into 4 tournedos and salt lightly. Heat the clarified butter in a sauté pan set over high heat, then put in the tournedos and cook on both sides until they are done to your liking. Arrange the tournedos in a silver or china dish and keep warm. Pour off the fat from the pan and deglaze with the white wine. Reduce until almost all the liquid has evaporated, then pour in the veal stock and reduce to a syrupy consistency.

Meanwhile, cream the butter with a wire whisk and beat in the 3 mustards and the Cognac. Take the pan off the heat and beat the flavoured butter into the sauce. Correct the seasoning, rub the sauce through a sieve and keep warm. Heat the watercress purée.

TO SERVE

Place the tournedos in the centre of the serving dish. Fill the warmed pastry cases with hot watercress purée and arrange them around the edge of the dish, alternating with the heated tomatoes. Pour the sauce over the tournedos, taking care not to spill any.

INGREDIENTS

800g (1lb 12oz) fillet of beef, trimmed

70g (2½oz) Puff pastry (see page 248)

pinch of flour

4 small tomatoes

250g (9oz) ceps, fresh or preserved

1 garlic clove

200g (7oz) butter

60g (2oz) clarified butter

500ml (1pt) Veal stock (see page 48)

50ml (2fl.oz) dry white wine

1 tsp tarragon mustard

1 tsp mustard flavoured with shallots

1 tsp mustard flavoured with green peppercorns

1 tbls Cognac

4 tbls Watercress purée (see page 220)

salt

freshly ground black pepper

Serves: 4 people
Preparation time: 50 minutes
Cooking time: about 10 minutes
Wine: Almost neighbours, but different in style, are the Pernand-Vergelesses, an earthy wine, preferably with some age, and the soft elegant Burgundy from Savigny-les-Beaune. Both wines would be perfect.

Above *Ris de veau ton sur ton (page 207)*
1 Beignets de légumes (choux-fleurs) (page 215)
2 Subrics de légumes (page 221)
3 Pommes de terre Darphin, Pommes de terre au porto (pages 218, 219)

1

2

3

CHAPTER ELEVEN

VEGETABLES

Vegetables are the most indispensable of foods. They must always be very fresh and plump and should not be kept for too long in the refrigerator, or they will lose their flavour. The variety of available vegetables changes with the seasons, so there is always something new on our table. Harmonizing the colours and textures of vegetables is like the painter's art. We regard vegetarians as gourmets whose tastes we wish to satisfy just as much as those of our meat-eating clientele.

BEIGNETS DE LEGUMES

(Vegetable fritters)

PREPARATION

Cut off the stem of the cauliflower and remove the outer leaves. Bring a saucepan of salted water to the boil, put in the cauliflower and half cook it, keeping it firm. Refresh immediately, drain and separate into florets. Pat dry with a cloth. Put the florets in a bowl, add the oil, vinegar or lemon juice and the chervil sprigs or snipped parsley. Carefully mix together, then leave the cauliflower to absorb the seasoning for 15 minutes before cooking.

DEEP FRYING THE CAULIFLOWER

Heat the oil in a deep fryer until it is very hot and almost smoking. Dip the cauliflower florets into the batter, one by one, then deep fry in the hot oil until they float to the surface and are golden brown. Drain on

INGREDIENTS

1 quantity fritter batter (see page 222)

800g (1lb 12oz) cauliflower

2 tbls olive oil

1 tbls vinegar *or* juice of ½ lemon

sprigs of chervil *or* 2 tbls snipped parsley

salt

oil for deep frying

Serves: 6 people
Preparation time: 8 minutes, plus 15 minutes marinating
Cooking time: 15 minutes
Picture: page 213

absorbent paper or a cloth. Sprinkle with a little salt and serve immediately.

TO SERVE

Pile the florets into a dome on a round silver or china dish, covered with a folded napkin or a paper doily. You can create a pretty effect with deep-fried parsley sprigs arranged round the base of the dome.

You can deep fry a variety of vegetables; some are cooked raw, like courgettes or aubergines cut into rounds, and onion rings.
   Other vegetables may need precooking in one of two ways:
PRE-COOKING IN SALTED WATER: Cauliflower or celeriac, cooked whole, then cut into quarters.
PRE-COOKING IN A WHITE COURT BOUILLON: ie 1 tbls flour, 2 tbls white wine vinegar, salt and 2L (3½ pts) water; beat with a wire whisk until smooth, then bring to the boil. Salsify, artichoke hearts and Chinese artichokes should be prepared in this way.

Those vegetables which are cooked raw should not be seasoned with oil and vinegar etc, but dipped into the batter unseasoned. All pre-cooked vegetables should be prepared in the same way as the cauliflower.

INGREDIENTS

250g (9oz) spinach

75g (2½oz) flour

1 egg

1 egg yolk

4 tbls oil, preferably corn oil

250ml (10fl.oz) milk

125g (5oz) sweetcorn, fresh or tinned

60g (2oz) butter

pinch of nutmeg

salt

pepper

CREPES AU MAIS ET AUX EPINARDS

(Spinach and sweetcorn pancakes)

Allow 2 pancakes per person for an original vegetable accompaniment; they go very well with grilled or white meats.

PREPARATION

THE SPINACH: Remove the stalks, wash the leaves and cook in boiling, salted water. Refresh, drain and press lightly between your hands to remove the excess moisture. Coarsely chop the spinach.
THE BATTER: In a bowl, mix together the flour, egg, egg yolk and oil, beating with a wire whisk. Stir in the milk. Add the sweetcorn kernels (cook them first if you are using fresh corn) and the spinach. Season with a pinch of nutmeg and salt and pepper. Set aside in a cool place for

at least 1 hour before using the batter.

Serves: 6 people (12 pancakes)
Preparation time: 20 minutes, plus 1 hour standing for the batter
Cooking time: 6 minutes

COOKING

Set 1 or 2 pancake pans, 11cm (4½in) diameter, over high heat with ½ tsp butter; pour in the batter to a depth of 5mm (¼in) and cook for 3 minutes on each side, until golden brown.

FEVES A LA CREME

(Broad beans in cream)

PREPARATION AND COOKING

Bring a saucepan of water to the boil. Plunge in the broad beans and blanch for 1 to 2 minutes, depending on their size. Refresh and drain. Pour the cream into a shallow pan set over medium heat, and bring to the boil. Meanwhile, squeeze the broad beans between your thumb and index finger, so that they pop out of their skins. Lightly salt the cream, then plunge in the skinned beans and cook gently for about 5 minutes. They should still be slightly crunchy.

Chop the sage very finely and stir it into the broad beans. Season to taste with salt and white pepper.

INGREDIENTS

500g (1lb 1oz) shelled broad beans

250ml (10fl.oz) double cream

5 sage leaves

salt

freshly ground white pepper

Serves: 4 to 6 people
Preparation time: 20 minutes
Cooking time: 7 minutes

TO SERVE

Serve in a vegetable dish or in little pastry cases. This recipe will give enough beans to fill about a dozen 7cm (2¾in) pastry cases.

ENDIVES MEUNIERES

(Chicory meunière)

The chicory will keep very well for several days in the refrigerator if left in the cooking liquid. It is a useful vegetable accompaniment as it is delicious and needs very little last-minute cooking.

INGREDIENTS

6 heads chicory, total weight 1.25kg (2lb 12oz)

1L (1¾pts) water

¼ lemon

160g (6oz) butter

pinch of caster sugar

salt and white pepper

PREPARATION

Preheat the oven to 200°C/400°F/Gas 6. Trim off any withered or

Serves: 6 people
Preparation time: 5 minutes
Cooking time: about 25 minutes

marked outer leaves from the chicory. Using a sharp knife, make a cross in each base to ensure even cooking. Wipe the chicory with a cloth and put into a saucepan with the water, lemon, 100g (4oz) butter and a pinch of salt. Set over high heat and bring to the boil, cover with greaseproof paper and the lid. Place the pan in the preheated oven for 20 minutes. Test the chicory with the point of a sharp knife; they are cooked if the knife goes in easily, meeting a very slight resistance. Tip the chicory and cooking liquid into a bowl.

TO SERVE

A few minutes before serving, heat 60g (2oz) butter in a frying pan. Sprinkle in the sugar and put in the well-drained chicory. Cook over medium heat for 3 minutes on each side, until the chicory is lightly browned. Season to taste and serve immediately.

INGREDIENTS

1kg (2lb 2oz) potatoes

240g (9oz) clarified butter

fine salt

Serves: 6 people
Preparation time: 10 minutes
Cooking time: 15 minutes

Picture: page 213

POMMES DE TERRE DARPHIN

(Potatoes Darphin)

If you only have 1 frying pan, you can cook the potatoes Darphin a little in advance and keep them warm in a slow oven. Inevitably, they will lose some of their crispness, so cook them at the last moment if you can.

It is better to use 2 frying pans at once, starting the cooking at 5 minute intervals, or you can make 1 large Darphin and cut it into portions with a knife or scissors. Vary the recipe by adding one-third quantity shredded courgettes to the potatoes.

PREPARATION

Peel the potatoes and cut into fine *julienne*, using a mandoline. Do not wash the potatoes, as the starch they contain is needed for holding the Darphin together during cooking. Salt the potatoes and divide into 6.

COOKING

Put 40g (1½oz) clarified butter in a frying pan about 12-15cm (5-6in) diameter and set over high heat. Arrange 1 serving of potatoes in the bottom of the pan, and press lightly with a palette knife to form a potato 'cake'. Fry until golden on the bottom, then lower the heat and cook gently for 7 or 8 minutes. Turn the potatoes with the palette knife and fry for a further 7 or 8 minutes. When both sides are cooked, remove the potatoes from the pan. Repeat the process with each serving.

POMMES DE TERRE AU PORTO

(Potatoes in port)

This light, appetizing potato dish is a derivation of potatoes Anna, but is much less greasy. It goes very well with grilled meat. It will be much quicker if you use 2 frying pans at once, starting to cook the potato cakes at 5 minute intervals. Serve the potatoes as soon as possible after cooking.

PREPARATION

Peel and wash the potatoes. Using a mandoline, cut them into 3mm (1/10in) slices. Pat dry with a cloth and sprinkle with salt. Divide into 6 portions.

COOKING

Put 30g (1oz) clarified butter in a small frying pan and set over high heat. Put in 1 portion of potato slices in overlapping circles and scatter over a few crumbs of truffle between each layer. Fry until the potatoes are golden on the bottom, then lower the heat and cook gently for 5 or 6 minutes. Using a palette knife, turn the potatoes and fry for a further 5 or 6 minutes. Sprinkle a few drops of port over the potato 'cake'. Remove the potatoes from the pan with a palette knife and keep warm. Repeat the process with each portion of potatoes.

INGREDIENTS

750g (1lb 9oz) potatoes

180g (6oz) clarified butter

25g (1oz) truffle peelings or broken pieces

100ml (4fl.oz) port

salt

pepper

Serves: 6 people
Preparation time: 10 minutes
Cooking time: 15 minutes

Picture: page 213

GRATIN SAVOYARD

(Savoyard potatoes)

One never grows tired of this potato dish, which goes particularly well with red meats, such as beef or lamb. It can be reheated very satisfactorily in a slow oven.

Serves: 4 people
Preparation time: 15 minutes
Cooking time: 45 minutes

INGREDIENTS

650g (1lb 6oz) medium potatoes

½ garlic clove

500ml (1pt) double cream

4 tbls milk

freshly grated nutmeg

salt

freshly ground white pepper

PREPARATION

THE POTATOES: Peel carefully, wash and slice on a mandoline; the slices should be only about 3mm (1/10in) thick. Spread them on a table and sprinkle lavishly with salt. Rub the slices together, then heap them up in a pile and leave for 5 or 10 minutes. The salt will extract the water and soften the potatoes.

THE CREAM: Combine the cream and milk in a saucepan large enough to take the potatoes later. Salt very lightly (remember that the potatoes are already salted). Add 2 turns of the pepper mill and grate in a little nutmeg. Set over high heat and bring to the boil for several minutes. Rub a medium gratin dish, preferably made of fine metal, with the half clove of garlic dipped in salt.

COOKING

Press the potatoes lightly between your hands to squeeze out the excess water. Add the potatoes to the boiling cream and bring the mixture back to the boil. Remove from the heat and, using a large spoon, spread the mixture evenly in the prepared dish. The *gratin* should be 5 or 6cm (about 2in) thick. Bake in a very slow oven, at 130°C/250°F/ Gas ½ for about 45 minutes.

INGREDIENTS

800g (1lb 12oz) water-cress

400ml (16fl.oz) Chicken stock (see page 48)

150ml (6fl.oz) double cream

1 tsp butter

salt

freshly ground black pepper

Serves: 4 people
Preparation time: 10 minutes
Cooking time: 5 minutes

Picture: page 213

PUREE DE CRESSON

(Watercress purée)

PREPARATION AND COOKING

Wash the watercress and remove the stalks and any yellow or withered leaves. Pour the chicken stock into a saucepan and bring to the boil. Put in the watercress and cook for 5 minutes. Drain in a sieve set over a saucepan to catch the chicken stock.

Set the pan over high heat and reduce the stock until syrupy. Rub the watercress through the sieve set over a saucepan. Set the pan over high heat and, using a small wire whisk, beat in the reduced stock, cream and butter and whisk until the mixture is very smooth. Season to taste with salt and pepper.

Make the purée in a blender or food processor if you wish. Process the cooked watercress with the reduced stock, cream and butter until smooth. Pass through a sieve and season to taste with salt and pepper.

You can make this delicate purée into watercress *subrics* with very little effort. Lightly butter 4 moulds, 6cm (2½in) diameter and 5.5cm (2¼in) deep. Stir 3 egg yolks, 1 whole egg and 1 tbls double cream into the watercress purée, then spoon the mixture into the moulds which can be lined with blanched ribbons of carrot, turnip or courgette. Place in a bain-marie lined with paper. Pour in boiling water to come halfway up the sides of the moulds. Cover with foil or greaseproof paper and bake in the oven at 190°C/375°F/Gas 5 for 15 minutes. Carefully turn out each mould onto a serving dish or plate. Brush the *subrics* with clarified butter to give them an attractive shine.

PUREE DE CELERI-RAVE

(Celeriac purée)

PREPARATION AND COOKING

Peel and wash the celeriac and cut into large dice. Place in a saucepan and pour in the chicken stock. Set the pan over high heat and bring to the boil. Lower the heat, cover the pan and simmer for about 15 minutes. Use the point of a knife to see if it is tender.

Drain the celeriac in a sieve set over a saucepan so as to catch the chicken stock. Set the pan over high heat and reduce the stock to a syrupy consistency. Rub the celeriac through a fine sieve into the saucepan containing the reduced stock. Using a small wire whisk, beat in the cream and the butter, whisking until the mixture is very smooth. Season to taste with salt and pepper.

INGREDIENTS

1kg (2lb 2oz) celeriac

500ml (1pt) Chicken stock (see page 48)

2 tbls double cream

50g (2oz) butter

salt

freshly ground black pepper

Makes: about 850g (2lb) purée
Preparation time: 8 minutes
Cooking time: 15 minutes

PUREE DE PANAIS A L'OSEILLE

(Parsnip purée with sorrel)

The addition of sorrel transforms the very humble parsnip into an elegant and colourful dish.

PREPARATION AND COOKING

Preheat the oven to 190°C/375°F/Gas 5. Peel, wash and finely dice the parsnips. Melt the butter in a casserole over gentle heat. Add the

INGREDIENTS

1kg (2lb 2oz) parsnips

100g (4oz) butter

100g (4oz) sorrel

500ml (1pt) double cream

salt

freshly ground white pepper

parsnips and sweat them for a few minutes. Season lightly with salt. Cover the casserole and place in the preheated oven for about 20 minutes, or until the parsnips are tender. Rub the parsnips through a fine sieve into a bowl and keep warm.

Meanwhile, remove the stalks from the sorrel, wash and snip the leaves. Pour the cream into the saucepan, and bring to the boil. Add the sorrel, lower the heat and simmer for 5 minutes. Using a spatula, stir the sorrel into the parsnip purée and then season with salt and pepper to suit your taste.

TO SERVE

Serve in a vegetable dish or in little pastry cases.

INGREDIENTS

1kg (2lb 2oz) leeks

200g (7oz) butter

3 tbls double cream

salt

freshly ground black pepper

Makes: 320g (11oz) purée
Preparation time: 8 minutes
Cooking time: 10 minutes

PUREE DE POIREAUX
(Leek Purée)

PREPARATION AND COOKING

Trim, wash and finely slice the leeks, discarding the greenest parts. Sweat them with the butter in a covered casserole for about 10 minutes, or until they are tender. Put in a blender or food processor with the cream and process until smooth. Rub through a fine sieve into a bowl. Season to taste with salt and pepper, then using a small wire whisk, beat until the purée is completely smooth.

TO SERVE

Serve in a vegetable dish or in pastry cases; or use the purée as a filling for choux buns.

INGREDIENTS

125g (4oz) flour

1½ eggs

1½ tbls olive oil

100ml (4fl.oz) light beer

½ tsp salt

PATE A BEIGNETS
(Fritter batter)

This is a crispy, light, dry fritter batter, which coats the food (vegetables, fish, fruit etc) only lightly, so as not to overwhelm it; that is why extra egg white is not used in this recipe.

For fruit fritters, add 15g (½oz) caster sugar to the batter. If it seems too thick when you come to use it, dilute it with 1 tbls cold water.

Makes: enough for 6 people
Preparation time: 5 minutes, plus 2 to 3 hours 'standing'

PREPARATION

Put the flour, eggs, oil and salt into a bowl and mix thoroughly with a wooden spatula. When everything is well mixed, stir in the beer. Leave the batter to stand in the refrigerator for at least 2 or 3 hours before you use it, so that it begins to ferment. The batter will relax and lose its elasticity according to how long you leave it.

PATE A NOUILLE

(Fresh noodle dough)

PREPARATION

Spread the flour on a wooden or marble work surface and make a well in the centre. Put the whole eggs, yolks, oil and salt in the middle. Using the fingertips of your right hand, work all the ingredients together. Use your left hand to mix in the flour to prevent it from falling into the well in little heaps. When the dough is very thoroughly mixed, knead it 2 or 3 times with the heel of your hand.

Leave the dough to rest in a cool place, covered with a dry cloth, for at least 10 minutes before cutting it into strips. You can roll it out either with a rolling pin or with a special pasta roller. The pasta should be about 3mm (1/10in) thick. Do not cook the noodles immediately after making them or they may be rubbery. It is better to let them rest for a few minutes so that they lose their elasticity.

Although fresh noodles are available commercially, it is much more satisfying to make your own and they do not take long to prepare. You can experiment endlessly with different shapes of noodles, macaroni and canneloni with various fillings.

Always stay by pasta when you are cooking it. It should never be overcooked or it will inevitably become gluey.

INGREDIENTS

250g (9oz) plain flour

2 whole eggs

3 egg yolks

1 tsp peanut oil

1 tsp salt

Serves: 8 people
Preparation time: 8 minutes

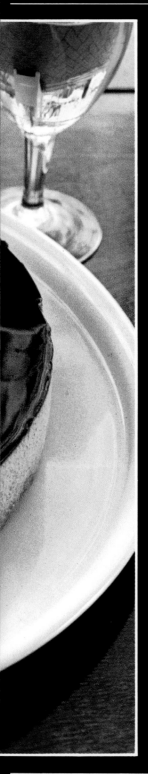

Left *Délice au cassis (page 229)*
Above *Sablé aux fraises (page 238)*

CHAPTER TWELVE

DESSERTS

Desserts should be light and delicate, with rich colours. They should set the final stamp on a meal, like a royal seal on a message, and therefore demand a great deal of attention and a touch of patience, too. By the end of the meal, your guests' appetites may be waning, but they will be tempted to eat your dessert if the presentation is restrained, original and rather special.

Although they sometimes take a long time to prepare, most desserts can be made several hours before your guests arrive. After weighing the dry ingredients for pastry or biscuit bases, set them out on individual sheets of greaseproof paper, so that they will be easier to mix; you can then tip them straight into the mixing bowl.

We think that sorbets are vital to the gourmet's dinner table. Flavoured with fresh fruits in season, they are a favourite dessert with almost everyone and they satisfy every taste, from the simplest to the most sophisticated. They are also very quick and easy to make.

COULIS DE FRUITS ROUGES

(*Coulis* of red fruits)

Any of the following fruits are suitable for this *coulis*, depending on the flavour you require: strawberries, raspberries, wild strawberries, redcurrants, blackberries. The quantities given here will yield 1.25L (2¼pts) of liquid. You will need at least 100ml (4fl.oz) of *coulis* per person to serve with a dessert. Add 2 tbls *coulis* to a glass of Champagne to make a most marvellous cocktail.

INGREDIENTS

800g (1lb 12oz) red soft fruits (eg strawberries, raspberries)

250ml (10fl.oz) Sorbet syrup (see page 242)

juice of 1 lemon

Preparation time: 15 minutes

PREPARATION

Hull, wash and drain the fruit and purée in a blender with the syrup and lemon juice. Rub the purée through a conical sieve and keep in the refrigerator until you are ready to use it. It will keep for several days.

INGREDIENTS

12 egg yolks

250g (9oz) caster sugar

1L (1¾pts) milk

1 vanilla pod

Makes: 1L (1¾pts)
Preparation time: 15 minutes
Cooking time: 8 minutes

CREME ANGLAISE

(Custard cream)

Custard cream is used as the base for numerous puddings, desserts and ice-creams. It can be served like a *coulis* or sauce with cakes or red fruits. Serve the custard very cold, it will keep for 2 or 3 days in the refrigerator. The vanilla pod can be omitted, depending on how the custard is going to be used.

PREPARATION

Using a wire whisk, work together the egg yolks and about one-third of the sugar in a bowl, until the whisk leaves a trail when lifted.

COOKING

Put the milk in a saucepan with the remaining sugar and the split vanilla pod and bring to the boil. Pour the boiling milk onto the egg mixture, whisking continuously. Pour the mixture back into the saucepan, set the pan over low heat and cook. Stir continuously with a spatula, until the custard is thick enough to coat it. On no account allow the mixture to boil. Pass the custard through a conical sieve and keep in a cool place until completely cold. Stir from time to time to prevent a skin from forming.

Serves: 10 people
Preparation time: 10 minutes plus 2 hours, resting time
Cooking time: 2 minutes for each pancake

CREPES PINAUDIER

(Daniel Pinaudier's pancakes)

This recipe was created by Daniel Pinaudier, who worked as a chef in private service in Paris from 1930 to 1960. He was very highly respected and we were privileged to work with him.

Choose your own favourite flavouring — vanilla, orange flower water, lemon zests or Grand Marnier, for instance. These *crêpes* can be used for lining terrines for fish pâtés; omit the sugar and add snipped chervil and chives instead.

PREPARATION

Combine the sifted flour, sugar and salt in a bowl. Add the eggs, one at a time, mixing well with a spatula. Pour in one-third of the milk, mixing continuously, until you have a smooth, homogenous batter. Pour in the cream and the rest of the milk and leave in a cool place for at least 2 hours before cooking the *crêpes*.

COOKING

Stir the batter and add your chosen flavouring. Brush a small, 12cm (15in) *crêpe* pan or 2 round, 30cm (12in) diameter, frying pans with clarified butter and set over medium heat. Using a ladle, pour in a little batter and cook for 1 or 2 minutes on each side, until done to your liking, tossing the *crêpe* or turning it with a palette knife.

TO SERVE

Roll the *crêpes* or fold into half or into four and eat them immediately.

INGREDIENTS

250g (9oz) plain flour, sifted

30g (1oz) caster sugar

pinch of salt

4 eggs

650ml (26fl.oz) cooled boiled milk

200ml (8fl.oz) double cream

flavouring of your choice

30g (1oz) clarified butter

DELICE AU CASSIS

(Blackcurrant delight)

PREPARATION

THE BLACKCURRANT PUREE: Reserve 8 blackcurrants for decoration. Purée the remainder in the blender with 50ml (2fl.oz) syrup. Rub the purée through a conical sieve, using the back of a ladle.
THE BLACKCURRANT CUSTARD: Soak 2 gelatine leaves in cold water. Reserve 2 tbls blackcurrant purée and put the remainder in a saucepan with the milk and vanilla pod. Bring to the boil. Using a wire whisk, work together the egg yolks and sugar in a bowl, until the whisk leaves a trail when lifted. Pour the boiling blackcurrant mixture onto the egg mixture, whisking continuously.
　　Pour the custard back into the saucepan and set over low heat. Do

Serves: 8 people
Preparation time: 40 minutes
Cooking time: 10 minutes
Wine: Choose a sweet wine produced in Vouvray in exceptional years. These can be compared in richness and sweetness with the finest from Sauternes and Barsac.

1 *Slice off one round slab from the sponge cake for the base of the flan.*
2 *Having put the base on a round cake board, brush it with the blackcurrant purée, to give it added flavour and moisture.*

1

2

3 *Using a wire whisk, gently stir the blackcurrant custard into the meringue.*
4 *After adding the crème de cassis liqueur and whisking in the partly-whipped cream, fold the mixture over with a spatula to ensure an even blend.*

3

4

5 *Pour the mixture into the sponge base and fill it up to the top of the flan ring.*
6 *Smooth over with a palette knife, leaving a completely flat surface. Put the mousse in the freezer or a very cold refrigerator for several hours.*

5

6

7 **To glaze** *Slowly pour the tepid glaze over the mousse, starting in the centre and spreading it to the outer edges with a palette knife.*
8 *Any bubbles that have formed in the glaze can be easily removed with the point of a knife to leave a perfectly smooth, mirror-like surface.*

7

8

not allow it to boil. Cook, stirring continuously with a spatula, until the custard is thick enough to coat the spatula. Take the pan off the heat and stir in the soaked gelatine leaves, then rub the mixture through a conical sieve into a bowl and leave to cool. Stir occasionally, to prevent a skin from forming.

THE BLACKCURRANT MOUSSE: When the custard is lukewarm, remove the vanilla pod and, using a wire whisk, gently fold in the meringue and the crème de cassis. Whip the cream until the whisk leaves a trail when lifted and, using a wooden spatula, stir it into the blackcurrant mixture. You must then assemble the pudding immediately, before the mousse sets.

ASSEMBLING THE DELICE

Place the biscuit base on a round 22cm (9in) cake board. Mix together 50ml (2fl.oz) syrup and 1 tbls reserved blackcurrant purée and brush the biscuit base with this mixture. Set a flan ring, 22cm (9in) diameter, 3.5cm (1½in) deep, round the biscuit and fill it with the mousse. Smooth over the top with a metal palette knife. Place in a freezer or a cold refrigerator for several hours. Remove 15 minutes before serving.

TO GLAZE: Combine 50ml (2fl.oz) syrup with 1 tbls blackcurrant purée and the 2 remaining gelatine leaves. Leave the mixture to cool, then, using a palette knife, spread it evenly over the top of the pudding. To remove the ring before serving, warm the outside over a gas flame for a few seconds, then slide the ring upwards.

TO DECORATE: Roll the 8 reserved blackcurrants in granulated sugar and arrange them on top of the pudding.

The unglazed *délice* will keep for several days in the refrigerator or for up to 2 weeks in the freezer. You can use a round of sponge cake, ½cm (¼in) thick, instead of the biscuit base.

INGREDIENTS

350g (12oz) blackcurrants, frozen or fresh

150ml (6fl.oz) Sorbet syrup (see page 242)

3 tsp powdered milk

¼ vanilla pod

3 egg yolks

25g (1oz) caster sugar

4 gelatine leaves

Italian Meringue, made with 1 egg white (see page 233)

200ml (8fl.oz) crème de cassis liqueur

400ml (16fl.oz) double cream

1 round sponge biscuit base, 20cm (8in) diameter, ½cm (¼in) thick (see recipe 1, page 244)

Picture: page 224

MACARONS

(Macaroons)

Makes: about 3 dozen
Preparation time: 15 minutes
Cooking time: 10 minutes

These *petits fours* are delicate both to make and to eat. They must be very shiny, smooth and, above all, very moist in the centre. Pack the macaroons in airtight containers; they freeze well.

INGREDIENTS

4 egg whites

225g (8oz) icing sugar

125g (4½oz) ground almonds

25g (1oz) caster sugar

Flavourings: ½ tsp vanilla essence *or* ½ tsp raspberry essence plus a few drops red food colouring (optional) *or* 20g (¾oz) unsweetened cocoa powder, finely sifted

This recipe uses the minimum quantity of egg white possible to obtain a good result. The macaroons will be even better if you double the amount. They can be filled, with a little raspberry jam or chocolate mousse for instance, or eaten plain.

PREPARATION

THE ICING SUGAR AND GROUND ALMONDS: Finely sift the icing sugar then sieve again with the ground almonds and the sifted cocoa powder if you are making chocolate macaroons. Keep the mixture on a sheet of paper.

THE EGG WHITES: Beat in an electric mixer until half-risen then add the caster sugar and beat until stiff. Add the desired flavouring, increase the speed and beat on high for 1 minute, until very stiff.

THE MACAROON MIXTURE: Sprinkle the icing sugar and ground almond mixture over the egg whites and fold in gently with a spatula. Mix together until thoroughly blended; the mixture should now be extremely smooth.

PIPING THE MACAROONS: Fill a piping bag with the mixture and pipe out small, even-sized rounds, about 2cm (¾in) diameter onto a baking sheet lined with greaseproof paper. Use a plain no.6 nozzle. Pipe the macaroons in staggered rows, about 2cm (1in) apart.

BAKING

METHOD 1: Preheat the oven to 180°C/350°F/Gas 4. Leave the macaroons at room temperature for about 15 minutes until a crust forms, then bake in the preheated oven for 10 minutes, leaving the oven door very slightly ajar (about 2cm/1in) to allow the steam to escape from the oven.

METHOD 2: Preheat the oven to 220-230°C/425-450°F/Gas 7-8. After piping, bake the macaroons immediately in the hot oven for 2 or 3 minutes, then quickly place them in another oven at 180°C/350°F/Gas 4, leaving the oven door very slightly ajar.

Whichever method you use, place an empty baking tray under the tray containing the macaroons to protect the bottom of the macaroons and prevent them from burning. As soon as the macaroons are cooked, run a little cold water between the greaseproof paper and the baking tray. After 2 or 3 minutes, lift off the macaroons with your fingers and gently stick them together in pairs. Leave to cool on a wire pastry rack.

MERINGUE ITALIENNE

(Italian meringue)

The glucose prevents crystals from forming in the egg whites or at the edge of the bowl when the sugar is added.

You can make an excellent buttercream using Italian meringue — make the meringue with 500g (1lb 2oz) sugar and 140ml (5½fl.oz) water plus 30g (1oz) glucose. When the mixture is almost cold, set the mixer on low and add 650g (1½lb) softened butter, a little at a time.

INGREDIENTS

300g (10oz) caster sugar

30g (1oz) glucose (optional)

80ml (3fl.oz) water

6 egg whites

Recipe for: 6 egg whites
Preparation time: 7 minutes
Cooking time: 15 to 20 minutes

PREPARATION

TO MAKE THE SYRUP: Put the sugar into a copper saucepan and add the water and glucose, if you are using it. Set over medium heat and bring to the boil, stirring occasionally with a slotted spoon. Skim the surface and, when the mixture boils, wash down the sugar crystals which form inside the pan with a brush dipped in cold water. Increase the heat to high and put in a sugar thermometer to check the temperature.

THE EGG WHITES: When the sugar reaches a temperature of 110°C (225°F), beat the egg whites in an electric mixer until stiff. Meanwhile, keep an eye on the syrup and stop cooking when it reaches 121°C (240°F).

MIXING THE SYRUP WITH THE EGG WHITES: When the egg whites are stiffly beaten, set the electric mixer to the lowest speed and gently pour in the syrup in a thin stream, taking care that it does not run onto the beaters. Continue to mix at low speed until the mixture has cooled to room temperature; this will take about 15 minutes. The meringue is now ready to use. It can also be stored in the refrigerator for several days in a bowl covered with a damp cloth.

MOUSSE AU CHOCOLAT ET MACARONS

(Chocolate mousse with macaroons)

This creamy mousse is rich without being sickly. Dry *petits fours*, *tuiles* or biscuit 'cigarettes' make an excellent accompaniment. You can always buy the macaroons from your patisserie to make the preparation of the dessert easier.

Serves: 6 people
Preparation time: 20 minutes
Wine: This is a very rich dessert and only the biggest and finest Sauternes will suffice. The finest sweet wine to come from Bordeaux is Château d'Yquem.

INGREDIENTS

100ml (4fl.oz) double cream

150g (5oz) bitter chocolate

125g (5oz) caster sugar

1 whole egg

5 egg yolks

12 Macaroons (see page 231)

2 tbls rum

PREPARATION

THE CREAM AND MACAROONS: Whip the cream until the whisk leaves a trail. Sprinkle the rum over 6 macaroons and leave to soak.

THE CHOCOLATE: Break into small pieces and put in a shallow pan or the top of a double boiler. Set in a bain-marie and melt the chocolate.

THE SUGAR: Put into a heavy-based pan with 4 tbls water and set over high heat. As soon as the mixture boils, skim the surface and cook until the syrup forms a hard crack (or reaches 140°C (275°F) on a sugar thermometer). Plunge the base of the pan into cold water for a few moments to prevent further cooking.

THE EGG AND YOLKS: Beat together in an electric mixer or with a wire whisk until pale and frothy. Pour in the hot, freshly-prepared syrup in a thin stream, whisking continuously. Beat the mixture at medium speed until barely lukewarm.

Using a wire whisk, beat the melted chocolate into the egg mixture until perfectly blended. Using a spatula, delicately fold in the whipped cream and blend well.

TO SERVE

Pour the mousse into 6 glass dishes, bowls or small deep plates to half-fill them. Crumble a plain macaroon over the surface of each mousse. Fill up the dishes with the remaining mousse and top with a rum-soaked macaroon. Chill in the refrigerator for several hours .

INGREDIENTS

4 very ripe white peaches

500ml (1pt) dry Champagne

350ml (14fl.oz) Sorbet syrup (see page 242)

1 small vanilla pod

250g (9oz) strawberries

150g (6oz) caster sugar

250ml (10fl.oz) double cream
Continued

PECHE AU CHAMPAGNE

(Peaches poached in Champagne)

PREPARATION

THE PEACHES: Make a very light incision all round the peach skins with the point of a knife. Plunge the peaches into boiling water, then into cold water and peel. Put them into a shallow pan, pour over the Champagne and syrup and add the vanilla pod. Set the pan over low heat and gently bring to the boil. Reduce the heat and poach the peaches at about 85°C (190°F). If they are very ripe, they will be cooked after 5 minutes. Take the pan off the heat, transfer the peaches to a dish and keep in a cool place, but do not refrigerate. Chill the poaching liquid in the refrigerator.

THE STRAWBERRIES: Rub through a fine sieve set over a bowl. Add the sugar to the strawberry pulp. Whip the cream until the whisk leaves a trail when lifted, then stir in the strawberry pulp and the lemon juice.

TO SERVE

Serve the peaches on attractively curved plates, or in glass dishes or small bowls. Pour the strawberry mousse over the bottom of the dishes and place a cold, but not chilled peach on top. Top each white peach with a mint leaf. Serve the chilled poaching Champagne separately in a sauceboat; it marries wonderfully well with the strawberry mousse.

juice of ½ lemon

4 fresh mint leaves

Serves: 4 people
Preparation time: 20 minutes
Cooking time: 5 minutes
Wine: A Demi Sec or Doux Champagne. These sweeter-than-Brut Champagnes are easily found and are produced by most Champagne houses.
Picture: page 246

SOUFFLE CHAUD AUX FRAMBOISES

(Hot raspberry soufflés)

PREPARATION

THE PASTRY CREAM: Combine the milk and 90g (3oz) sugar in a saucepan and bring to the boil. Put the egg yolks and 50g (2oz) sugar in a bowl and work together with a wire whisk for several minutes. Stir in the flour and beat until the mixture is very smooth. Pour in the boiling milk, whisking continuously.

Pour the mixture back into the pan. Set over high heat and boil for 3 minutes, stirring continuously. Dot a few flakes of butter over the surface, to prevent a skin forming and keep in a cool place.

THE RASPBERRIES: Pick out 18 nice raspberries and put them in a small bowl. Sprinkle over 1 tbls Framboise *eau-de-vie*, cover the bowl with a saucer and set aside. Put the remaining raspberries into a saucepan with 300g (12oz) sugar and 1L (1¾pts) water. Set over high heat and bring to the boil. Cook for 5 minutes, then purée the mixture in a blender or food processor and rub through a fine sieve.

Return two-thirds of the purée to the pan. Set over low heat and cook until it has the consistency of jam. Set aside. Add 1 tbls *eau-de-vie* and the lemon juice to the remaining one-third of the raspberry purée and set this *coulis* in a bain-marie.

THE SOUFFLE DISHES: You need 6 individual dishes; 10cm (4in) diameter and 6cm (2½in) deep. Brush the inside of each with melted butter. Pour 70g (2½oz) sugar into one of the dishes and rotate the

INGREDIENTS

1.1kg (2lb 5oz) raspberries, fresh or frozen

500ml (1pt) milk

450g (1lb) caster sugar

6 egg yolks

50g (2oz) flour

30g (1oz) butter

2 tbls Framboise *eau-de-vie*

juice of 1 lemon

10 egg whites

12 vanilla-flavoured macaroons (see page 231) (optional)

For the soufflé dishes

30g (1oz) melted butter

70g (1½oz) caster sugar

icing sugar, to serve

Above *Mille-feuilles aux framboises (page 240)*

dish so that the whole surface is well coated with sugar. Pour the remaining sugar into the next dish and repeat the process with each.
ASSEMBLING THE SOUFFLES: Preheat the oven to 220°C/425°F/Gas 7. Fold the raspberry 'jam' into the pastry cream and pour the mixture into a wide-mouthed bowl. Beat the 10 egg whites until frothy. Add a pinch of sugar and beat until they form soft peaks. Using a whisk, quickly beat one-third of the egg whites into the pastry cream then, using a spatula, gently fold in the remaining egg whites.

Pour the mixture into the soufflé dishes so that it comes halfway up the sides. Put 3 of the reserved raspberries into each dish, then add 2 lightly crushed macaroons to each. Fill up the dishes with the soufflé mixture and level the surface with a palette knife. With the point of a knife, push the mixture away from the edges of each dish.

Serves: 6 people
Preparation time: 25 minutes
Cooking time: 10 minutes
Wine: The Chenin Blanc grape grown in the Coteaux du Layon produces fine rich wines of velvet smooth texture which would suit this soufflé.

Picture: page 246

COOKING

Bake for 10 minutes. Then dust with icing sugar and serve at once. Pass round the lukewarm raspberry *coulis* in a sauceboat.

SOUFFLES TIEDES AUX PECHES

(Warm peach soufflés)

PREPARATION

THE FRUIT: Finely dice the strawberries and put in a bowl with the passion fruit flesh. Finely dice 50g (2oz) peaches and add ⅓ to the bowl. Pour kirsch over the remainder.
THE SOUFFLE MIXTURE: Purée 250g (10oz) peaches in a blender or food processor. Place the purée in a saucepan, set over low heat and cook for 45 minutes, stirring occasionally with a spatula.

Put 100g (4oz) sugar with 50ml (2fl.oz) water in a heavy-based saucepan and heat to 160°C (315°F), then pour the syrup into the peach purée, stirring with a spatula. Add the arrowroot and bring to the boil for 2 minutes. Take the pan off the heat and transfer the peach mixture to a bowl. Keep at room temperature.

INGREDIENTS

300g (10oz) peaches in syrup, drained and syrup reserved

1 passion fruit

3 strawberries

1 tbls kirsch

150g (5oz) caster sugar

1 tsp arrowroot

100g (4oz) butter

6 egg whites

6 small mint leaves

ASSEMBLING THE SOUFFLES

Preheat the oven to 220°C/450°F/Gas 8. Thickly brush the insides of

Serves: 6 people
Preparation time: 35 minutes
Cooking time: 3 minutes
Wine: A wine produced across the river from Sauternes, which is not so well known, is the charming and elegant wine from St Croix du Mont.

Picture: page 246

the moulds with melted butter and coat with the remaining sugar. Beat the egg whites until well-risen and quickly mix one-third into the peach purée. Gently fold in the remainder with a wooden spatula. Half-fill 6 metal moulds with this mixture. They should be 7cm (2½in) diameter, 5cm (2in) deep, and 6cm (2¼in) at the base. Spoon the diced peaches in kirsch into the middle, then fill up the moulds with soufflé mixture and smooth over the tops with a palette knife. Set the moulds on a baking sheet and bake for 3 minutes.

TO SERVE

Divide the fruit *brunoise* between 6 warmed plates and add 1 tbls syrup from the peaches to each. Carefully unmould the soufflés onto the plates, place a mint leaf on each and serve at once.

If you prefer, you can use larger, china soufflé dishes, in which case do not unmould the soufflés. The given quantities will only fill 3 10cm (4in) moulds, 6cm (2¼in) deep. Bake at 220°C/450°F/Gas 8 for 6 minutes, then carefully spoon the fruit *brunoise* over the top of the soufflés. Omit the peach syrup.

INGREDIENTS

800g (1lb 12oz) strawberries

500ml (1pt) Strawberry *coulis* (see page 227)

800g (1lb 12oz) Shortbread dough (see page 251)

pinch of flour

1 egg yolk, beaten with 1 tbls milk, to glaze

Serves: 6 people
Preparation time: 25 minutes
Cooking time: 8 minutes
Wine: A wine from the region of Sauternes would match this dish. A fine Grand Cru which is not as sweet as a Château d'Yquem would be suitable.

SABLES AUX FRAISES

(Strawberry shortbread)

You can use either wild strawberries or raspberries instead of strawberries, depending on their availability and on your preference. This recipe may be prepared well in advance of the meal, but do not assemble the shortbreads until just before serving, as the *coulis* will soften the pastry and it will lose its wonderful crumbliness.

If you prefer, instead of glazing the pastry tops, you can sift a little icing sugar over them and garnish each with a strawberry.

PREPARATION

THE SHORTBREAD BASES: Preheat the oven to 200°C/400°F/Gas 6. On a lightly floured marble or wooden surface, roll out the pastry to a thickness of about 2mm (1/12in). Cut out 18 circles with a plain round 10cm (4in) pastry cutter and arrange them on a baking sheet.

Brush 6 circles with the egg wash. Decorate them as you like, or draw lines with the back of a small knife or a fork.

Picture: page 225

COOKING

Bake all the shortbread circles in the preheated oven for about 8 minutes. When they are cooked, allow to cool slightly, then use a palette knife to transfer them to a wire pastry rack and keep cool.
THE STRAWBERRIES: Wash if necessary, hull and either halve them or leave whole, depending on their size. Roll in two-thirds of the strawberry *coulis*, then keep in the refrigerator.

TO SERVE

Place an unglazed shortbread base on each plate. Spread over a few strawberries, place a second shortbread circle on top, add another layer of strawberries and top with a glazed shortbread circle.
Serve the remaining strawberry *coulis* separately in a sauceboat.

FEUILLETES TIEDES AUX RAISINS, SABAYON AU KIRSCH

(Warm *feuilletés* with grapes and kirsch-flavoured *sabayon* sauce)

INGREDIENTS

400g (15oz) white grapes

150ml (6fl.oz) fine quality kirsch

350g (12oz) Puff pastry (see page 248)

40g (1½oz) icing sugar

120g (4½oz) caster sugar

6 egg yolks

4 mint leaves

100ml (4fl.oz) water

PREPARATION

THE GRAPES: Peel them and, using a small knife, scoop out the seeds, taking care not to spoil the grapes, which should remain whole. Put into a bowl and pour over a little of the kirsch. Set aside.
THE *FEUILLETES:* Dust a pastry board with icing sugar not flour, and roll out the pastry to a thickness of 5mm (⅛in). Cut out 4 circles with a plain round 9cm (3½in) pastry cutter and place on a baking sheet brushed with cold water. Leave in a cool place for at least 30 minutes.

COOKING

Meanwhile, preheat the oven to 220°C/450°F/Gas 8. Bake the *feuilletés* in the preheated oven for 10 minutes. The icing sugar should have given the tops a lovely glaze. Using a palette knife, transfer the *feuilletés* to a wire rack. With the point of a knife, mark out a circle 1.5cm (½in) in from the edge of each *feuilleté*. Slip in the point of the

Serves: 4 people
Preparation time: 40 minutes
Cooking time: 10 minutes
Wine: In exceptional years Alsace produces a naturally sweet Riesling. It is very rare and lucky are those who find it. More commonly available would be the Riesling Beerenauslese from Germany.

knife and lift off these 'lids'. Keep warm.

THE *SABAYON* SAUCE: Combine the caster sugar and the water in a small saucepan and boil to make a syrup. Leave to cool, then stir in the egg yolks and 100ml (4fl.oz) kirsch. Set the pan over very low heat and beat continuously with a wire whisk until you have a smooth, rich mousse. Increase the heat slightly and continue to beat until the whisk leaves a trail when lifted. Stir in the remaining kirsch and take the pan off the heat.

TO SERVE

Gently warm the grapes. Place the *feuilletés* on individual serving plates and put a spoonful of *sabayon* in each cavity. Drain the warmed grapes and divide them between the *feuilletés*. Cover with a spoonful of *sabayon* and pour a ribbon of sauce round the edge of each *feuilleté*.

Put a mint leaf in the centre of each one and prop the lids against the *feuilletés* at an angle, with one side on the edge of the plate.

To keep the pastry crisp and light, do not fill the *feuilletés* until the last moment. Make the *sabayon* sauce immediately before serving, otherwise the flavour will be spoilt. If you have any Sorbet syrup (see page 242) in the refrigerator, use it to make the *sabayon* instead of boiling the sugar and water.

INGREDIENTS

350g (12oz) Puff pastry (see page 248)

400g (14oz) strawberries or raspberries

700ml (28fl.oz) Red fruit *coulis* (see page 227)

500ml (1pt) double cream

150ml (6fl.oz) Sorbet syrup (see page 242) chilled

60g (2oz) icing sugar

MILLE-FEUILLES, FRAISES OU FRAMBOISES

(Strawberry or raspberry mille-feuilles)

This is a light, delicate, crispy dessert. To keep the mille-feuilles crisp, never bake them more than 1 or 2 hours before the meal and only fill them with fruit and cream just before serving.

PREPARATION

THE STRAWBERRIES OR RASPBERRIES: Wash, drain and hull the fruit and cut into halves or quarters, or leave whole, depending on the size. Put into a bowl with 300ml (12fl.oz) red fruit *coulis* and mix well. Place in the refrigerator.

THE DOUBLE CREAM: Pour the cream into a well-chilled bowl and

whip until the whisk leaves a trail when lifted. Stir in the chilled sorbet syrup and whip until almost stiff. Chill in the refrigerator. Assemble a piping bag and medium plain or fluted nozzle and chill.
THE PUFF PASTRY: Preheat the oven to 220°C/425°F/Gas 7. Dust the pastry board and the pastry with icing sugar, not flour, and roll out the pastry to a thickness of about 4mm (¼in). Cut out 8 circles with a plain round pastry cutter, 9cm (3½in) diameter and place them on a baking sheet brushed with cold water. Leave to rest in a cold place for 30 minutes before baking.

Serves: 4 people
Preparation time: 25 minutes
Cooking time: 10 minutes
Wine: With the pastry we feel something fresh like a glass of well chilled Doux (sweet) Champagne would be delicious.

Picture: page 236

COOKING

Bake the pastry circles in the preheated oven for about 10 minutes. The icing sugar from the pastry board should give the tops a lovely glaze. Using a palette knife, transfer the pastry circles to a wire rack .

TO SERVE

Using a small, sharp knife, hollow out a small cavity in the centre of 4 of the pastry circles. Spread a little whipped cream over the bottom of each cavity, then fill generously with strawberries or raspberries. Pipe a pretty border of whipped cream around the outside edge of each filled circle, then top with the second pastry circle. Place on individual plates, pour about 100ml (4fl.oz) red fruit *coulis* around each mille-feuille and pipe a rosette of cream on top of each one. Decorate with a raspberry or small strawberry.

GLACE AMANDINE

(Hazelnut praliné ice-cream with hot chocolate sauce)

Serves: 4 people
Preparation time: 15 minutes

INGREDIENTS

60g (2oz) whole hazelnuts

60g (2oz) caster sugar

1 tsp peanut oil

1 tsp instant coffee powder

½L (1pt) Custard cream (see page 228)
Continued overleaf

PREPARATION

THE HAZELNUTS: Place on a baking tray and put in a very hot oven or under a hot grill until the skin blisters and the hazelnuts turn golden brown. Rub them with a cloth to remove the skins and keep warm.
THE *NOUGATINE:* Heat the sugar in a heavy-based saucepan, without adding any liquid. Stir continunously with a wooden spatula until the sugar has completely dissolved and is a lovely pale golden colour. Throw in the hazelnuts and cook for 1 minute. Pour into a lightly oiled

200ml (8fl.oz) double cream

150g (5oz) bitter chocolate

25g (1oz) butter

baking tray and keep in a cold place.

FREEZING THE ICE-CREAM: Put the coffee powder and custard cream in a bowl and beat together with a wire whisk. Stir in 50ml (2fl.oz) cream and pour the mixture into an ice-cream maker.

Meanwhile, crush the cold *nougatine* with a rolling pin. When the ice-cream is ready, stir in the crushed *nougatine* with a wooden spatula. Serve at once or keep in the freezer.

THE CHOCOLATE SAUCE: Break the chocolate into the top of a double boiler or a saucepan and place over hot water. Add 150m (6fl.oz) double cream and melt the chocolate. Stir in the butter with a wooden spatula. Serve the hot sauce separately in a sauceboat.

INGREDIENTS

1kg (2lb 2oz) granulated or caster sugar

1.4L (2½pts) water

175g (6oz) glucose

Preparation time: 5 minutes
Cooking time: 20 minutes

SIROP A SORBET

(Sorbet syrup)

COOKING

Combine all the ingredients in a heavy-based pan and set over high heat, stirring occasionally with a wooden spatula. Bring the mixture to the boil and leave to bubble for several minutes, skimming the surface if necessary. Pass through a conical sieve into a bowl and leave to cool. Once cold, the syrup can be used in any fruit sorbet, or it will keep for up to 2 weeks in the refrigerator.

INGREDIENTS

½ bottle dry Champagne, preferably pink

300ml (12fl.oz) Sorbet syrup (see page 242)

½ lemon

½ egg white

Serves: 6 people
Preparation time: 10 minutes

Picture: page 247

SORBET AU CHAMPAGNE

(Champagne sorbet)

Serve this sorbet in well-chilled glass dishes. Add a few wild strawberries in season to make it look pretty; their flavour marries very well with the Champagne.

PREPARATION

Put the sorbet syrup in a bowl, pour over the Champagne and stir with a spatula. Add the lemon zest and juice. Beat the egg white with a fork and add it to the Champagne. Stir well, transfer to a sorbetière or ice-cream maker and freeze.

TARTE AU CITRON

(Lemon tart)

This tart tastes much better if it is made 1 or 2 days before you eat it, so you have the bonus of being able to prepare it in advance. Thickly powder the top of the tart with icing sugar just before serving.

PREPARATION

THE PASTRY BASE: Preheat the oven to 170°C/325°F/Gas 3. On a lightly floured marble or wooden surface, roll out the pastry to a thickness of about 4mm (1/6in). Butter a flan ring, 22cm (9in) diameter, 3.5cm (1½in) deep, place on a buttered baking sheet and line with the pastry. Put a circle of greaseproof paper in the bottom, fill with dried beans and bake in the preheated oven for 10 minutes. Remove from the oven, take out the beans and paper and keep the pastry shell at room temperature. Lower the oven temperature to 150°C/300°F/Gas 2.

THE LEMONS: Wash, grate the zests and squeeze the lemons, reserving the zests and juice together.

THE EGGS: Break them into a bowl, add the sugar and beat lightly with a wire whisk until the mixture is smooth and well blended.

THE CREAM: Pour the cream onto the egg mixture and mix very lightly with a wire whisk. Stir in the lemon juice and zests and pour the filling onto the pastry case.

COOKING

Place immediately in the preheated oven and bake for 40 minutes. If the top of the tart becomes too brown before the end of the cooking time, cover with foil. When the tart is cooked, remove the flan ring before it cools completely.

INGREDIENTS

650g (1lb 6oz) Shortbread dough (see page 251)
pinch of flour
butter for greasing
4 lemons
9 eggs
375g (14oz) caster sugar
300ml (12fl.oz) double cream
icing sugar, to serve

Serves: 6 people
Preparation time: 40 minutes
Cooking time: 1 hour
Wine: This dessert needs a wine not as sweet as Sauternes. Such a wine comes from Barsac in Bordeaux.

Picture: page 246

TARTE CHAUDE AUX DEUX FRUITS

(Hot two-fruit tart, with *sabayon* sauce)

This delicate dessert is quick and easy to make. Never make the *sabayon* sauce more than 10 minutes before serving, or it will lose its lightness. If you prefer, you can make small tartlets instead of

INGREDIENTS

220g (8oz Puff pastry trimmings (see page 248) or Short pastry (see page 250)

pinch of flour

5 medium crisp eating apples, (about 500g/1lb 2oz)

75g (2½oz) butter

30g (1oz) caster sugar

75ml (3fl. oz) Calvados

80g (3½oz) (drained weight) bilberries in syrup

4 egg yolks

Serves: 4 people
Preparation time: 35 minutes
Cooking time: 15 minutes
Wine: From the Loire Valley comes sweet, utterly charming wine from Anjou and Touraine. Two perfect examples for this dish would be Quarts de Chaume or Bonnezeaux.

Picture: page 246

one large tart. Serve these on individual plates.

PREPARATION

THE PASTRY: On a lightly floured marble or wooden surface, roll out the pastry to a thickness of 2mm (1/12in). Place on a baking sheet brushed with cold water and cut out a circle 22cm (9in) diameter. Prick the pastry with a fork or a small knife and keep in a cool place.
THE APPLES: Peel, halve and core them, then cut each half into 8 or 10 evenly sized segments. Put them in a frying pan with the butter, set over high heat and sauté quickly for 2 minutes. Add the sugar, then pour in 15ml (2 tbls) Calvados and ignite. Leave to cool.
ASSEMBLING THE TART: Arrange the cold apple segments on the pastry base in an attractive rosette pattern.

COOKING

Preheat the oven to 240°C/475°F/Gas 9. Bake the tart in the very hot oven for 12 minutes. Drain the bilberries thoroughly; remove the tart from the oven and arrange the bilberries in little heaps on top of the apples. Return the tart to the oven and cook for a further 3 minutes.
THE *SABAYON* SAUCE: Combine the egg yolks, the remaining Calvados, 1 tbls water and the cooking juice from the apples in a shallow pan. Place the pan in a bain-marie or over a saucepan of hot water. Set over low heat and beat the mixture continuously with a small wire whisk until you have a lukewarm (50°C/120°F) froth, which is very smooth and thick enough to coat the back of a spoon.

TO SERVE

Serve the tart on a round china plate. Pour a little *sabayon* around the edge and serve the rest separately in a sauceboat.

LES BISCUITS
(Sponge biscuits)

These sponge biscuits may be used as the basis for numerous puddings, from the simplest to the most elaborate. Serve them filled with jam or fruit purée, or with *crème chantilly* (sweetened whipped cream) sprinkled with red fruits; or use them for almost all charlottes or in certain decorative *pièces montées*, like the classic *pièces Bretonnes*. Sponge fingers must be eaten on the day they are made, otherwise they will lose their texture; after 2 or 3 days, they dry out and crumble.

PREPARATION

THE EGGS: Separate them and put the whites in the bowl of an electric mixer. Add three-quarters of the sugar to the yolks and beat until the whisk leaves a trail when lifted. Beat the whites until well-risen. Add the remaining sugar and beat for 1 minute at high speed until very stiff.
MIXING THE YOLKS AND WHITES: Using a flat perforated spoon, stir about one-third of the whites into the yolks. The mixture must be completely homogenous. Tip in the remaining egg whites all at once, and very carefully fold them into the mixture. Before it becomes thoroughly mixed, lightly sprinkle over the sifted flour and potato flour, if you are using it. Lightly mix everything together until well blended, then stop mixing, or the mixture will become heavy.

SHAPING AND COOKING THE SPONGE MIXTURE

Cooking time will depend on the shape, thickness and size.
TO PIPE A ROLLED BISCUIT (USE INGREDIENTS I): Use a plain round nozzle, No. 3 or 4, or a ridged nozzle or palette knife. Line a baking sheet with buttered, floured greaseproof paper and pipe or spread the mixture onto the paper. Bake in a hot oven at 220°C/425°F/Gas 7 for about 3 minutes. Invert the cooked biscuit (which should now be about 5mm/1/5in thick) onto a tea-towel and immediately and carefully peel off the paper. Fill and roll the biscuit as soon as possible.
TO PIPE SPONGE FINGERS (USE INGREDIENTS II): Use a plain nozzle, No. 10. Pipe the mixture onto a baking sheet lined with lightly buttered and floured greaseproof paper. The 'fingers' should be about 10cm (4in) long. Lightly dust them twice with icing sugar, at 5 minute intervals. Bake in a moderate oven at 190°C/375°F/Gas 5 for 8 to 10 minutes. Before the sponge fingers have cooled completely, lift them off the paper with a palette knife and place on a wire pastry rack.
TO MAKE BASES FOR DECORATIVE PUDDINGS OR DESSERTS (USE INGREDIENTS II): Pour the mixture into a lightly buttered and floured sponge tin and bake in a moderate oven at 190°C/375°F/Gas 5. Depending on the diameter of the tin and hence on the thickness of the

INGREDIENTS I

4 whole eggs

3 egg yolks

85g (3oz) caster sugar

35g (1oz) flour

40g (1½oz) potato flour

INGREDIENTS II

6 eggs

190g (7oz) caster sugar

225g (8oz) flour

Recipe for: 6 or 7 eggs
Preparation time: 20 minutes
Cooking time: depends on the thickness of the biscuits

1

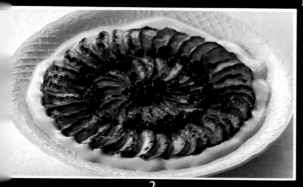

2

3

4

5

1 *Pêche au Champagne (page 234)*
2 *Tarte chaude aux deux fruits (page 243)*
3 *Tarte au citron (page 243)*
4 *Soufflé chaud aux framboises (page 235)*
5 *Soufflé tiède aux pêches (page 237)*
Above *Sorbet au Champagne (page 242)*

biscuit, the cooking time will be between 15 and 25 minutes. As soon as the biscuit is cooked, unmould and invert it onto a wire pastry rack.

INGREDIENTS

500g (1lb 1oz) plain flour, plus flour for 'turning' the pastry

200ml (8fl.oz) water

2 tsp fine salt

2 tbls white wine vinegar

450g (1lb) very firm, dry butter

Makes: 1.2kg (2lb 10oz) dough
Preparation time: 1 hour 10 minutes plus about 5 hours, resting time

FEUILLETAGE JEAN MILLET

(Puff pastry Jean Millet)

PREPARATION

PREPARING THE PASTE: Put the 500g (1lb 2oz) flour on the work surface and make a well in the centre. Pour in the water, salt, vinegar and 50g (2oz) melted butter. Work all the ingredients together with the fingertips of your right hand. Use your left hand to push small quantities of flour into the centre of the well, as it will tend to spread out.

When all the ingredients are well mixed, work the dough lightly with the palm of your hand until it is completely smooth. Roll it into a ball and lightly prick the surface with a knife to break up the elasticity. Wrap the dough in a polythene bag or greaseproof paper and chill in the refrigerator for 2 to 3 hours.

INCORPORATING THE BUTTER: Flour the work surface. Roll out the ball of dough in four different places, so that it looks rather like four large ears around a small head. Put the butter, beaten into 1 slab if necessary, into the centre; it must be supple, firm and very cold. Fold up the four 'ears', making sure that the dough completely encloses the butter. Chill for 30 minutes.

TURNING AND FOLDING: Lightly flour the work surface then gently and progressively roll the dough away from you into a rectangle, about 70 x 40cm (25 x 16in). Flour the work surface as you roll. Mark out the dough into 3 equal parts, and fold the 2 end thirds on to the centre third. This is the first 'turn'.

SECOND TURN: Turn the rectangle through 90° and again roll it out gently and progressively away from you, flouring the work surface as you roll. Roll the dough into a rectangle 70 x 40cm (25 x 16in). Fold over the dough once more into 3 equal parts. At this stage, wrap the pastry in the polythene bag or greaseproof paper and place in the refrigerator for 30 minutes to 1 hour to rest and firm up.

Repeat both the turns exactly as described above. You will now have given the pastry 4 turns. Chill in the refrigerator for 30 minutes to 1 hour. Finally, give the pastry 2 more turns, so that it has had 6 turns in all. The puff pastry is now ready to use. If well-wrapped in polythene or greaseproof paper, it will keep for 3 days in the refrigerator, or for several weeks in the freezer.

To use puff pastry, roll it out, then cut into the desired shape (*bouchée, vol-au-vent, fleurons, feuilletés*, palm hearts and so on), and leave to rest for at least 30 minutes before baking; this will prevent the pastry from shrinking and spoiling its shape.

Always bake puff pastry in a hot or very hot oven (220-240°C/ 425-475°F/Gas 7-9). People are often obsessed by the horrors of making puff pastry, quite without cause. It is true that it is a very lengthy process, but it really is not at all difficult to make. This recipe was created by Jean Millet, the president of the Confederation de la Pâtisserie-Confiserie-Glacerie de France and an M.O.F. in pastry.

PATE A CHOUX

(Choux paste)

The versatility of choux paste makes it an enormously important element of patisserie and cooking. If stored in an airtight container, it will keep well in the refrigerator or freezer.

PREPARATION

COOKING THE PASTE: Cut the butter into small pieces and put it in the saucepan with the water, milk, salt and sugar. Set over high heat and bring to the boil, stirring with a wooden spatula. Take the pan off the heat and, stirring all the time, quickly scatter in the sifted flour.

The next stage, which is called 'drying out' is absolutely vital if you want to make good choux paste. When the mixture is smooth, return the pan to the heat for 1 minute, stirring with the spatula. This will dry out the paste and cause some of the water to evaporate. Tip the mixture into a bowl.

FINISHING THE PASTE: Using a spatula, beat in the eggs, one at a time and stir vigorously until the paste is very smooth. It is now ready to use. If the paste is not for immediate use, spread one-third of a beaten egg over the surface; this will prevent a skin or crust from forming, which often happens after a few hours.

PIPING THE CHOUX PASTE: Choose an appropriate nozzle to pipe the desired shape — small or large choux buns, éclairs, swans, gâteau

INGREDIENTS

100g (4oz) butter
125ml (5fl.oz) water
125ml (5fl.oz) milk
½ tsp fine salt
1 tsp caster sugar
150g (6oz) flour, sifted
4 eggs

Makes: 250ml (10fl.oz) paste (enough for 22-25 choux buns or éclairs)
Preparation time: 20 minutes
Cooking time: 10 to 20 minutes

Paris-Brest or whatever. A piping bag is really essential for this, although it is possible to shape the paste with a tablespoon. Butter a baking sheet and pipe on the choux paste shapes. Glaze each shape with beaten egg and milk before baking.

COOKING

Bake in a preheated oven at 200°C/400°F/Gas 6, but open the oven door 2cm (1in) after 4 or 5 minutes to let the steam escape, otherwise the choux buns may go soft instead of remaining crisp. Depending on the size of the shapes, cooking time will vary from 10 to 20 minutes.

INGREDIENTS

250g (9oz) plain flour

160g (6oz) butter

1 egg

pinch of caster sugar

1 tsp fine salt

1 tbls milk

Makes: 475g (1lb) pastry
Preparation time: 15 minutes

PATE BRISEE

(Short pastry)

PREPARATION

Put the flour on the pastry board and make a well in the centre. Cut the slightly softened butter into small pieces and put into the well, together with the egg, sugar and salt. Rub in all the ingredients with the fingertips of your right hand. Use your left hand to push small quantities of flour into the centre of the well, as it will tend to spread.

When the ingredients are well mixed, add the cold milk. Knead the pastry 2 or 3 times to mix very thoroughly. Wrap in greaseproof paper or a polythene bag and chill in the refrigerator for several hours.

You can use this crumbly, light, delicate pastry as a substitute for puff pastry; it is especially good for meat or fish *en croûte*. It can also be used as the crust for pâté *en croûte*, in place of the pâté dough. Traditionally, however, it is used as a base for flans and tartlets. Short pastry will keep for several days in the refrigerator.

Makes: 885g (about 2lb)
Preparation time: 10 minutes

PATE A PATE

(Pâté crust)

The dough will keep for several days in the refrigerator. This is the crust which is normally used for pâtés *en croûte*, but short pastry may be used instead.

PREPARATION

Put the flour on the pastry board and make a well in the centre. Cut the butter into small pieces and put into the well, together with the salt. Work together for 1 minute, then add the egg yolks and knead for 1 or 2 minutes. Add the water.

Knead the dough 2 or 3 times with the palm of your hand, so that all the ingredients are perfectly blended. Wrap in greaseproof paper or a polythene bag and leave to rest in the refrigerator for several hours.

INGREDIENTS

500g (1lb 1oz) plain flour

200g (7oz) butter, slightly softened

1½ tsp fine salt

125g (4½ oz) egg yolks

50ml (2fl.oz) water

PATE SABLEE

(Shortbread dough)

PREPARATION

Cut the butter into small pieces and place it on the marble or wooden surface. Work the butter with your fingertips until it is very soft. Sift the icing sugar and add it to the butter with a pinch of salt.

Work the mixture with your fingertips until the ingredients are thoroughly blended, then add the egg yolks (or the whole egg) and lightly mix all the ingredients together. Sift the flour and, using your right hand, amalgamate it evenly into the mixture together with the ground almonds if you are making recipe II. Use your left hand to push any flour which spreads out into the centre. When the pastry is thoroughly mixed, add the vanilla or lemon essence, if you are using it.

Rub the pastry gently 2 or 3 times using the palm of your hand. Do not overwork it. Roll it into a ball and flatten it out lightly. Wrap in greaseproof paper or a polythene bag and chill for several hours.

Always add the flour to a shortbread dough at the last minute so that the pastry remains crumbly and 'short'. Once the flour is added, the pastry must never be overworked, but mixed only until all the ingredients are amalgamated; overworking will ruin the pastry.

Recipe I is very delicate; when using the pastry to line a flan dish or to make *sablés* etc, this must be done very quickly and without handling the dough too much, as it will soften very rapidly. Recipe II is easier to make, roll out and handle, but because it contains less butter, it is less rich and delicate. The two recipes are made in the exactly the same way. Both doughs keep very well for several days in the refrigerator.

INGREDIENTS I

200g (7oz) butter

pinch of salt

100g (4oz) icing sugar

2 egg yolks

250g (9oz) flour

1 drop vanilla or lemon essence (optional)

INGREDIENTS II

140g (5oz) butter

pinch of salt

100g (4oz) icing sugar

1 whole egg

250g (9oz) flour

1 drop vanilla or lemon essence (optional)

30g (1oz) ground almonds

Makes: about 600g (1lb 6oz)
Preparation time: 15 minutes

APPENDICES

The recipes in this book were created using metric measurements, which both Michel and Albert prefer. However, for those who are accustomed to working in imperial, conversions have been given.

It is impractical to give exact equivalents when converting from metric to imperial measurements. 1 ounce is actually equal to 28.352 grammes so that it is not really possible to measure accurately 25 or 30 grammes if you are using imperial measuring spoons, jugs and scales.

The same is true of liquid measurements so, in order to avoid complications, we have rounded the conversions up or down to the nearest ounce or fluid ounce. Thus, 30 grammes equals 1 ounce and 25 millilitres equals 1 fluid ounce. There are, however, certain recipes (eg pastry) where the exact proportions of liquids to solids is critically important. In these cases, we have used absolutely accurate conversions.

It is imperative to use *either* metric *or* imperial measurements, *but not a mixture of both*.

CONVERSION CHART

ABBREVIATIONS

kg	kilogramme	lb	pound	ml	millilitre	in	inch
g	gramme	oz	ounce	cm	centimetre	tbls	tablespoon
L	litre	fl.oz	fluid ounce	mm	millimetre	tsp	teaspoon
		pt	pint	°C	Centigrade	°F	Fahrenheit

WEIGHTS AND MEASURES

For the sake of simplicity, we have measured certain ingredients in tablespoons and teaspoons. One level tablespoon or teaspoon is roughly equivalent to the following weights:

1 tbls butter	= 30g (1oz)		1 tbls fine salt	= 25g (1oz)	
1 tsp butter	= 15g (½oz)		1 tsp fine salt	= 8g (¼oz)	
1 tbls sugar	= 30g (1oz)		1 tbls flour	= 20g (¾oz)	
1 tsp sugar	= 10g (⅓oz)		1 tsp flour	= 6g (1/5oz)	

OVEN TEMPERATURES

NB It is essential to preheat the oven for at least 20 minutes so that it reaches the desired temperature before you put the dish in the oven to cook.

	°C	°F	Gas		°C	°F	Gas
Very slow	120°	230°	¼	**Fairly hot**	190°	375°	5
	130°	205°	½		200°	400°	6
	140°	275°	1	**Hot**	220°	425°	7
Slow	160°	300°	2		220°	450°	8
	170°	325°	3	**Very hot**	240°	475°	9
Moderate	180°	350°	4		250°	500°	10

GLOSSARY
253

GLOSSARY AND INDEX

ABAISSER: To roll out pastry with a rolling pin.

APPAREIL: The mixture of ingredients which go into the making of a dish (eg *appareil à soufflé = soufflé mixture*).

BAIN-MARIE: A water bath designed to keep liquids, stews etc hot at below boiling point. A bowl or saucepan is placed in a larger pan which is then filled with hot water. It is used to keep custards, sauces etc warm without overcooking or spoiling the texture.

BAKE BLIND (CUIRE A BLANC): To bake pastry shells, flan cases etc without a filling; the empty shell is filled with rice, dried beans or fruit stones to prevent it from collapsing or bubbling up.

BEURRE MANIÉ: Kneaded butter, used for thickening certain sauces, soups and casserole dishes. It is made by mashing together equal quantities of softened butter and flour; the mixture is then stirred into the preparation, a little at a time.

BI-METAL: A copper serving platter lined with silver or stainless steel.

BLANCH (BLANCHIR): To boil meat, offal or vegetables for a few minutes to preserve their colour or to prepare them for subsequent cooking.

BRUNOISE: Vegetables, meats, shellfish, etc cut into very small, even-sized dice.

CHEMISER: To line a dish with pancakes, thin slices of fat, bacon etc; or to line an ice-cream mould with one flavour of sorbet before filling the centre (eg with a *bombe* mixture).

CIVET: A rich stew.

CLARIFY (CLARIFIER): To clear a liquid by beating it over high heat with egg whites, blood, tomatoes or chopped lean meat. To clarify butter; melt it very gently and ladle it through a muslin cloth, leaving the milky deposit in the bottom of the pan.

CLOUTER: To stud meat, poultry, etc with small pieces of barding fat, truffle, scarlet tongue, ham, vegetables, etc.

COAT (NAPPER): When referring to cooked sauces, such as custard, the sauce is

cooked when it is thick enough to coat the back of a wooden spoon.

CONCASSER: To chop roughly or pound in a mortar.

DE-BEARD: See ebarber.

DECANT (DECANTER): To pour liquid delicately from one container to another so as not to disturb the sediment.

DEGLAZE (DEGLACER): To add liquid to the pan in which meat has been cooking so that the concentrated juices and crusty bits from the bottom of the pan are incorporated into the gravy.

DEGORGER: To soak food in cold running water to eliminate any impurities.

DEGRAISSER: To skim the fat off the surface of a liquid using a spoon or ladle.

DESSECHER: To evaporate moisture from choux paste, *duchesse* potatoes, etc by stirring the mixture in gentle heat.

DORER (TO GILD): To brush certain foods, such as pastry, with beaten egg before baking in the oven.

DRESSER: To arrange a prepared dish and its garnishes on a platter or plates just before serving.

EBARBER: To remove the 'beard' from mussels, oysters, etc; to cut off the fins of a fish with scissors.

EGG WASH: A glaze for pastry, made by beating together 1 egg yolk and 1 tbls milk.

EMINCER: To cut into very fine slices.

EMONDER: To skin tomatoes or fruits such as peaches, nectarines, etc, by plunging them into boiling water for a few seconds and then dipping them into cold water.

ESCALOPER: To cut food slantways to give a larger surface area.

ETUVER: To cook food in a covered pan, either with or without fat, but without the addition of liquid.

FLEURONS: Puff pastry crescents, used as a garnish.

FONCER: To line a flan dish, tartlet tins, etc with pastry; to put a layer of bacon, carrots, onions, etc in the bottom of a braising pan.

FOULER: To rub a purée through a conical sieve using the back of a ladle, in order to extract as much liquid as possible.

FRAISER: To work pastry with the palm of your hand so that all the ingredients are very thoroughly mixed.

GLACE: Liquid, such as stock reduced to a syrupy consistency.

GLACER: To glaze various foods in the following ways: by rolling cooked 'turned' vegetables in the butter in which they were cooked; by dusting patisserie with icing sugar and baking in an intensely hot oven; to caramelize a crème Chiboust or to refrigerate a prepared dish.

JULIENNE: To cut into strips or 'matchsticks' of varying thickness, using a knife or a mandoline.

LEVER: To lift one or more fish fillets from the bone, or the breast fillets from a chicken, etc.

LIER (or LIAISON): A thickening agent, such as a roux, starch, egg white, blood, etc.

LUSTRER: To coat slices of truffle, pastry *fleurons* etc, with clarified butter; to glaze cold dishes, such as fish, pâtés, poultry, eggs, etc, with half-set aspic, using a brush or a spoon.

MASK (MASQUER): To cover cooked poultry with sauce, or a pudding with cream, etc.

MIREPOIX: Coarsely diced vegetables; a mixture of carrots, celery and sometimes lean ham, all coarsely diced and simmered gently in butter.

MONDER: To skin almonds, hazelnuts, pistachios, etc, by pouring boiling water over them.

MONTER: To mix butter into a sauce by beating or whisking; to beat egg whites lightly or stiffly.

MOUILLER: To add liquid to a dish.

PARE (PARER): To cut away all unappetizing or inedible parts.

PINCER: To pinch up the edges of a tart, etc; to brown vegetables or meat over high heat.

POACH (POCHER): To cook gently in liquid at below boiling point (between 80°C/175°F and 90°C/195°F).

POT ROAST (POELER): To cook food in fat in a covered pan.

RAGOUT: A robust casserole, in which the meat is browned, then sprinkled with flour and braised in stock or wine.

REDUCE (REDUIRE): To reduce a liquid by evaporation over high heat until it reaches the desired consistency.

REFRESH (RAFRAICHIR): To soak or plunge in cold water until completely cooled.

RESERVE (RESERVER): To set aside certain ingredients as they are prepared, ready for later use.

REVENIR: To brown or sear meat in fat on all sides.

RIBBON (RUBAN): A mixture of ingredients beaten together until it forms folds like a ribbon and holds this shape for a few moments.

SAUTE: Like a ragoût, but a thickened sauce is added to the diluted juices in the sauté pan and the meat is braised in this sauce.

SEAL (RAIDIR): To sear the surface of meat without allowing it to brown.

SINGER: To sprinkle with flour.

SNIP (CISELER): To cut finely, without chopping, using scissors or a knife.

SUBRIC: A purée of vegetables baked in a bain-marie (see 'watercress purée' page 221).

SWEAT (SUER): To cook very gently until drops of moisture form.

TOURER: To fold and refold puff pastry, turning and rolling it several times.

TURN (TOURNER): To cut vegetables into different shapes with a small knife, (eg olive-, almond- and barrel-shapes).

VANNER: To stir a sauce or custard occasionally with a wooden spatula while it is cooling — this prevents a skin from forming.